1999

THE 100

BEST MUTUAL FUNDS

YOU CAN BUY

Gordon K. Williamson

Adams Media Corporation
Holbrook, Massachusetts

Also by Gordon K. Williamson

Big Decisions, Small Investor

Low Risk Investing

Making the Most of Your 401(k)

Dedication

This book is dedicated to all of my clients.
I would be nowhere without their trust and support.

Acknowledgments

Special thanks to Cynthia Shaffer for her computer skills. This is a truly
thankless job, and I appreciate everything she has done.

Published by Adams Media Corporation
260 Center Street, Holbrook, MA 02343

ISBN: 1-58062-065-5

Printed in the United States of America.

J I H G F E D C B A

This publication is designed to provide accurate and authoritative information with regard to the
subject matter covered. It is sold with the understanding that the publisher is not engaged in rendering legal, accounting, or other professional advice. If legal advice or other expert assistance
is required, the services of a competent professional person should be sought.
    — From a *Declaration of Principles* jointly adopted by a Committee of the
American Bar Association and a Committee of Publishers and Associations

While due care has been taken to ensure accurate and current data, the ideas, principles, conclusions, and general suggestions contained in this volume are subject to the laws and regulations
of local, state, and federal authorities, as well as to court cases and any revisions of court cases.
Due to the magnitude of the database and the complexity of the subject matter, occasional errors
are possible; the publisher assumes no liability direct or incidental for any actions or investments
made by readers of this book, and strongly suggests that readers seek consultation with legal,
financial, or accounting professionals before making any investment.

The data used to analyze the funds is current through June 30, 1998.

This book is available at quantity discounts for bulk purchases.
For information, call 1-800-872-5627 (in Massachusetts, 781-767-8100).

Visit our home page at http://www.adamsmedia.com

Contents

I.
About This Book

There are 5.4 million business entities operating in the United States; 13,000 of these businesses are publicly held (meaning they have issued stock to the public). Of the 13,000 publicly traded companies, 2,700 are listed on the New York Stock Exchange.

There are over 10,000 mutual funds. There are well over three times as many mutual funds as there are stocks listed on the New York Stock Exchange! The mutual fund industry is now the second largest financial institution in the nation, with assets exceeding $5 trillion, up from $1 trillion in 1991. Over the past five years, the percentage of U.S. households that invest in mutual funds has risen from 25 percent to 45 percent.

Mutual funds are the *best* investment vehicle that has been developed in the twentieth century. When properly selected, these vehicles combine professional management, ease of purchase and redemption, simple record keeping, risk reduction, and superb performance, all in one type of investment. There are dozens of other types of investments, but none match the overall versatility of mutual funds.

A mutual fund is simply one method of investing. When you invest in a fund, your money is pooled with thousands of other investors' monies. This large pool of money is overseen by the fund's management. These managers invest this pool of money in one or more types of investments. The universe of investments includes common stocks, preferred stocks, corporate bonds, tax-free municipal bonds, U.S. government obligations, zero-coupon bonds, convertible securities, gold, silver, foreign securities, and even real estate. The amount of money invested in one or more of these categories depends upon the fund's objectives and restrictions and on the management's perception of the economy.

The beauty of mutual funds is that once the investor decides upon the *type* of investment desired there are several funds that fulfill that criterion. As an example, someone who needs current income would be attracted to bond funds (or a series of equity-oriented funds coupled with what is known as a "systematic withdrawal plan"—a monthly income program described in Appendix D). A person interested in appreciation would focus on an aggressive growth, growth and income, and/or international stock fund. A person who wanted some current income plus some growth to offset the effects of inflation should consider a balanced fund.

The track records of these funds can easily be obtained, as contrasted to the track records of stockbrokers, who are not ranked at all. A few mutual fund sources even look at a fund's risk-adjusted return, a standard of measurement that has not been sufficiently emphasized in the past.

This book was written to fill a void. There are already several mutual fund books and directories, but none deal exclusively with the very best funds. More important, *none of these publications measure risk properly*.

This is the ninth edition of this book. If you have read one or more of the previous editions, you will notice that this edition includes many funds not previously listed and that several of the *previous* "100 Best" are not included here. This does not mean that you should sell or transfer from a previous recommendation to one that appears in this edition. For the most part, mutual funds described in past editions are still excellent choices and should not be moved. There are a number of reasons why a fund no longer appears in this, or previous, editions. These reasons will be detailed in Chapter 10.

Moving from one fund to another can often spell trouble. Consider a recent Morningstar study that compared the performance of its growth fund index with the average investor's return during the five-year period ending 5/31/94. While the overall market gained, on average, 12.5 percent a year, the average investor *lost* 2.5 percent a year. Volatility can make it easy for investors to forget about the long-term case for stocks.

Other sources give almost endless numbers and performance statistics for hundreds and hundreds of mutual funds, leaving readers to draw their own conclusions as to what are the best funds. This book will save you a great deal of time because it has taken the over 10,000 existing funds and narrowed them down to the best 100, ranked by specific category and risk level. Even money market funds are included, a category rarely covered by any other publication.

Investors and financial advisors are not concerned with mediocre or poor performers; they simply want the best funds, *given certain parameters*. Personal investment considerations should include (in order of priority) your time horizon, risk tolerance, financial goals, existing portfolio, and tax bracket. Parameters within a given fund category include risk, performance, and consistency.

Current books and periodicals that cover funds focus on how a fund has performed in the past. Studies clearly point out that a fund whose performance is in the top half one year has a 50–50 chance of being in the bottom half the next year, or the year after that. Since there is little correlation between the past and the future when it comes to market returns, this book concentrates on consistency in management and the amount of risk assumed.

The model used to rank the 100 best is fully described in a later chapter. It is a logical, common-sense approach that cuts through the statistical jargon; it is also easy to understand. As my dad used to say, "There is nothing as uncommon as common sense."

II.
What Is a Mutual Fund?

A mutual fund is an investment company—an entity that makes investments on behalf of individuals and institutions who share common financial goals. The fund pools the money of many people, each with a different amount to invest. Professional money managers then use the pool of money to buy a variety of stocks, bonds, or money market instruments that, in their judgment, will help the fund's shareholders achieve their financial objectives.

Each fund has an investment objective, described in the fund's prospectus, that is important to both the manager and the potential investor. The fund manager uses it as a guide when choosing investments for the fund's portfolio. Prospective investors use it to determine which funds are suitable for their own needs. Mutual funds' investment objectives cover a wide range. Some follow aggressive investment policies, involving greater risk, in search of higher returns; others seek current income from more conservative investments.

When the fund earns money, it distributes the earnings to its shareholders. Earnings come from stock dividends, interest paid by bonds or money market instruments, and gains from the sale of securities in the fund's portfolio. Dividends and capital gains produced are paid out in proportion to the number of fund shares owned. Thus, shareholders who invest a few hundred dollars get the same investment return per dollar as those who invest hundreds of thousands.

Mutual funds remain popular because they are convenient and efficient investment vehicles that give all individuals—even those with small sums to invest—access to a splendid array of opportunities. Mutual funds are uniquely democratic institutions. They can take a portfolio of giant blue-chip companies like IBM, General Electric, and General Motors, and slice it into small enough pieces so that almost anyone can buy.

Mutual funds allow you to participate in foreign stock and bond markets that might otherwise demand too much time, expertise, or expense to be worthwhile. International funds make investing across national borders no more difficult than investing across state lines. Over the next decade, as securities markets develop in the former Iron Curtain countries, mutual funds will no doubt give investors many opportunities to participate in those markets as well.

Mutual funds have opened up a world of fixed-income investing to people who, until recently, had few choices apart from passbook accounts and savings bonds. Through bond funds, shareholders can tap into the interest payments from any kind of fixed-income security you can imagine—and many you have never heard of. The range goes from U.S. Treasury bonds (T-bonds) to collateralized mortgage obligations (CMOs), adjustable-rate preferred stock, floating-rate notes, and even to other countries' debts—denominated both in U.S. dollars and in other currencies.

What is heavily marketed is not necessarily what is appropriate for you to invest in. A global biotechnology fund may be a great investment, but it may not be the right mutual fund for you. Buying what is "hot" rather than what is appropriate is one of the most common mistakes made by investors and an issue that is addressed throughout this book.

III.
How to Invest in a Mutual Fund

Investing in a mutual fund means buying shares of the fund. An investor becomes an owner of shares in the fund just as he or she might be an owner of shares of stock in a large corporation. The difference is that a fund's only business is investing in securities, and the price of its shares is directly related to the value of the securities held by the fund.

Mutual funds continually issue new shares for purchase by the public. The price per share for existing fund investors is not decreased by the ongoing issuance of new shares, since each share created is offset by the amount of new money coming in. Phrased another way, new money that comes into the fund is used to purchase additional securities in order not to dilute the income or value for existing shareholders.

A fund's share price can change from day to day, depending on the daily value of the securities held by the fund. The share price is called the net asset value (NAV), which is calculated as follows. The total value of the fund's investments at the end of the day, after expenses, is divided by the number of shares outstanding.

Newspapers report mutual fund activity every day. An example from the *Wall Street Journal* is shown below.

Everett Funds:			
Evrt r	12.38	NL	−.01
MaxRtn	18.39	NL	+.06
ValTr	12.33	NL	−.01
LtdSl	17.71	NL	−.14
ExtrMid	2.82	2.95	−.02
ExJY p	7.24	7.60	+.01
FBK Gth t	11.06	11.06	..
FJA Funds:			
Capit f	14.67	15.69	−.02
NwHrz	9.65	10.10	..
Permt	12.91	13.81	..
Perrin	20.96	22.42	−.02

The first column in the table is the fund's abbreviated name. Several funds under a single heading indicate a family of funds.

The second column is the net asset value (NAV) per share as of the close of the preceding business day. In some newspapers, the NAV is identified as the sell or the bid price—the amount per share you would receive if you sold your shares. Each mutual fund determines its net asset value every business day by dividing the market value of its total assets, less liabilities, by the number of shares outstanding. On any given day, you can determine the value of your holdings by multiplying the NAV by the number of shares you own.

The third column is usually the offering price or, in some papers, the buy or the asked price—the price you would pay if you purchased shares. The buy price is the NAV plus any sales charges. If there are no sales charges, an NL for no load appears in this column. In such a case, the buy price would be the same as the NAV.

The next column shows the change, if any, in the net asset value (NAV) from the preceding quotation—in other words, the change over the most recent one-day trading period. Thus, if you see a "+.06" in the newspaper next to your fund, *each* of your shares in the fund went up in value by six cents during the previous day.

A *p* following the abbreviated name of the fund denotes a fund that charges a fee that is subtracted from assets for marketing and distribution costs, also known as a 12b-1 plan (named after the federal government rule that permits such an expense). If the fund name is followed by an *r*, the fund has a contingent deferred sales load (CDSL) or a redemption fee. A CDSL is a charge incurred if shares are sold within a certain period; a redemption fee is a cost you would pay *whenever* shares are sold. An *f* indicates a fund that habitually enters the previous day's prices, instead of the current day's. A *t* designates a fund that has both a CDSL or a redemption fee and a 12b-1 plan.

IV.
How a Mutual Fund Operates

A mutual fund is owned by all of its shareholders, the people who purchased shares of the fund. The day-to-day operation of a fund is delegated to a management company.

The management company, often the organization that created the fund, may offer other mutual funds, financial products, and financial services as well. The management company usually serves as the fund's investment advisor.

The investment advisor manages the fund's portfolio of securities. The advisor is paid for its services in the form of a fee that is based on the total value of the fund's assets; fees average 0.5 percent. The advisor employs professional portfolio managers who invest the fund's money by purchasing a number of stocks or bonds or money market instruments, depending on what type of fund it is.

These fund professionals decide where to invest the fund's assets. The money managers make their investment decisions based on extensive, ongoing research into the financial performance of individual companies, taking into account general economic and market trends. In addition, they are backed up by economic and statistical resources. On the basis of their research, money managers decide what and when to buy, sell, or hold for the fund's portfolio, in light of the fund's specific investment objective.

In addition to the investment advisor, the fund may also contract with an underwriter that arranges for the distribution of the fund's shares to the investing public. The underwriter may act as a wholesaler, selling fund shares to security dealers, or it may retail directly to the public.

V.
Different Categories of Mutual Funds

Aggressive Growth. The investment objective of aggressive growth funds is maximum capital gains, with little or no concern for dividends or income of any kind. What makes this category of mutual funds unique is that fund managers often have the ability to use borrowed money (leverage) to increase positions. Sometimes they deal in stock options and futures contracts (commodities). These trading techniques sound, and can be, scary, but such activities represent only a minor portion of the funds' holdings.

Because of their bullish dispositions, these funds will usually stay fully invested in the stock market. For investors, this means better-than-expected results during good (bull) markets and worse-than-average losses during bad (bear) market periods. Fortunately, the average bull market is almost four times as long as the typical bear market.

Do not be confused by economic conditions and stock market performance. There have been eight recessions since World War II. During seven of those eight recessions, U.S. stocks went up. During all eight recessions, stocks posted impressive gains in the second half of every recession. By the same token, do not underestimate the impact of a loss. A 20 percent decline means that you must make 25 percent to break even. A loss of 20 percent does not happen very often to aggressive growth funds, particularly on a calendar year basis, but you should be aware that such extreme downward moves are possible. Often brokers like to focus on the +45 percent and +50 percent years, such as 1980 and 1991, while glossing over a bad year, such as 1984, when aggressive growth funds were down almost 13 percent on average.

One of the great wonders of the stock market is how volatility of returns is reduced when one's holding period is increased. Because of this, aggressive growth funds should only be owned by one of two kinds of investors: those who can live with high levels of daily, monthly, quarterly and/or annual price per share fluctuations, and those who realize the importance of a diversified portfolio that cuts across several investment categories—the investor who looks at how the entire package is performing, not just one segment.

The top ten holdings of aggressive growth funds are: Concertra Managed Care, Applied Graphics Techs, Network Appliance, American Disposal Services, CMAC Investment, Interface Class A, Pride International, Enhance Financial Services Group, Quanex, and PXRE. The typical price-earnings (p/e) ratio for stocks in this category is 35, a figure that is about 17% higher than the S&P 500 Index (which has an average p/e ratio of 30). This group of funds has an average beta of 1.0, making its *market-related* risk identical to that of the S&P 500 (which always has a beta of 1.0, no matter what market conditions or levels are).

The standard deviation for aggressive growth funds is 21 percent. This means that one's expected return for any given year may vary either way by 21 percent. In other words, since aggressive growth funds have averaged 19.3% over the past three years, annual returns are expected to range from –1.7 percent (19.3 – 21) to 40.3 percent (19.3 + 21). This would represent *one* standard deviation (20 percent in the case of aggressive growth funds). A single standard deviation accounts for what you can expect every two out of three months (67 percent of the time or roughly two out of every three years). If you are looking for greater assurance, then two standard deviations must be used (2 x 21 percent in this case). This means that returns for about 95 percent of the months (two standard deviations) would be 19.3 percent plus or minus 42 percent. In other words, a range of –22.7 percent to +61.3 percent.

Small-company stocks have an average p/e ratio of 28. (The price-earnings ratio refers to the selling price of a stock in relation to its annual earnings. Thus a fund category that has a p/e ratio of, say, 10 is comprised of mutual funds whose typical stock in the portfolio is selling for ten times what the corporation's earnings are for the year.) Small-company stock funds have a standard deviation of 20 percent and a beta of 0.8 percent, figures that support the view that this category is slightly less volatile than aggressive growth funds.

Historical returns over the past three, five, ten, and fifteen years for aggressive growth and small-company stock funds are shown below. All of the figures shown are average *annual* rates of return (all periods ending 6/30/98).

category	3 years	5 years	10 years	15 years
aggressive growth	19%	16%	15%	11%
small-company stocks	20%	17%	15%	12%
S&P 500	30%	23%	19%	17%
T-bills	5%	5%	6%	6%
CPI (rate of inflation)	2%	2%	3%	3%

The aggressive growth fund category is dominated by technology and service stocks. These two groups represents over 46 percent of the typical aggressive growth fund's portfolio. The other three top sectors are health, financial, and retail stocks. Small-company stocks are also dominated by technology and service issues.

Balanced. This kind of fund invests in common stocks and corporate bonds. The weighting given to stocks depends upon the fund manager's perception of, or belief in, the market. The more bullish the manager is, the more likely the portfolio will be loaded up with equities. Yet no matter how strongly management feels about the stock market, it would be very rare to see stocks equal more than 75 percent of the portfolio. Similarly, no matter how bearish one becomes, it would be unlikely for a balanced fund to have more than 70 percent of its holdings represented by bonds. Often a fund's prospectus will outline the weighting ranges: The fund's managers must stay within these wide boundaries at all times. A small portion of these funds is made up of cash equivalents (T-bills, CDs, commercial paper, etc.) with a very small amount sometimes dedicated to preferred stocks and convertible securities.

Three other categories, "multi-asset global," "convertible," and "asset allocation" have been combined with balanced funds for the purposes of this book. This grouping together is logical; since overall objectives are largely similar, general portfolio composition can be virtually identical in many cases, and the fund managers in each of these categories have the flexibility to load up heavily on stocks, bonds, preferreds, or convertible securities.

Multi-asset global funds typically emphasize bonds more than stocks or cash. It is not uncommon to see a multi-asset global fund that has 60 percent of its holdings in bonds, with 10 to 20 percent in stocks, and the remainder in foreign equities, preferred stocks, and cash. For the *stock* portion of this category, the p/e ratio is 27 and the standard deviation 8 percent. On the bond side, the average maturity of debt instruments in the portfolio is nine years.

Convertible funds, as the name implies, are made up mostly of convertible preferred stocks and convertible bonds. The conversion feature allows the owner, the fund in this case, to convert or exchange securities for the corporation's common stock. Conversion and price appreciation take place during bull-market periods. Uncertain or down markets make conversion much less likely; instead, management falls back on the comparatively high dividend or interest payments that convertibles enjoy. The typical convertible fund has somewhere between two-thirds and three-quarters of its holdings in convertibles; the balance is in cash, stocks, and preferreds. For the stock portion of this category, the p/e ratio is 24 and the standard deviation is 8 percent. On the bond side, the average maturity of debt instruments in the portfolio is eight years.

Asset allocation funds, like other categories that fall under the broad definition of "balanced," are hybrid in nature, part equity and part debt. These funds have a tendency to emphasize stocks over bonds. A fund manager who wants to take a defensive posture may stay on the sidelines by converting moderate or large parts of the portfolio into cash equivalents. The average asset allocation fund has somewhere between 50 and 65 percent of its portfolio in common stocks, with the remainder in bonds, foreign stocks, and cash. For the stock portion of this category, the p/e ratio is 24 and the standard deviation is 8 percent. On the bond side, the average maturity of debt instruments in the portfolio is ten years.

The top ten holdings of balanced funds are: Philip Morris, GE, U.S. Treasury Notes, Bristol-Myers Squibb, American Home Products, IBM, DuPont, Exxon, Intel, and Merck. The typical price-earnings (p/e) ratio for stocks in this category is 23, a figure that is lower than that of the S&P 500. This group of funds has an average beta of 0.7, making its *market-related risk* 30 percent less than the S&P 500. Keep in mind that beta refers to a portfolio's *stock market-related* risk—it is not a meaningful way to measure bond or foreign security risk. The typical bond in these funds has an average maturity of nine years.

The standard deviation for balanced funds is 8 percent, less than half the level of aggressive growth funds. This means that one's expected return for any given year will vary by 8 percent. (For example, if you were expecting an annualized return of 12 percent, your actual return would range from 4 percent to 20 percent most of the time.)

Historical returns over the past three, five, ten, and fifteen years for balanced, multi-asset global, convertible, and asset allocation funds are shown below. All of the figures shown are average *annual* rates of return (all periods ending 6/30/98).

category	3 years	5 years	10 years	15 years
balanced	17%	13%	13%	13%
multi-asset global	12%	8%	7%	9%
convertible	16%	13%	12%	11%
asset allocation	16%	13%	12%	11%
Corp./Gov't Bond Index	8%	7%	9%	10%

The equity portion of the balanced fund category is dominated by industrial and financial stocks. These two groups represent a third of the typical balanced fund's stock portfolio. The other four top equity sectors are: service, technology, health, and energy stocks.

Like other hybrid funds, balanced funds provide an income stream. The average yield of balanced and asset allocation funds is under 3 percent. The typical yield for both multi-asset global and convertible securities funds is about 3 percent. High-tax-bracket investors who want to invest in these funds should consider using tax-sheltered money, if possible. Balanced, multi-asset global, asset allocation, and convertible bond funds are particularly attractive within an IRA, other qualified retirement plans, or variable annuities. (For more information about both fixed-rate and variable annuities, see two of my other books, *The 100 Best Annuities* and *All About Annuities*.)

Corporate Bonds. These funds invest in debt instruments (IOUs) issued by corporations, governments, and agencies of the U.S. government. Perhaps the typical corporate bond fund should be called a "government-corporate" fund. Bond funds have a wide range of maturities. The name of the fund will often indicate whether it is made up of short-term or medium-term obligations. If the name of the fund does not include the words "short-term" or "intermediate," then the fund most likely invests in bonds with average maturities over ten years. The greater the maturity, the more the fund's share value can change. There is an inverse relationship between interest rates and the value of a bond; when one moves up, the other goes down.

The top ten holdings of corporate bond funds are: U.S. Treasury Bonds, FNMA, Province British Columbia, Time Warner, GNMA, Paine Webber Group, FHLMC, U.S. Treasury Notes, Canadian Imperial Bank, and Norfolk Southern. The weighted maturity date of the bonds within this group averages eight years, with a typical coupon rate of 7.2 percent. (The coupon rate represents what the corporation or government pays out annually on a per-bond basis.)

All bonds have a maturity date—a date when the issuer (the government, municipality, or corporation) pays back the *face value* of the bond (which is almost always $1,000 per bond) and stops paying interest. There are often hundreds of different securities in any given bond fund. Each one of these securities (bonds in this case) has a maturity date; these maturity dates can range anywhere from a few days to up to thirty years. "Weighted maturity" refers to the time left until the average bond in the portfolio comes due (matures).

The standard deviation for corporate bonds is 3 percent, less than half the level of balanced funds. This means that one's expected return for any given month, quarter, or year will be more predictable than almost any other category of mutual funds.

Using a beta measurement for bonds is of little value, since beta defines *stock market* risk and has nothing to do with interest-rate or financial risk. Historical returns over the past three, five, ten, and fifteen years for corporate bond funds are shown below. All of the figures shown are average *annual* rates of return (all periods ending 6/30/98).

category	3 years	5 years	10 years	15 years
corporate bond funds	7%	6%	9%	10%
government bond funds	6%	5%	8%	9%
municipal bond funds	7%	6%	8%	8%
world bond funds	8%	6%	7%	11%
CPI (rate of inflation)	2%	2%	3%	3%

Like income funds, corporate funds provide a high yield that is fully taxable and should be sheltered whenever possible. The average yield of these bond funds is just over 6 percent.

Global Stock. This category of mutual funds invests in equities issued by domestic and foreign firms. Fifteen of the twenty largest corporations in the world are located outside of the United States. It makes sense to be able to invest in these and other corporations and industries—to be able to take advantage of opportunities wherever they appear. Global, also known as world, stock funds have the ability to invest in any country. The more countries a fund is able to invest in, the lower its overall risk level will be; often return potential will also increase.

For the purposes of this book, the global stock category includes foreign and international equity funds. When it comes to investing in mutual funds, the words "foreign" and "international" are interchangeable. A foreign, or international, fund invests in securities outside of the United States. Some foreign funds are broadly diversified, including stocks from European as well as Pacific Basin economies. Other international funds specialize in a particular region or country. A global fund invests in domestic as well as foreign securities. The portfolio manager of a global fund generally has more latitude in the securities selected, since either U.S. or foreign securities can end up representing 50 percent or more of the portfolio, depending upon management's view of the different markets, whereas a foreign or international fund may not be allowed to invest in U.S. stocks or bonds.

To get an idea of the return potential of global stocks, take a look at how the United States has fared compared to stock markets in other countries. The table below shows the best-performing market for each of the past 12 years (ending 12/31/97), its total return in U.S. dollars, and performance figures for the U.S. stock market. All of the figures shown below are adjusted for any good or bad foreign currency swings (meaning that these percentage figures reflect those times when the U.S. dollar has been strong or weak).

year	best major market	best emerging market	U.S. returns
1986	Spain (123%)	n/a	+18%
1987	Japan (43%)	n/a	+5%
1988	Belgium (55%)	Indonesia (258%)	+17%
1989	Austria (105%)	Turkey (547%)	+31%
1990	United Kingdom (10%)	Greece (90%)	−3%
1991	Hong Kong (50%)	Argentina (405%)	+31%
1992	Hong Kong (32%)	Jordan (40%)	+8%
1993	Hong Kong (117%)	Poland (754%)	+10%
1994	Finland (52%)	Brazil (66%)	+1%
1995	Switzerland (45%)	Israel (24%)	+37%
1996	Spain (39%)	Venezuela (228%)	+26%
1997	Portugal (47%)	Russia (+209%)	+ 33%

The top ten holdings of global (world) stock funds are: Sony, Novartis, Telecom Italia, ING Groep, Telebras, Philips Electronics, Alcatel Alsthom, Shell Transport & Trading, National Bank of Cananda, and Enso. The typical price-earnings (p/e) ratio for stocks in this category is 26, a figure that is virtually identical to that of the S&P 500. This group of funds has an average beta of 0.7, meaning that its *U.S. market-related* risk is about 30 percent less than that of the general market, as measured by the S&P 500. The standard deviation for global stock funds is 11 percent, versus 14 percent for growth funds.

Foreign stock funds, which are exclusive of U.S. investments, have a p/e ratio of 26. Their standard deviation over the past three years has been 12 percent. Pacific Basin funds, a more narrowly focused type of foreign fund, have an average p/e ratio of 26 and a standard deviation of 16 percent. European funds, another type of specialized international fund, have a price-earnings ratio of 24 and a standard deviation of 11 percent.

Historical returns over the past three, five, ten, and fifteen years for global stocks are shown below. All of the figures shown are average *annual* rates of return (all periods ending 6/30/98).

category	3 years	5 years	10 years	15 years
global stock funds	17%	15%	12%	13%
foreign stock funds	12%	11%	10%	14%
S&P 500	30%	23%	19%	17%
world bond funds	8%	6%	7%	11%
CPI (rate of inflation)	2%	2%	3%	3%

The four areas that dominate world stock funds are the United States, Europe, Japan, and the Pacific Rim. Stocks from U.S. and European markets account for over two-thirds of a typical global equity fund's portfolio.

Government Bonds. These funds invest in securities issued by the U.S. government or one of its agencies (or former affiliates), such as GNMA, FHLMC, or FNMA. Investors are attracted to bond funds of all kinds for two reasons. First, bond funds have monthly distributions; individual bonds pay interest only semiannually. Second, effective management can control interest rate risk by varying the average maturity of the fund's portfolio. If management believes that interest rates are moving downward, the fund will load up heavily on long-term obligations. If rates do decline, long-term bonds will appreciate more than their short- and medium-term counterparts. Conversely, if the manager anticipates rate hikes, average portfolio maturity can be pared down so that there will be only modest principal deterioration if rates do go up.

Bond funds have portfolios with a wide range of maturities. Many funds use their names to characterize their maturity structure. Generally, "short term" means that the portfolio has a weighted average maturity of less than five years. "Intermediate" implies an average maturity of five to ten years, and "long term" is over ten years. The longer the maturity, the greater the change in the fund's price per share (your principal) when interest rates change. Longer-term bond funds are riskier than short-term funds but tend to offer higher yields. The top holdings of government bond funds are GNMAs and U.S. Treasury notes (T-notes) of varying maturities.

The weighted maturity date of the bonds within this group averages just under eight years, with a typical coupon rate of 7 percent (the coupon rate represents what is paid out annually on a per bond basis)—figures that are virtually identical to the corporate bond category. These funds have a standard deviation of 4 percent—again the figure is almost identical to that for corporate bonds. This means that corporate and government bonds have similar volatilities.

The top eight holdings for government bond: are REFCORP zeros, U.S. Treasury Strips, U.S. Treasury Bonds, U.S. Treasury Notes, Norwest Asset Securities CMO, GNMA, FNMA CMO, FHLMC CMO.

Historical returns over the past three, five, ten, and fifteen years for government bond funds are shown below (all periods ending 6/30/98).

category	3 years	5 years	10 years	15 years
government bond funds	7%	6%	8%	9%
high-yield bond funds	12%	10%	10%	11%
CPI (rate of inflation)	2%	2%	3%	3%
utility funds	19%	12%	13%	14%
convertible bond funds	16%	13%	12%	11%

Like corporate bond funds, government funds provide a high yield that is fully taxable on the federal level and should be sheltered whenever possible. Interest from direct obligations of the U.S. government—T-bonds, T-notes, T-bills, EE bonds, and HH bonds—are exempt from state and local income taxes. This means that a part of the income you receive from funds that include such securities is exempt from *state* taxes.

Corporate bonds are rated as to their safety. The two major rating services are Moody's and Standard and Poor's. By reading the fund's prospectus or by telephoning the mutual fund company, you can find out how safe a corporate bond fund is. The vast majority of these funds are extremely conservative and safety (default) is not really an issue. U.S. government bonds are not rated since it is believed that there is no chance of default—unlike a corporation, the federal government can print money.

Growth. These funds seek capital appreciation with dividend income as a distant secondary concern. Indeed, the average annual income stream from growth funds is just 0.5 percent. Investors who are attracted to growth funds are aiming to sell stock at a profit; they are not normally income oriented. If you are interested in current income you will want to look at Appendix D, "Systematic Withdrawal Plan."

Growth funds are attracted to equities from large, well established corporations. Unlike aggressive growth funds, growth funds may end up holding large cash positions during market declines or when investors are nervous about recent economic or market activities. The top ten holdings of growth funds are: Intel, GE, Pfizer, Microsoft, Merck, Philip Morris, Citicorp, Johnson & Johnson, Eli Lily, and Coca-Cola. The typical price-earnings (p/e) ratio for stocks in this category is 27, compared to 26 for the S&P 500. This group of funds has an average beta of 1.0, the same as the S&P 500.

The standard deviation for growth funds is 14 percent. This means that one's expected return for any given year will vary by 14 percentage points. As an example, if you were expecting a 15 percent annual return, annual returns would probably range between 1 percent and 29 percent (15 percent plus or minus 14 percent).

Historical returns over the past three, five, ten, and fifteen years for growth and small-company stock funds are shown below. All of the figures shown are average *annual* rates of return (all periods ending 6/30/98).

category	3 years	5 years	10 years	15 years
growth funds	24%	19%	16%	14%
small-company stock funds	20%	17%	15%	12%
S&P 500	30%	23%	19%	17%
growth & income funds	25%	19%	15%	14%
global stock funds	17%	15%	12%	13%

Technology, industrial cyclicals, financial, and service stocks dominate growth funds. The balance is fairly evenly divided up among health, utility, retail, and consumer staple issues.

Growth and Income. With a name like this, one would think that this category of mutual funds is almost equally as concerned with income as it is with growth. The fact is, growth and income funds have an average dividend yield of just one percent. This boost in income is due to the small holdings in bonds and convertibles possessed by most growth and income funds.

The top ten holdings of growth and income funds are: Philip Morris, Mobil, IBM, Ford, Bristol-Myers Squibb, Exxon, Atlantic Richfield, Chase Manhattan, American Home Products, and GTE. The typical price-earnings (p/e) ratio for stocks in this category is 24, versus 26 for the S&P 500. This group of funds has an average beta of just under 0.9, meaning that its *market-related risk* is 10 percent less than that of the general market, as measured by the S&P 500.

The standard deviation for growth and income funds is 12 percent, about 15 percent less than that found with the average growth fund. This means that, as a group, growth and income funds have slightly more predictable returns than growth funds.

For the purposes of this book, a second category, "equity-income funds," has been combined with growth and income. Equity-income funds have a lower standard deviation (10 percent compared to 12 percent for growth and income funds), a higher yield (2.0 percent compared to 1.0 percent), and a lower beta (0.8 percent compared to 0.9 percent for growth and income funds).

The typical growth and income fund is divided as follows: 90 percent in common stocks (5 percent of which is in foreign stock), 6 percent in cash, 2 percent in bonds, and 2 percent in other assets. The average equity-income fund is divided as follows: 83 percent in common stocks (6 percent of which is in foreign stock), 6 percent in cash, 4 percent in bonds, and 7 percent in other assets. The typical price-earnings (p/e) ratio for stocks in this category is 22.

Historical returns over the past three, five, ten, and fifteen years for growth and income funds are shown below. All of the figures shown are average *annual* rates of return (all periods ending 6/30/98).

category	3 years	5 years	10 years	15 years
growth and income funds	25%	19%	15%	14%
equity-income funds	23%	18%	15%	15%
growth funds	24%	19%	16%	14%
balanced funds	17%	13%	13%	13%
foreign stock funds	12%	11%	10%	14%

Industrial cyclicals and financial stocks dominate growth and income funds, representing over a third of the typical portfolio. Service, health, technology, and consumer stocks represent the other major industry groups for this category.

High-Yield. These funds generally invest in lower-rated corporate debt instruments. Bonds are characterized as either "bank quality," also known as "investment grade," or "junk." Investment-grade bonds are bonds rated AAA, AA, A, or BAA; junk bonds are instruments rated less than BAA: BA, B, CCC, CC, C, and D. High-yield bonds, also referred to as junk bonds, offer investors higher yields in exchange for the additional risk of default. High-yield bonds are subject to less *interest-rate risk* than regular corporate or government bonds. However, when the economy slows or people panic, these bonds can quickly drop in value.

The top ten holdings of high-yield bonds funds are: Trump Holdings Funding, Gaylord Container, Affiliated News Step, Commodore Media Reset, U.S. Treasury Notes, Riverwood Holdings, Republic of Brazil, FNMA, Neodata Services, and First Nationwide. The average weighted maturity date of the bonds within this group is eight years, a figure similar to that for high-quality corporate and government bond funds. The typical coupon rate is 9 percent. (The coupon rate represents what the corporation pays out annually on a per bond basis.) When it comes to high-yield bonds, investors would be wise to accept a lower yield in return for more stability of principal and appreciation potential. As with income funds, corporate funds provide a high yield that is fully taxable and should be sheltered whenever possible.

The standard deviation for high-yield bond funds is 4 percent, a figure very similar to that of corporate and government bond funds as a whole but 4 percent less than balanced and global bond funds. Historical returns over the past three, five, ten, and fifteen years for high-yield corporate bond funds are shown below. All of the figures shown are average *annual* rates of return (all periods ending 6/30/98).

category	3 years	5 years	10 years	15 years
high-yield bond funds	12%	10%	10%	11%
corporate bond funds	7%	6%	8%	10%
government bond funds	7%	6%	8%	9%
world bond funds	8%	6%	7%	11%
balanced funds	17%	13%	13%	13%

Metals and Natural Resources. Metals funds invest in precious metals and mining stocks from around the world. The majority of these stocks are located in North America; South Africa and Australia are the only other major players. Most of these companies specialize in gold mining. Some funds own gold and silver bullion outright. Direct ownership of the metal is considered to be a more conservative posture than owning stocks of mining companies; these stocks are more volatile than the metal itself.

Metals funds, also known as gold funds, are the most speculative group represented in this book. They are considered to be a sector or specialty fund, in that they are only able to invest in a single industry or country. Metals funds enjoy international diversification but are still narrowly focused; the limitations of the fund are what make it so unpredictable. Usually, fund management can invest in only three things: mining stocks, direct metal ownership (bullion or coins), and cash equivalents.

Despite their volatile nature, gold funds are included in the book because they can actually reduce portfolio risk. Why? Because gold and other investments often move in opposite directions. For example, when government bonds are moving down in value, gold funds often increase in value. What could otherwise be viewed as a wild investment becomes somewhat tame when included as part of a diversified portfolio.

The typical dividend for metal funds is 0.6 percent. The typical price-earnings (p/e) ratio for stocks in this category is 32, about 20 percent more than the p/e ratio for the S&P 500.

This group of funds has an average beta of 0.6, meaning that its stock market-related risk is modest—but do not let this fool you. We are only talking about *stock market risk*. Beta focuses on that portion of risk that investors cannot reduce by further diversification in U.S. stocks. Metals funds, as shown by their wild track record, are anything but conservative. A 0.6 beta indicates that movement in this category has a fair amount to do with the direction of the S&P 500, and therefore risk can be reduced by further diversification. The standard deviation for metals funds is 23 percent, higher than any other mutual fund category in this book.

Another category, natural resources, has been combined with metals funds for this book. As the name implies, natural resources funds are commodity-driven, just as metals funds are heavily influenced by two commodities, gold and silver. In the case of natural resources funds, the prices of oil, gas, and timber are the driving force. Natural resources funds invest in companies that are involved with the discovery, exploration, development, refinement, storage, and transportation of one or more of these three natural resources. The standard deviation for this group is 17 percent, beta is 0.7, and the p/e ratio is 26. The top ten holdings for metals and natural resources funds are: Newmont Mining, ALCOA, Schlumberger, United Meridian, Noble Drilling, Placer Dome, Getchell Gold, Barrick Gold, Euro-Nevada Mining, Placer Dome.

Historical returns over the past three, five, ten, and fifteen years for metals funds are shown below. All of the figures shown are average *annual* rates of return (all periods ending 6/30/98).

category	3 years	5 years	10 years	15 years
metals funds	−18%	−11%	−5%	−4%
aggressive growth funds	19%	16%	15%	11%
natural resources funds	10%	8%	8%	10%
emerging markets funds	−5%	0%	4%	4%
CPI (rate of inflation)	2%	2%	3%	3%

Money Market. These funds invest in short-term money market instruments such as bank CDs, T-bills, and commercial paper. By maintaining a short average maturity and investing in high-quality instruments, money market funds are able to maintain a stable $1 net asset value. Since money market funds offer higher yields than a bank's insured money market deposit accounts, they are a very attractive haven for savings or temporary investment dollars. Like bond funds, money market funds come in both taxable and tax-free versions. Reflecting their tax-free status, municipal money market funds pay lower *before-tax* yields than taxable money market funds but can offer higher returns on an *after-tax* basis.

Since the price per share of taxable money market funds always stays at $1, interest is shown by the accumulation of additional shares. (For example, at the beginning of the year, you may have 1,000 shares and, by the end of the year, 1,050. The 50-share increase, or $50, represents interest.) There are no such things as capital gains or unrecognized gains in a money market fund. The entire return, or yield, is fully taxable (except in the case of a tax-free money market fund, where your gain or return would always be exempt from federal taxes and possibly state income taxes as well).

These funds are designed as a place to park your money for a relatively short period of time, in anticipation of a major purchase such as a car or house, or until conditions appear more favorable for stocks, bonds, and/or real estate. There has only been one, now defunct, money market fund that has ever lost money for its investors (most of whom were bankers).

There are approximately 900 taxable money market funds and 450 tax-exempt money funds. By far the largest money market fund is the Merrill Lynch CMA Money Fund ($41 billion). As of 6/30/98, the ten largest money market funds controlled close to $200 billion and had an average maturity of 64 days. The five highest-yielding taxable money market funds as of the middle of 1997 were: Strong Heritage Money Fund (5.7% over the past 12 months), OLDE Premium Plus MM Series (5.6%), Strategist Money Market Fund (5.6%), E Fund (5.4%), and Kiewit Mutual Fund/MMP (5.4%).

The standard deviation for money market funds is lower than any other category of mutual funds. Historical returns over the past three, five, ten, and fifteen years for taxable and tax-free money market funds are shown below. All of the figures shown are average *annual* rates of return (all periods ending 6/30/98).

category	3 years	5 years	10 years	15 years
money market funds	5%	4%	6%	6%
tax-free money market funds	3%	3%	4%	4%
municipal bond funds	7%	6%	8%	8%
government bond funds	7%	6%	8%	9%
CPI (rate of inflation)	2%	2%	3%	3%

Municipal Bonds. Also known as tax-free, these funds are made up of tax-free debt instruments issued by states, counties, districts, or political subdivisions. Interest from municipal bonds is normally exempt from federal income tax. In almost all states, interest is also exempt from state and local income taxes if the portfolio is made up of issues from the investor's state of residence, a U.S territory (Puerto Rico, the U.S. Virgin Islands, etc.), or the District of Columbia.

The top ten holdings of municipal bond funds are: NY NYC GO, NJ Turnpike, MA Water Resource, DC GO, MA State, GA State, TX Muni Power, MI Detroit Resource Rec, AK North Slope, CA San Joaquin Hills Transportation.

Until the early 1980s, municipal bonds were almost as sensitive to interest rate changes as corporate and government bonds. During the last several years, however, tax-free bonds have taken on a new personality. Now when interest rates change, municipal bonds exhibit only one-half to one-third the price change that occurs with similar funds comprised of corporate or government issues. This decreased volatility is due to a smaller supply of municipal bonds and the elimination of almost all tax shelters, which has increased the popularity of tax-free bonds.

Three kinds of events may result in tax liability for every mutual fund except money market funds. The first two events described below cannot be controlled by the investor. The final event is determined solely by you, the shareholder (investor).

First, when bonds or stocks are sold in the fund portfolio for a profit (or loss), a capital gain (or capital loss) occurs. These gains and losses are passed down to the shareholder. Tax-free bond funds are not immune from capital gains taxes (or capital losses).

Second, interest and/or dividends paid by the securities within the fund are also passed on to shareholders (investors). As already mentioned, interest from municipal bonds is free from federal income taxes and, depending on the fund, may also be exempt from state income taxes. Municipal bond funds do not own stocks or convertibles, so they never throw off dividends.

Third, a taxable event may occur when you sell or exchange shares of a fund for cash or to go into another fund. As an example, suppose you bought into the fund at X dollars and cents per share. If shares are sold (or exchanged) by you for X plus Y, then there will a taxable gain (on Y, in this example). If shares are sold or exchanged for a loss (X minus Y), then there will be a capital loss. Municipal bond funds are subject to such capital gains or losses. Fortunately, you are never required to sell off shares in any mutual fund; the decision as to when and how much is always yours.

The standard deviation for municipal bond funds is 5 percent, meaning that this category's volatility is a little greater than that of high-yield bonds and government securities. Historical returns over the past three, five, ten, and fifteen years for municipal funds are shown below. All of the figures shown are average *annual* rates of return (all periods ending 6/30/98).

category	3 years	5 years	10 years	15 years
municipal bond funds	7%	6%	8%	8%
CA municipal bond funds	7%	6%	8%	9%
NY municipal bond funds	7%	6%	7%	8%
government bond funds	7%	6%	8%	9%
T-bills (90-day maturity)	5%	5%	6%	6%

Utilities. These funds invest in common stocks of utility companies. A small percentage of the funds' assets are invested in bonds. Investors opposed to or in favor of nuclear power can seek out funds that avoid or buy into such utility companies by reviewing a fund's semiannual report or by telephoning the fund, using its toll-free phone number.

If you like the usual stability of a bond fund but want more appreciation potential, then utility funds are for you. Since these funds are interest-rate sensitive, their performance somewhat parallels that of bonds but is also influenced by the stock market. The large dividend stream provided by utility funds makes them less risky than other categories of stock funds. Recession-resistant demand for electricity, gas, and other utilities translates into a comparatively steady stream of returns.

Since a healthy portion of the total return for utility funds (dividends) cannot be controlled by the investor, these funds are best suited for retirement plans or as part of some other tax-sheltered vehicle. But even if you do not have a qualified retirement plan such as an IRA, pension plan, or TSA, utility funds can be a wise choice to lower overall portfolio volatility.

The standard deviation for utility funds is 12 percent, a figure that is about 15 percent lower than that of growth and income funds. Utility funds have a beta of 0.6. The top ten holdings for this category are: GTE, CINergy, BellSouth, Texas Utilities, Southern, SBC Communications, Pinnacle West Capital, MCI, Ameritech, and FPL Group.

Historical returns over the past three, five, ten, and fifteen years for utilities funds are shown below. All of the figures shown are average *annual* rates of return (all periods ending 6/30/98).

category	3 years	5 years	10 years	15 years
utility funds	19%	12%	13%	14%
convertible funds	16%	13%	12%	11%
multi-asset global funds	12%	8%	7%	9%
asset allocation funds	16%	13%	12%	11%
growth & income funds	25%	19%	15%	14%

World Bonds. Although the United States leads the world in outstanding debt, other countries and foreign corporations also issue IOUs as a way of financing projects and operations. As high as our debt seems, it is not out of line when compared to our GNP (now called GDP—gross domestic product). The ratio of our debt to GDP is lower than any other member of the group of seven. (The other G-7 members are: Germany, Japan, Canada, Italy, the United Kingdom, and France.)

International, also known as foreign, bond funds invest in fixed-income securities outside of the United States. Global, or world, bond funds invest around the world, including the United States. Foreign bond funds normally offer higher yields than their U.S. counterparts but also provide additional risk. Global bonds, on the other hand, provide less risk than a pure U.S. bond portfolio and also enjoy greater rates of return.

Global diversification reduces risk because the major economies around the world do not move up and down at the same time. As we climb out of a recession, Japan may be just entering one, and Germany may still be in the middle of one. When Italy is trying to stimulate its economy by lowering interest rates, Canada may be raising its rates in order to curtail inflation. By investing in different world bond markets, you ensure that you will not be at the mercy of any one country's political environment or fiscal policy.

The top ten holdings of world (global) bond funds are: Republic of Argentina FRN, Republic of Germany, U.S. Treasury Notes, U.K. Treasury, Government of New Zealand, Republic of Brazil FRN, Republic of Italy, Government of Canada, Kingdom of Denmark, and Republic of Venezuela FRN.

The weighted maturity date of the bonds within this group is nine years, about one year longer than U.S. government bond funds. Global bond funds have an average coupon rate of 8 percent. As with any investment that throws off a high current income, global and foreign bond funds should be part of a qualified retirement plan or variable annuity whenever possible.

The standard deviation for world bond funds is 6 percent, a low figure but one that is still about twice as great as the typical U.S. government bond fund. Historical returns over the past three, five, ten, and fifteen years for world bond funds are shown below. All of the figures shown are average *annual* rates of return (all periods ending 6/30/98).

category	3 years	5 years	10 years	15 years
world bond funds	8%	6%	7%	11%
government bond funds	7%	6%	8%	9%
corporate bond funds	7%	6%	8%	10%
high-yield bond funds	12%	10%	10%	11%
global stock funds	17%	15%	12%	13%

All Categories. An inescapable conclusion drawn from these different tables is that patience usually pays off. The single-digit performers over the past fifteen years have been emerging markets, government bonds, metals (the only negative category), money market funds, multi-asset global, municipal bond. What the tables do not take into account, moreover, are the tax advantages of certain investments. Government bonds are exempt from state and local income taxes. (Note: this is only true with direct obligations of the United States, it does not apply to GNMAs, FNMAs, or other government-agency issues.) Municipal bonds are exempt from federal income taxes and, depending upon the type of tax-free fund as well as your state of residency, may also be exempt from any state or local taxes.

Money market funds should never be considered an investment. Money market funds, T-bills, and bank CDs should be viewed as places to park your money temporarily. Such accounts are best used to earn interest before you make a major purchase, while you are becoming educated about investing in general, or until market conditions change.

Average Annual Returns for the 15-Year Period Ending 6/30/98

category	15 years	category	15 years
aggressive growth	11%	growth & income	14%
asset allocation	11%	high-yield	11%
balanced	13%	metals (only)	−4%
convertible bond	11%	money market	6%
corporate bond	10%	multi-asset global	9%
emerging markets	4%	municipal bond	8%
equity-income	15%	natural resources	10%
European (stock)	n/a	Pacific (stock)	10%
foreign	14%	small company	12%
global equity	13%	utilities	14%
government bond	9%	world bond	11%
growth	14%	average for all categories	10%

A common theme throughout this book is that, given time, equity (the different stock categories) always outperforms debt (the different bond categories). This does not mean that all of your money should be in the equity categories. Not everyone has the same level of patience or time horizon. It does mean that the great majority of investors need to review their portfolios and perhaps begin to emphasize domestic and foreign stocks more.

VI.
Which Funds Are Best for You?

When asked what they are looking for, investors typically say "I want the best." This could mean that they are looking for the most safety and greatest current income or the highest total return. There is no single "best" fund. The top-performing fund may have incredible volatility, causing shareholders to redeem their shares at the first sign of trouble. The "safest" fund may be devastated by risks not previously thought of: inflation and taxes.

As you have already seen, there are several different categories of mutual funds, ranging from tax-free money market accounts to precious metals. During one period or another, each of these categories has dominated some periodical's "ten best funds" list. These impressive scores may only last a quarter, six months, or a year. The fact is that no one knows what will be the *next* best-performing category or individual fund.

For some fund groups, such as international stocks, growth, growth and income, and aggressive growth, the reign at the top may last for several years. For other categories, such as money market, government bond, and precious metals, the glory may last a year or even less. Trying to outguess, chart, or follow a financial guru in order to determine the next trend is a fool's paradise. The notion that anyone has special insights into the marketplace is sheer nonsense. Countless neutral and lengthy studies attest to this fact. If this is the case, what should we do?

Step 1: Categories That Have Historically Done Well
First we should look at those generic categories of investments that have historically done well over long periods of time. A time frame of at least fifteen or twenty years is recommended. True, your investment horizon may be a fraction of this, but keep in mind two points. First, fifteen or twenty years includes good as well as bad times. Second, bad results cannot be hidden when you are studying the long term. Even the investor looking at a one- or two-year holding period should ask, "Do I want something that does phenomenally well one out of every five years, or do I want something that has a very good return in eight or nine out of every ten years?" Unless you are a gambler, the answer is obvious.

All investments can be categorized as either debt or equity instruments. Debt instruments in this book include corporate bonds, government bonds, high-yield bonds, international bonds, money market accounts, and municipal bonds. Equity instruments include growth, growth and income, international stocks, metals, and utility funds. Four other categories are hybrid instruments: asset allocation, balanced, convertible, and multi-asset global funds. In this book, these four categories are combined under the heading "balanced."

Throughout history, *equity has outperformed debt*. The longer the time frame reviewed, the better equity vehicles look. Over the past half century, the worst fifteen-year holding period performance for stocks (+4.3% a year) was very similar to the average fifteen-year holding period performance for long-term government bonds (+4.9% a year). For twenty-year holding periods, the worst period for common stocks has been more than 40 percent better than the average for long-term government bonds. Indeed, stocks have outperformed bonds in every decade. Look at it this way: would you rather have loaned Henry Ford or Bill Gates the money to start their companies, or would you rather have given them money in return for a piece of the action?

Step 2: Review Your Objectives

Decide what you are trying to do with your portfolio. Everyone wants one of the following: growth, current income, or a combination of growth and income. Don't assume that if you are looking for current income your money should go into a bond or money market fund. There is a way to set up an equity fund so that it will give you a high monthly income. This is known as a "systematic withdrawal program" and is discussed in Appendix D. The growth-oriented investor, on the other hand, should consider certain categories of debt instruments or hybrid securities to help add more stability to a portfolio.

Objectives are certainly important, but so is the element of time. The shorter the time frame and the greater the need for assurances, the greater the likelihood that debt instruments should be used. A growth investor who is looking at a single-year time frame and wants a degree of safety is probably better off in a series of bond and/or money market accounts. On the other hand, the longer the commitment, the better equities look. Thus, even a cautious investor who has a life expectancy (or whose spouse has a life expectancy) of ten years or more should seriously consider having at least a moderate portion of his or her portfolio in equities.

A retired couple in their sixties should realize that one or both of them will probably live at least fifteen more years. Since this is the case, and since we know that equities have almost always outperformed bonds when looking at a horizon of ten years or more, their emphasis should be in this area.

The conservative investor may say that stocks are too risky. True, the day-to-day or year-to-year volatility of equities can be quite disturbing. However, it is also true that the medium- and long-term effects of inflation and the resulting diminished purchasing power of a fixed-income investment are even more devastating. At least with an equity there is a better than 50–50 chance that it will go up in value. In the case of inflation, what do you think are the chances that the cost of goods and services will go *down* during the next one, three, five, or ten years? The answer is "not likely."

Step 3: Ascertain Your Risk Level

No investment is worthwhile if you stay awake at night worrying about it. If you do not already know or are uncertain about your risk level, contact your financial advisor. These professionals usually have some kind of questionnaire that you can answer. Your responses will give a good indication of which investments are proper for you and which should be avoided. If you do not deal with a financial advisor, try the test below. Your score, and what it means, are shown at the end of the questionnaire.

Test for Determining Your Risk Level

1. "I invest for the long term, five to ten years or more. The final result is more important than daily, monthly, or annual fluctuations in value."

(10) Totally disagree. (20) Willing to accept some volatility, but not loss of principal. (30) Could accept a moderate amount of yearly fluctuation in return for a good *total* return. (40) Would accept an *occasional* negative year if the final results were good. (50) Agree.

2. Rank the importance of current income.

(10) Crucial, the exact amount must be known. (20) Important, but I am willing to have the amount vary each period. (30) Fairly important, but other aspects of investing are also of concern. (40) Only a modest amount of income is needed. (50) Current income is unimportant.

3. Rank the amount of loss you could tolerate in a single *quarter*.

(10) None. (20) A little, but over a year's time the total value of the investment should not decline. (30) Consistency of total return is more important than trying to get big gains. (40) One or two quarters of negative returns are the price you must pay when looking at the total picture. (50) Unimportant.

4. Rank the importance of beating inflation.

(10) Factors such as preservation of principal and current income are much more important. (20) I am willing to have a slight variance in my returns, *on a quarterly basis only*, in order to have at least a partial hedge against inflation. (30) Could accept some annual volatility in order to offset inflation. (40) I consider inflation to be important, but have mixed feelings about how much volatility I could accept from one year to the next. (50) The long-term effects of inflation are devastating and should not be ignored by anyone.

5. Rank the importance of beating the stock market over any given two-to-three-year period.

(10) Irrelevant. (20) A small concern. (30) Fairly important. (40) Very important. (50) Absolutely crucial.

Add up your score from questions 1 through 5. Your risk, as defined by your total point score, is as follows: 0–50 points = extremely conservative; 50–100 points = somewhat conservative; 100–150 points = moderate; 150–200 points = somewhat aggressive; 200–250 points = very aggressive.

Step 4: Review Your Current Holdings

Everyone has heard the expression, "Don't put all your eggs in one basket." This advice also applies to investing. No matter how much we like investment X, if a third of our net worth is already in X, we probably should not add any more to this investment. After all, there is more than one good investment.

Since no single investment category is the top performer every year, it makes sense to diversify into several *fundamentally* good categories. By using *proper* diversification, we have an excellent chance of being number one with a portion of our portfolio every year. Babe Ruth may have hit more home runs than almost anyone, but he also struck out more. As investors, we should be content with consistently hitting doubles and triples.

Trying to hit a homer every time may result in financial ruin. Never lose track of the fact that losses always have a greater impact than gains. An investment that goes up 50 percent the first year and falls 50 percent the next year still has a net loss of 25 percent. This philosophy is emphasized throughout the book.

Step 5: Implementation

There is no such thing as the perfect time to invest. No matter how strongly you or some "expert" individual or publication believes that the market is going to go up or down, no one actually knows.

Once you have properly educated yourself, *now* is the right time to invest. If you are afraid to make the big plunge, consider some form of dollar-cost averaging (see Appendix C). This is a disciplined approach to investing; it also reduces your risk exposure significantly.

Reading investment books and attending classes are encouraged, but some people may be tempted to remain on the sidelines indefinitely. For such people, there is no perfect time to invest. If the stock market drops two hundred points, they are waiting for the next hundred-point drop. If stocks or bonds are up 15 percent, they say things are peaking and they will invest as soon as it drops by 10 percent. If the stock or bond market does drop by that magical figure, these same investors are now certain that it will drop another 10 percent.

The "strategy" described above is frustrating. More important, it is wrong. One can look back in history and find lots of reasons not to have invested. But the fact is that all of the investments in this book have gone up almost every year. The "wait and see" approach is a poor one; the same reasons for not investing will still exist in the present and throughout the future.

Remember, your money is doing something right now. It is invested somewhere. If it is under the mattress, it is being eaten away by inflation. If it is in a "risk-free" investment, such as an insured savings account, bank CD, or U.S. Treasury bill, it is being subjected to taxation and the cumulative effects of reduced purchasing power. Do not think you can hide by having your money in some safe haven. Once you understand that there can be things worse than market swings, you will become an educated investor who knows there is no such thing as a truly risk-free place or investment.

If you are still not convinced, consider the story of Louie the loser. There is only one thing you can say about Louie's timing: It is *always* awful. So it is no surprise that when he decided to invest $5,000 a year in New Perspective, a fund featured in this book, he managed to pick the *worst* possible times. *Every year* for the past twenty years (1977–1996), he has invested on the very day that the stock market *peaked*. How has he done? He has over $523,000, which means his money has grown at an average rate of 14.7 percent a year (a cumulative investment of $100,000; twenty years times $5,000 invested each year).

If, perchance, Louie had managed to pick the best day each year for the last twenty years (ending 12/31/96) to make his investments, the day the market bottomed each year, his account would have been worth $636,000 (16.1 percent a year) by the beginning of 1997. Yet even by picking the *worst* possible days, Louie still came out way ahead of the $218,000 he would have had if he had put his money in U.S. Treasury bills each year. Even though his timing was terrible, he still fared much better than if he had done what many people are doing today: waiting for the "perfect" time to invest.

After asking you a series of questions, your investment advisor can give you a framework within which to operate. Investors who do not have a good advisor may wish to look at the different sample portfolios below. These general recommendations will provide you with a sense of direction.

The Conservative Investor
   15 percent balanced
   10 percent utilities
   15 percent growth & income
   10 percent world bond
   10 percent international equities
   10 percent money market or short-term bonds
   30 percent intermediate-term municipal or government bonds
      (depending upon your tax bracket)

This portfolio would give you a weighting of 43 percent in equities (stocks) and 57 percent in debt instruments (bonds and cash equivalents). Investors who are not in a high federal income tax bracket may wish to avoid municipal bonds completely and use government bonds instead.

If your tax bracket is such that you are not sure whether you should own tax-free or taxable bonds (if, that is, the after-tax return on government bonds is similar to what a similarly maturing, high-quality municipal bond pays), lean toward a municipal bond fund—they are almost always less volatile than a government bond fund that has the same or a similar average maturity.

The Moderate Investor
>   10 percent small-company growth
>   5 percent balanced/convertibles
>   15 percent growth
>   15 percent growth & income
>   15 percent high yield
>   10 percent world bond
>   25 percent global equities
>   5 percent natural resources

This portfolio would give you a weighting of 75 percent in equities (common stocks) and 25 percent in debt instruments. The figures are a little misleading since high-yield bonds are more of a hybrid investment—part stock and part bond. The price, or value, of high-yield bonds is influenced by economic (macro and micro) news as well as interest rate changes. Whereas government, municipal, and high-quality corporate bonds often react favorably to bad economic news such as a recession, increases in the jobless rate, a slowdown in housing starts, and so on, high-yield bonds have a tendency to view such news positively. Thus, taking into account that high-yield bonds are about halfway between traditional bonds and stocks, the weighting distribution is more in the range of 82.5 percent equities and 17.5 percent bonds.

The Aggressive Investor
>   20 percent aggressive growth
>   20 percent small-company growth
>   10 percent growth
>   5 percent growth & income
>   20 percent international equities
>   15 percent emerging markets
>   10 percent natural resources

This portfolio would give you a weighting of 100 percent in equities. Bond fund categories, with the possible exception of high-yield and international, are not recommended for the aggressive investor because they usually do not have enough appreciation potential.

Readers of the previous editions of this book may notice that this edition weighs equities (the different stock categories) more heavily than it has in the past. This is because bonds cannot experience the appreciation or total return for the balance of the 1990s that they saw in the 1980s and very early 1990s. For the most part, bonds increase in value because of falling interest rates. In 1981, the prime interest rate briefly peaked at 21.5 percent; for more than a dozen years this benchmark figure dropped. During the balance of the 1990s, it would be literally impossible for prime to drop 13 points (it cannot drop below zero).

Stocks, on the other hand, could end up doing worse than bonds, the same, or better. At least conceptually, however, equities have the possibility of exceeding their performance over the past ten years. The 1980s and early 1990s (whatever ten-year period you wish to use during this time horizon) were not the best ten years in a row for stocks. It is certainly possible that the next ten years, or the ten years beginning in 1998 or 1999, will be the best. When you look at the state of the world, the conditions certainly seem more favorable now for tremendous economic and stock market growth for the next several decades.

Step 6: Review

After implementation, it is important that you keep track of how you are doing. One of the beauties of mutual funds is that, if you choose a fund with good management, managers will do their job and you can spend your time on something else. Nevertheless, review your situation at least quarterly. Once you feel comfortable with your portfolio, only semiannual or annual reviews are recommended.

Daily or weekly tracking is pointless. If a particular investment goes up or down 5 percent, that does not mean you should rush out and buy more or sell off. That same investment may do just the opposite the following week or month. By watching your investments too closely, you will be defeating a major attribute of mutual funds: professional management. Presumably these fund managers know a lot more about their particular investments than you do. If they do not, you should either choose another fund or start your own mutual fund.

Step 7: Relax

If you do your homework by reading this book, you will be in fine shape. There are several thousand mutual funds. Some funds are just plain bad. Most mutual funds are mediocre. And, as with everything else in this world, a small portion are truly excellent. This book has taken those thousands of funds and eliminated all of the bad, mediocre, and fairly good. What are left are only excellent mutual funds.

If you would like help in designing a portfolio or picking a specific fund, telephone the Institute of Business & Finance (800/848-2029). The institute will be able to give you the names and telephone numbers of Certified Fund Specialists (CFS) in your area. To become a CFS, one must complete a rigorous, one-year educational program, pass a comprehensive exam, adhere to a professional code of ethics, and meet annual continuing education requirements.

VII.
Fund Features

Advantages of Mutual Funds

Listed below are some of the features of mutual funds—advantages not found in other kinds of investments.

Ease of Purchase. Mutual fund shares are easy to buy. For those who prefer to make investment decisions themselves, mutual funds are as close as the telephone or the mailbox. Those who would like help in choosing a fund can draw upon a wide variety of sources.

Many funds sell their shares through stockbrokers, financial planners, or insurance agents. These representatives can help you analyze your financial needs and objectives and recommend appropriate funds. For these professional services, you may be charged a sales commission, usually referred to as a "load." This charge is expressed as a percentage of the total purchase price of the fund shares. In some cases, there is no initial sales charge, or load, but there may be an annual fee and/or another charge if shares are redeemed during the first few years of ownership.

Other funds distribute their shares directly to the public. They may advertise in magazines and newspapers; most can be reached through toll-free telephone numbers. Because there are no sales agents involved, most of these funds, often called "no loads," charge a much lower fee or no sales commission at all. With these funds it is generally up to you to do your investment homework.

In order to attract new shareholders, some funds have adopted 12b-1 plans (named after a federal government rule). These plans enable the fund to pay its own distribution costs. Distribution costs are those costs associated with marketing the fund, either through sales agents or through advertising. The 12b-1 fee is charged against fund assets and is paid indirectly by existing shareholders. Annual distribution fees of this type usually range between 0.1 percent and 1.25 percent of the value of the account.

Fees charged by a fund are described in the prospectus. In addition, a fee table listing all transactional fees and all annual fund expenses can be found at the front of the prospectus.

Access to Your Money (Marketability). Mutual funds, by law, must stand ready on any business day to redeem any or all of your shares at their current net asset value (NAV). Of course, the value may be greater or less than the price you originally paid, depending on the market.

To sell shares back to the fund, all you need to do is give the fund proper notification, as explained in the prospectus. Most funds will accept such notification by telephone; some funds require a written request. The fund will then send your check promptly. In most instances the fund will issue a check when it receives the notification; by law it must send you the check within seven business days. You receive the price your shares are worth *on the day* the fund gets proper notice of redemption from you. If you own a money market fund, you can also redeem shares by writing checks directly against your fund balance.

Disciplined Investment. The majority of funds allow you to set up what is known as a "check-o-matic plan." Under such a program a set amount of money is automatically deducted from your checking account each month and sent directly to the mutual fund of your choice. Your bank (or credit union) will not charge you for this service. Mutual funds also offer such programs free of charge. Automatic investment plans can be changed or terminated at any time, again at no charge.

Exchange Privileges. As the economy or your own personal circumstances change, the kinds of funds you hold may no longer be the ones you need. Many mutual funds are part of a "family of funds" and offer a feature called an exchange privilege. Within a family of funds there may be several choices, each with a different investment objective, varying from highly conservative funds to more aggressive funds that carry a higher degree of risk. An exchange privilege allows you to transfer all or part of your money from one of these funds to another. Exchange policies vary from fund to fund. The fee for an exchange is nominal, five dollars or less. For the specifics about a fund's exchange privilege, check the prospectus.

Automatic Reinvestment. You can elect to have any dividends and capital gains distributions from your mutual fund investment turned back into the fund, automatically buying new shares and expanding your current holdings. Most shareholders opt for the reinvestment privilege. There is usually no cost or fee involved.

Automatic Withdrawal. You can make arrangements with the fund to automatically send you, or anyone you designate, checks from the fund's earnings or principal. This system works well for retirees, families who want to arrange for payments to their children at college, or anyone needing monthly income checks. See Appendix D for a more detailed example as to how a systematic withdrawal plan (SWP) works.

Detailed Record Keeping. The fund will handle all the paperwork and record keeping necessary to keep track of your investment transactions. A typical statement will note such items as your most recent investment or withdrawal and any dividends or capital gains paid to you in cash or reinvested in the fund. The fund will also report to you on the tax status of your earnings. If you lose any paperwork, the fund will send you copies of current or past statements.

Retirement Plans. Financial experts have long viewed mutual funds as appropriate vehicles for retirement investing; indeed, they are quite commonly used for this purpose. For retirees over the age of seventy and a half, mutual fund companies will recompute the minimum amount that needs to be taken out each year, as dictated by the IRS. Mutual funds are ideal for Keoghs, IRAs, 401(k) plans, and other employer-sponsored retirement plans. Many funds offer prototype retirement plans and standard IRA agreements. Having your own retirement plan drafted by a law firm would cost you thousands of dollars, not to mention what you would be charged for the updates that would be needed every time the laws change. Mutual funds offer these plans and required updates for free.

Accountability. There are literally dozens of sources that track and monitor mutual funds. It is easy for you to determine a fund's track record and volatility over several different time periods. Federal regulatory bodies such as the NASD (National Association of Securities Dealers) and SEC (Securities and Exchange Commission) have strict rules concerning performance figures and what appears in advertisements, brochures, and prospectuses.

Flexibility. Investment choices are almost endless: domestic stocks, foreign debt, international equities, government obligations, money market instruments, convertible securities, short- and intermediate-term bonds, real estate, gold, and natural resources. Your only limitation is the choices offered by the fund family or families you are invested in. And because you can move part or all of your money from one mutual fund to another fund within the same family, usually for only a minimal transfer fee, your portfolio can become more aggressive, conservative, or moderate with a simple phone call.

Economies of Scale. As a shareholder (investor) in a fund, you automatically get the benefit of reduced transaction charges. Since a fund is often buying or selling thousands of shares of stock at a time, it is able to conduct its transactions at dramatically reduced costs. The fees a fund pays are far lower than what you would pay even if you were buying several hundred shares of a stock from a discount broker. The same thing is true when it comes to bonds. Funds are able to add them to their portfolio without any markup. When you buy a bond through a broker, even a discounter, there is always a markup; it is hidden in the price you pay and sell the bond for. The savings for bond investors ranges anywhere from less than 1 percent all the way up to 5 percent.

Risk Reduction: Importance of Diversification

If there is one ingredient to successful investing that is universally agreed upon, it is the benefit of diversification. This concept is also backed by a great deal of research and market experience. The benefit provided by diversification is risk reduction. Risk to investors is frequently defined as volatility of return—in other words, how much an investment's return might vary. Investors prefer returns that are relatively predictable, which is to say, less volatile. On the other hand, they want returns to be high. Diversification eliminates most of the risk without reducing potential returns.

A fund's portfolio manager(s) will normally invest the fund's pool of money in 50 to 150 different securities to spread the fund's holdings over a number of investments. This diversification is an important principle in lessening the fund's overall investment risk. Such diversification is typically beyond the financial capacity of most individual investors. The table below shows the relationship between diversification and investment risk, defined as the variability of annual returns of a stock portfolio.

number of stocks	risk ratio
1	6.6
2	3.8
4	2.4
10	1.6
50	1.1
100	1.0

Note that the variability of return, or risk, associated with holding just one stock is more than six times that of a hundred-stock portfolio. Yet the *increased* potential return found in a portfolio made up of a small number of stocks is minimal.

VIII.
Reading a Mutual Fund Prospectus

The purpose of the fund's prospectus is to provide the reader with full and complete disclosure. The prospectus covers the following key points:

- The fund's investment objective: what the managers are trying to achieve.
- The investment methods it uses in trying to achieve this objective.
- The name and address of its investment advisor and a brief description of the advisor's experience.
- The level of investment risk the fund is willing to assume in pursuit of its investment objective.
- Any investments the fund will *not* make (for example, real estate, options, or commodities).
- Tax consequences of the investment for the shareholder.
- How to purchase shares of the fund, including the cost of investing.
- How to redeem shares.
- Services provided, such as IRAs, automatic investment of dividends and capital gains distributions, check writing, withdrawal plans, and any other features.
- A condensed financial statement (in tabular form, covering the last ten years, or the period the fund has been in existence, if less than ten years) called "Per Share Income and Capital Changes." The fund's performance may be calculated from the information given in this table.
- A tabular statement of any fees charged by the fund and their effect on earnings over time.

IX.
Commonly Asked Questions

Q. Are mutual funds a new kind of investment?
No. In fact, they have roots in eighteenth-century Scotland. The first U.S. mutual fund was organized in Boston in 1924. This fund, Massachusetts Investors Trust, is still in existence today. Several mutual fund companies have been in operation for over half a century.

Q. How much money do you need to invest in a mutual fund?
Literally anywhere from a few dollars to several million. Many funds have no minimum requirements for investing. A few funds are open to large institutional accounts only. The vast majority of funds require a minimum investment of between $250 and $1,000.

Q. Do mutual funds offer a fixed rate of return?
No. Mutual funds invest in securities such as stocks, bonds, and money market accounts whose yields and values fluctuate with market conditions.

Mutual funds can make money for their shareholders in three ways. First, they pay their shareholders dividends earned from the fund's investments. Second, if a security held by a fund is sold at a profit, funds pay their shareholders capital gains distributions. And third, if the value of the securities held by the fund increases, the value of each mutual fund share also increases.

In none of these cases, however, can a return be guaranteed. In fact, it is against the law for a mutual fund to make a claim as to its future performance. Ads quoting returns are based on past performance and should not be interpreted as a fixed rate yield. Past performance should not be taken as a predictor of future earnings.

Q. What are the risks of mutual fund investing?
Mutual funds are investments in financial securities with fluctuating values. The value of the securities in a fund's portfolio, for example, will rise and fall according to general economic conditions and the fortunes of the particular companies that issue those securities. Even the most conservative assets, such as U.S. government obligations, will fluctuate in value as interest rates change. These are risks that investors should be aware of when purchasing mutual fund shares.

Q. How can I evaluate a fund's long-term performance?
You can calculate a fund's performance by referring to the section in the prospectus headed "Per Share Income and Capital Changes." This section will give

you the figures needed to compute the annual rates of return earned by the fund each year for the past ten years (or for the life of the fund if less than ten years). There are also several periodicals that track the performance of funds on a regular basis. You can also telephone the fund, and they will give you performance figures.

Q. What's the difference between *yield* and *total return*?

Yield is the income per share paid to a shareholder from the dividends and interest over a specified period of time. Yield is expressed as a percent of the current offering price per share.

Total return is a measure of the per-share change in total value from the beginning to the end of a specified period, usually a year, including distributions paid to shareholders. This measure includes income received from dividends and interest, capital gains distributions, and any unrealized capital gains or losses. Total return looks at the whole picture: appreciation (or loss) of principal plus any dividends or income. Total return provides the best measure of overall fund performance; *do not be misled by an enticing yield.*

Q. How much does it cost to invest in a mutual fund?

A mutual fund normally contracts with its management company to provide for most of the needs of a normal business. The management company is paid a fee for these services, which usually include managing the fund's investments.

In addition, the fund may pay directly for some of its costs, such as printing, mailing, accounting, and legal services. Typically, these two annual charges average 1.5 percent. In such a fund you would be paying $10 to $15 a year on every $1,000 invested.

Some fund directors have adopted plans (with the approval of the fund's shareholders) that allow them to pay certain distribution costs (the costs of advertising, for example) directly from fund assets. These costs may range from 0.1 percent to 1.25 percent annually.

There may also be other charges involved—for example, in exchanging shares. Some funds may charge a redemption fee when a shareholder redeems his or her shares, usually within five years of purchasing them. All costs and charges assessed by the fund organization are disclosed in its prospectus.

Q. Is the management fee part of the sales charge?

No, the management fee paid by the fund to its investment advisor is for services rendered in managing the fund's portfolio. An average fee ranges from 0.5 percent to 1 percent of the fund's total assets each year. As described above, the management fee and other business expenses generally total somewhere between 1 percent and 1.5 percent. These expenses are paid from the fund's assets and are reflected in the price of the fund shares. In contrast, most sales charges are deducted from your initial investment.

Q. Is my money locked up for a certain period of time in a mutual fund?

Unlike some other types of financial accounts, mutual funds are liquid investments. That means that any shares an investor owns may be redeemed freely on any day the fund is open for business. Since a mutual fund stands ready to buy back its shares at their current net asset value, you always have a buyer for your shares at current market value.

Q. How often do I get statements from a mutual fund?
Mutual funds ordinarily send immediate confirmation statements when an investor purchases or redeems (sells) shares. Statements alerting shareholders to reinvested dividends are sent out periodically. At least semiannually, investors also receive statements on the status of the fund's investments. Tax statements, referred to as "substitute 1099s," are mailed annually. Some funds automatically send out quarterly reports.

Q. I've already purchased shares of a mutual fund. How can I tell how well my investment is doing?
Figuring out how well your fund is faring is a two-step procedure. First you need to know how many shares you *now* own. The "now" is emphasized because if you have asked the fund to plow any dividends and capital gains distributions back into the fund for you, it will do so by issuing you more shares, thereby increasing the value of your investment. Once you know how many shares you own, look up the fund's net assets value (sometimes called the sell or bid price) in the financial section of a major metropolitan daily newspaper. Next, multiply the net asset value by the number of shares you own to figure out the value of your investment as of that date. Compare today's value against your beginning value.

You will need to keep the confirmation statements you receive when you first purchase shares and as you make subsequent purchases in order to compare present value to the original purchase value. You will also need these statements for tax purposes.

Q. Do investment experts recommend mutual funds for IRAs and other qualified plans?
Financial experts view many mutual funds as compatible with the long-term objectives of saving for retirement. Indeed, fund shareholders cite this reason for investing more than any other. Many kinds of funds work best when allowed to ride out the ups and downs of market cycles over long periods of time.

Funds can also offer the owner of an IRA, Keogh, pension plan, 401(k), or 403(b) flexibility. By using the exchange privilege within a family of funds, the investor can shift investments from one kind of security to another in response to changes in personal finances or the economic outlook, or as retirement approaches.

Q. Are money market funds a good investment?
No. If I were to recommend an investment to you that lost money in 17 of the last 25 calendar years (adjusted for income taxes and inflation), you would probably balk. Yet, this is the track record of CDs, money market accounts, and T-bills. Money market funds are an excellent place to park your money for the short-term—some period less than two years.

Q. Why don't more people invest in foreign (international) securities?
Ignorance. The reality is that foreign securities (stocks and bonds), when added to domestic investments, actually reduce the portfolio's level of risk. Stock and bond markets around the world rarely move up and down at the same time. This random correlation is what helps lower risk and volatility: When U.S. stocks (or bonds) are going down, securities in other parts of the world may well be moving sideways or going up.

Q. Is standard deviation the correct way to measure risk?
No. Standard deviation measures volatility (or predictability) of returns. The standard deviation for each of the mutual funds in this book is ranked under the star system next to the heading "predictability of returns." The system used in this book for measuring risk is different, punishing funds for performance that is less than that offered by T-bills, a figure commonly referred to as the "risk-free rate of return." To me this makes more sense than a system that punishes a fund for volatility by translating its high standard deviation figure as "high risk." This is what most financial writers do, whether the volatility the fund experienced was upward or downward volatility. I have yet to meet an investor who is upset that he or she did better than expected. No one minds *upward* volatility.

Q. Why not simply invest in those funds that were the best performers over the past one, three, five, or ten years?
This would be a big mistake. There is little relationship (or correlation) between the performance of one fund or fund category from one year to the next. This, by the way, is the way most investors and advisors select investments—making this one of the biggest and costliest mistakes one could make. Unfortunately, no one knows what the next best performing fund or category will be.

Q. What are you referring to when you talk about "common stocks"?
Whenever you see the words "common stocks," they refer to the Standard & Poor's 500 (S&P 500). The S&P 500 is comprised of 500 of many of the largest corporations in the United States, representing several industry groups. As of the middle of 1998, there had been 75 changes made to the S&P 500 since the beginning of 1995. The purpose of changes is to make the index more representative of the U.S. economy and the stock market. As an example, financial stocks now represent 15% of the S&P 500 capitalization, up from 8% in 1990; technology stocks represent 14%, up from 7% in 1990 (Microsoft, which was added to the index in 1994, makes up 2.3% of the index). In short, the S&P 500 is higher growth, more global, less cyclical, and more diversified than it has ever been (and therefore deserves a higher p/e ratio than in the past).

X.
How the 100 Best Funds Were Determined

With an entry field that numbers over 10,000, it is no easy task to determine the 100 best mutual funds. Magazines and newspapers report on the "best" by relying on performance figures over a specific period, usually one, three, five, or ten years. Investors often rely on these sources and invest accordingly, only to be disappointed later.

Studies from around the world bear out what investors typically experience: that there is no correlation between the performance of a stock or bond from one year to the next. The same can be said for individual money managers—and sadly, for most mutual funds.

The criteria used to determine the 100 best mutual funds are unique and far-reaching. In order for a fund to be considered for this book, it must pass several tests. First, all stock and bond funds that have had managers for less than five years were excluded; in the case of money market funds, the only remaining category, the criterion was liberalized since overhead costs have a much greater bearing on net returns than management's expertise.

This first step alone eliminated well over half the contenders. The reasoning for the cutoff is simple: a fund is often only as good as its manager. An outstanding ten-year track record may be cited in a periodical, but how relevant is this performance if the manager who oversaw the fund left a year or two ago? This criterion was liberalized in selecting money market funds because this category of funds normally requires less expertise.

Second, any fund that places in the bottom (worst) half of its *category's* risk ranking is excluded. No matter how profitable the finish line looks, the number of investors will be sparse if the fund demonstrates too much negative activity. In most cases, a little performance was gladly given up if a great deal of risk was eliminated. This reflects the book's philosophy that returns must be viewed in relation to the amount of risk that was taken. In most cases the funds described in the book possess outstanding risk management. Those few selected funds where risk control has been less than stellar have shown tremendous performance, and their risky nature has been highlighted to warn the reader.

Virtually all sources measure risk by something known as *standard deviation.* Determining an investment's standard deviation is not as difficult as you might imagine. First you calculate the asset's average annual return. Usually, the most recent three years are used, updated each quarter. Once an average annual rate of return is determined, a line is drawn on a graph, representing this return.

Next, the monthly returns are plotted on the graph. Since three years is a commonly accepted time period for such calculations, a total of thirty-six individual points are plotted—one for each month over the past three years. After all of these points are plotted, the standard deviation can be determined. Quite simply, standard deviation measures the variance of returns from the norm (the line drawn on a graph).

There is a problem in using standard deviation to determine the risk level of any investment, including a mutual fund. The shortcoming of this method is that standard deviation punishes *good* as well as bad results. An example will help expose the problem.

Suppose there were two different investments, X and Y. Investment X went up almost every month by exactly 1.5 percent but had a few months each year when it went down 1 percent. Investment Y went up only 1 percent most months, but it always went up 6 percent for each of the final months of the year. The standard deviation of Y would be substantially higher than X. It might be so high that we would avoid it because it was classified as "high risk." The fact is that we would love to own such an investment. No one ever minds *upward* volatility or surprises; it is only negative or downward volatility that is cause for alarm.

The system used for determining risk in this book is not widely used, but it is certainly a fairer and more meaningful measurement. The book's method for determining risk is to see how many months over the past three years a fund underperformed what is popularly referred to as a "risk-free vehicle," something like a bank CD or U.S. Treasury bill. The more months a fund falls below this safe return, the greater the fund will be punished in its risk ranking.

Third, the fund must have performed well for the last three and five years. A one- or two-year time horizon could be attributed to luck or nonrecurring events. A ten- or fifteen-year period would certainly be better, if not for the reality that the overwhelming majority of funds are managed by a different person today than they were even six years ago.

Finally, the fund must either possess an excellent risk-adjusted return or have had superior returns with no more than average levels of risk. It is assumed that most readers are equally concerned with risk and reward. Thus, the foundation of the text is based on which mutual funds have the best *risk-adjusted returns*.

Sadly, some funds were excluded, despite their superior performance and risk control, because they were either less than five years old, had new management, or were closed to new investors.

XI.
The 100 Best Funds

This section describes the 100 very best funds out of a universe that now numbers over 10,000. As discussed, the methodology used to narrow down the universe of funds is based on performance, risk, and management.

Every one of these 100 funds is a superlative choice. However, there must still be a means to compare and rank each of the funds within its peer group. Each one of the 100 funds is first categorized by its investment objective. The category breakdown is as follows:

category of mutual fund	number
aggressive growth	10
balanced	10
corporate bond	5
global equity	13
government bond	5
growth	14
growth & income	11
high-yield bonds	5
metals/natural resources	4
money market	6
municipal bonds	8
utilities	5
world bonds	4
total	**100 funds**

The funds were ranked based on data through June 30, 1998. They were ranked in five areas: (1) total return, (2) risk/volatility, (3) management, (4) tax minimization (*current income* in the case of bond, hybrid, and money market funds), and (5) expense control. Of these five classifications, management, risk/volatility, and total return are the most important.

The track record of a fund is only as good as its management, which is why extensive space is given to this section for each fund. The areas of concern are management tenure, background and investment philosophy.

The risk/volatility of the fund is the second biggest concern but is more often than not *the* major screening criteria used in selecting those portfolios that appear in this book. Investors like to be in things that have somewhat predictable results—securities that are not up 60 percent one year and down 25 percent the next. When a highly volatile fund is included in any edition of the book, the risk associated with such a fund is clearly highlighted, informing the prospective investor.

Total return was the third concern. When all is said and done, people like to make lots of money with an acceptable level of risk, or at least get decent returns by taking little, if any, risk. This is also known as the *risk-adjusted return*. So, although the very safest funds within each category were preferred, this safety had to be combined with impressive returns.

The fourth category, current income, was of lesser importance. Income is important to a lot of people but often gets in the way of selecting the proper investment; preservation of capital should also be considered. There is a better way to get current income than to rely on monthly dividend or interest checks. This is known as a systematic withdrawal plan (SWP). A sixty-four-year example of a SWP is shown in Appendix D. Current-income-oriented investors will truly be amazed when they see how such a system works.

In the case of equity funds, "tax minimization" (how much of the total return is not currently taxed) was substituted for the category "current income." This was done for two reasons. First, there is no reason why a fund whose objective is capital appreciation should be punished simply because it does not throw off a high dividend. Once you are familiar with the benefits of using a systematic withdrawal plan, you will no longer care whether or not a certain stock fund pays much in the form of dividends. Second, unless your money is sheltered in a qualified retirement plan (IRA, pension plan, etc.), income taxes are a real concern. Funds should be rewarded for minimizing shareholder tax liability. This is why every mutual fund (except money market funds) in the book is rated, one way or another, when it comes to personal income taxes.

Tax-conscious investors want to downplay current income as much as possible. For them, a high current income simply means paying more in taxes. For other categories, such as utilities and balanced, a healthy current income stream often translates into lower risk. And for still other categories, such as corporate bonds, government bonds, international bonds, money market, and municipal bonds, current income is, and rightfully should be, a major determinant for selection.

According to the mutual fund tracking service Morningstar, in 1997 fund investors paid more than $150 billion from their investment gains. Strategies vary for keeping the tax bill low, but one simple method is for a fund manager to buy and hold. Funds bearing the Morningstar "tax-efficent" label (21 funds by the beginning of 1998, from fund families such as Vanguard, T. Rowe Price, Charles Schwab, Stein Roe, and Eaton Vance) generally have turnover rates of less than 20% a year. Most of these funds will only buy stocks that pay small or no dividends.

To give you an idea as to how good and bad it gets when it comes to tax minimization, look at the table below. The table shows how five of the best and five of the worst tax efficient funds fared on a pre- and after-tax basis for the three-year period ending February 1998.

tax-efficient funds	pre-tax total return	tax-adjusted total return
White Oak Growth Stock	40.6%	40.4%
Montaq & Caldwell Growth	36.9%	36.7%
Baron Growth & Income	33.9%	33.6%
Muhlenkamp	33.2%	32.8%
Depositors of Boston	33.1%	32.6%

tax-inefficent funds	pre-tax total return	tax-adjusted total return
Fiduciary Mgmt. Growth	33.1%	19.4%
Mosaic Mid-Cap Growth	15.6%	5.0%
GMO U.S. Sector III	29.6%	19.8%
Dresdner RCM Growth Equity	25.4%	15.6%
Morgan Stanley Inst. Emer. Gr.	17.6%	8.1%

The final category, expenses, rates how effective management is in operating the fund. High expense ratios for a given category mean that the advisors are either too greedy or simply do not know or care about running an efficient operation. The actual expenses incurred by a fund are not directly seen by the client (although there are detailed in the fund's prospectus), but such costs are deducted from the portfolio's gross returns, which is important since such a deduction affects the fund's actual performance—its net return.

In addition to looking at the expense ratio of a fund, the turnover rate is also factored into the rating. The turnover rate shows how often the fund buys and sells its securities; the lower the turnover rate, the less trading in the portfolio. There is a real cost when such a transaction occurs. These transaction costs, also known as commissions, are borne by the fund and eat into the gross return figure. Expense ratios do not include transaction costs or the spread between the buy and the sell price of any securities being traded. Thus, expense ratios do not tell the whole story. By scrutinizing the turnover rate, the rankings take into account excessive trading. A fund's turnover rate may represent a cost to the investor that is greater than its published expense ratio.

Each fund is ranked in each one of these five categories. The rating ranges from zero to five points (stars) in each category. The points can be transcribed as follows: zero points = poor, one point = fair, two points = good, three points = very good, four points = superior, and five points = excellent.

All of the rankings for each fund are based on how such a fund fared against its peer group category in the book. Thus, even though a given rating may only be fair or even poor, it is within the context of the category and its peers that have made the book—a category that only includes the very best. There is a strong likelihood that a fund in the book that is given a low score in one category would still rate as great when compared to the entire universe of funds or even compared to other funds within the same category but not included in this book.

Do not be fooled by a low rating for any fund in any of the five areas. All 100 of these funds are true winners. Keep in mind that only one in one hundred funds can appear in the book. The purpose of the ratings is to show the best of the best.

Aggressive Growth Funds

These funds focus strictly on appreciation, with no concern about generating income. Aggressive growth funds strive for maximum capital growth, frequently using such trading strategies as leveraging, purchasing restricted securities, or buying stocks of emerging growth companies. Portfolio composition is almost exclusively U.S. stocks.

Aggressive growth funds can go up in value quite rapidly during favorable market conditions. These funds will often outperform other categories of U.S. stocks during bull markets but suffer greater percentage losses during bear markets.

Over the past fifteen years, small stocks, which are included in the aggressive growth category, have underperformed common stocks by 3.4 percent per year, as measured by the Standard & Poor's 500 Stock Index. From 1983 to 1998, small stocks averaged 14.1 percent, while common stocks averaged 17.5 percent compounded per year. A $10,000 investment in small stocks grew to $62,270 over the past fifteen years; a similar initial investment in the S&P 500 grew to $102,700.

During the past twenty years, there have been sixteen five-year periods (1978–1982, 1979–1983, etc.). The Small Stock Index, made up from the smallest 20 percent of companies listed on the NYSE, as measured by market capitalization, *outperformed* the S&P 500 in just seven of those sixteen five-year periods. During these same twenty years, there have been eleven ten-year periods (1978–1987, 1979–1988, etc.). The Small Stock Index *outperformed* the S&P 500 in just two of those eleven ten-year periods.

During the past thirty years, there have been eleven twenty-year periods (1968–1987, 1969–1988, etc.). The Small Stock Index *outperformed* the S&P 500 in every twenty-year period.

Over the past fifty years, there have been forty-six five-year periods (1948–1952, 1949–1953, etc.). The Small Stock Index outperformed the S&P 500 in nineteen of those forty-six five-year periods. Over the past fifty years, there have been forty-one ten-year periods (1948–1957, 1949–1958, etc.). The Small Stock Index outperformed the S&P 500 in twenty-six of those forty-one ten-year periods, the last such period being 1979–1988.

A dollar invested in small stocks for the past fifty years grew to $1,034 by the end of 1997 (versus $474 for $1 invested in the S&P 500). This translates into an average compound return of 14.9 percent per year for small stocks and 13.1 percent for the S&P 500. Over the past fifty years, the worst year for small stocks was 1973, when a loss of 31 percent was suffered. Two years later these same stocks posted a gain of almost 53 percent in one year. The best year so far has been 1967,

Acorn

227 W. Monroe Street, Suite 3000
Chicago, IL 60606
(800) 922-6769

total return	★★★
risk reduction	★★★
management	★★★★
tax minimization	★★
expense control	★★★★★
symbol ACRNX	17 points
up-market performance	excellent
down-market performance	poor
predictability of returns	excellent

Total Return   ★★★

Over the past five years (all periods ending 6/30/98), Acorn has taken $10,000 and turned it into $21,640 ($18,550 over three years and $50,080 over the past ten years). This translates into an average annual return of 16.7 percent over the past five years, 22.9 percent over the past three years, and 17.5 percent for the decade. Over the past five years, this fund has outperformed 65 percent of all mutual funds; within its general category it has done better than 50 percent of its peers. Aggressive growth funds have averaged 16 percent annually over these same five years.

Risk/Volatility   ★★★

Over the past five years, Acorn has been safer than 75 percent of all aggressive growth funds. Over the past decade, the fund has had two negative years, while the S&P 500 has had one (off 3 percent in 1990); the Russell 2000 fell twice (off 20 percent in 1990 and two percent in 1994). The fund has underperformed the S&P 500 six times and the Russell 2000 three times in the last ten years.

	last 5 years		last 10 years	
worst year	7%	1994	−18%	1990
best year	32%	1993	32%	1993

In the past, Acorn has done better than 99 percent of its peer group in up markets but outperformed only 10 percent of its competition in down markets. Consistency, or predictability, of returns for Acorn can be described as excellent.

Management   ★★★★

There are 255 stocks in this $3.9 billion portfolio. The average aggressive growth fund today is $340 million in size. Close to 94 percent of fund's holdings are in stocks. The stocks in this portfolio have an average price-earnings (p/e) ratio of 30 and a median market capitalization of $1.5 billion. The portfolio's equity holdings can be categorized as mid-cap and value-oriented issues.

Ralph Wanger and Charles P. McQuaid have managed this fund for the past 16 years. There are two funds besides Acorn within the Acorn Investment Trust family. Overall, the fund family's risk-adjusted performance can be described as very good.

Tax Minimization   ★★
During the past five years, a $10,000 initial investment grew to $19,320 after taxes, assuming a 39.6 percent income tax bracket (state and federal combined) and a capital gains rate of 28 percent. This means that investors in this fund were able to preserve 82 percent of their total returns. Compared to other equity funds, this fund's tax savings are considered to be fair.

Expenses   ★★★★★
Acorn's expense ratio is 0.6 percent; it has also averaged 0.6 percent annually over the past three calendar years. The average expense ratio for the 800 funds in this category is 1.5 percent. This fund's turnover rate over the past year has been 32 percent, while its peer group average has been 100 percent.

Summary
Acorn's ratings look even more impressive over longer periods of time: ranked in the top 10% over the past decade and number one for small cap stock funds for the past 15 years. Like its peers, this fund has its fair share of technology issues, but volatility is reduced by going into the service side of technology. When categorized as a "global equity fund," as it is by some sources, return rankings for the past three and five years are in the top 15% and 25%, respectively. However, the fund's real strength is its control over expenses and predictability of returns. Other funds within the small Acorn family are also recommended.

Profile
minimum initial investment $1,000	IRA accounts available . . . . yes
subsequent minimum investment . . $100	IRA minimum investment $1,000
available in all 50 states. . . . . yes	date of inception. . . . . June 1970
telephone exchanges. . . . . yes	dividend/income paid . . . . annually
number of funds in family 3	quality of annual reports . . . . excellent

Ariel Growth

307 North Michigan Avenue, Suite 500
Chicago, IL 60601
(800) 292-7435

total return	★★★★
risk reduction	★★★★★
management	★★★★★
tax minimization	★★★★
expense control	★★★★
symbol ARGFX	22 points
up-market performance	fair
down-market performance	fair
predictability of returns	very good

Total Return   ★★★★

Over the past five years (all periods ending 6/30/98), Ariel Growth has taken $10,000 and turned it into $23,260 ($20,160 over three years and $36,170 over the past ten years). This translates into an average annual return of 18.4 percent over the past five years, 26.3 percent over the past three years, and 13.7 percent for the decade. Over the past five years, this fund has outperformed 70 percent of all mutual funds; within its general category it has done better than 55 percent of its peers. Aggressive growth funds have averaged 16 percent annually over these same five years.

Risk/Volatility   ★★★★★

Over the past five years, Ariel Growth has been safer than 35 percent of all aggressive growth funds. Over the past decade, the fund has had two negative years, while the S&P 500 has had one (off 3 percent in 1990); the Russell 2000 fell twice (off 20 percent in 1990 and 2 percent in 1994). The fund has underperformed the S&P 500 five times and the Russell 2000 four times in the last ten years.

	last 5 years		last 10 years	
worst year	−4%	1994	−16%	1990
best year	36%	1997	36%	1997

In the past, Ariel Growth has done better than 30 percent of its peer group in up markets and outperformed 40 percent of its competition in down markets. Consistency, or predictability, of returns for Ariel Growth can be described as very good.

Management   ★★★★★

There are 35 stocks in this $200 million portfolio. The average aggressive growth fund today is $340 million in size. Close to 96 percent of the fund's holdings are in stocks. The stocks in this portfolio have an average price-earnings (p/e) ratio of

27 and a median market capitalization of $1.4 billion. The portfolio's equity holdings can be categorized as mid-cap and value-oriented issues.

John W. Rogers Jr. has managed this fund for the past 12 years. There are three funds besides Growth within the Ariel Mutual Funds family. Overall, the fund family's risk-adjusted performance can be described as very good.

Tax Minimization ★★★★
During the past five years, a $10,000 initial investment grew to $23,210 after taxes, assuming a 39.6 percent income tax bracket (state and federal combined) and a capital gains rate of 28 percent. This means that investors in this fund were able to preserve 89 percent of their total returns. Compared to other equity funds, this fund's tax savings are considered to be very good.

Expenses ★★★★
Ariel Growth's expense ratio is 1.3 percent; it has also averaged 1.3 percent annually over the past three calendar years. The average expense ratio for the 800 funds in this category is 1.5 percent. This fund's turnover rate over the past year has been 20 percent, while its peer group average has been 100 percent.

Summary
Ariel Growth ranks extremely well in every single category; no other fund in its category receives an overall higher score. Management is well-heeled, making sure that shareholders are happy whether it comes to risk reduction or returns. Due to the fund's ability to minimize taxes, this small company growth portfolio is very well suited for non-qualified money as well as sheltered retirement accounts. Other funds within the small Ariel family are also recommended.

Profile

minimum initial investment $1,000	*IRA accounts available* . . . . yes
subsequent minimum investment . . . $50	*IRA minimum investment* $250
available in all 50 states. . . . . yes	*date of inception* . . . . Sept. 1986
telephone exchanges. . . . . yes	*dividend/income paid* . . . . annually
number of funds in family 4	*quality of annual reports* . . . . excellent

Babson Enterprise II

700 Kames Boulevard
Kansas City, MO 64108
(800) 422-2766

total return	★★★
risk reduction	★★
management	★★★★
tax minimization	★★★★★
expense control	★★★★
symbol BAETX	18 points
up-market performance	good
down-market performance	poor
predictability of returns	good

Total Return ★★★

Over the past five years (all periods ending 6/30/98), Babson Enterprise II has taken $10,000 and turned it into $22,360 ($19,140 over three years). This translates into an average annual return of 17.5 percent over the past five years and 24.2 percent over the past three years. Over the past five years, this fund has outperformed 60 percent of all mutual funds; within its general category it has done better than 50 percent of its peers. Aggressive growth funds have averaged 16 percent annually over these same five years.

Risk/Volatility ★★

Over the past five years, Babson Enterprise II has been safer than 40 percent of all aggressive growth funds. Over the past decade, the fund has had one negative year, while the S&P 500 has had one (off 3 percent in 1990); the Russell 2000 fell twice (off 20 percent in 1990 and 2 percent in 1994). The fund has underperformed the S&P 500 three times and the Russell 2000 three times in the last ten years.

	last 5 years		since inception	
worst year	–7%	1994	–7%	1994
best year	33%	1997	33%	1997

In the past, Enterprise II has done better than 60 percent of its peer group in up markets and outperformed just 20 percent of its competition in down markets. Consistency, or predictability, of returns for Babson Enterprise II can be described as good.

Management ★★★★

There are 50 stocks in this $95 million portfolio. The average aggressive growth fund today is $340 million in size. Close to 100 percent of the fund's holdings are in stocks. The stocks in this portfolio have an average price-earnings (p/e) ratio of

25 and a median market capitalization of $700 million. The portfolio's equity holdings can be categorized as small-cap and value-oriented issues.

Lance F. James and Peter C. Schlieman have managed this fund for the past seven years. There are 9 funds besides Enterprise II within the Babson Fund Group family. Overall, the fund family's risk-adjusted performance can be described as very good.

Tax Minimization   ★★★★★
During the past five years, a $10,000 initial investment grew to $22,290 after taxes, assuming a 39.6 percent income tax bracket (state and federal combined) and a capital gains rate of 28 percent. This means that investors in this fund were able to preserve 94 percent of their total returns. Compared to other equity funds, this fund's tax savings are considered to be excellent.

Expenses   ★★★★
Enterprise II's expense ratio is 1.3 percent; it has also averaged 1.3 percent annually over the past three calendar years. The average expense ratio for the 800 funds in this category is 1.5 percent. This fund's turnover rate over the past year has been 21 percent, while its peer group average has been 100 percent.

Summary
Babson Enterprise II favors inexpensive companies that are not widely held by insititutional money managers. Current and near-future profitability are what management focuses on. Risk and return ratings are misleadingly low since performance in the last 2–3 years has been much higher than in earlier years. Tax minimization is superb and management's ability to keep overhead expenses low also make this an attractive choice for the investor looking for a small company growth fund. Other funds within the Babson family are also recommended.

Profile
minimum initial investment $1,000	*IRA accounts available* . . . . yes
subsequent minimum investment . . $100	*IRA minimum investment* $250
available in all 50 states. . . . . yes	*date of inception* . . . . Aug. 1991
telephone exchanges. . . . . yes	*dividend/income paid* . . . . annually
number of funds in family 10	*quality of annual reports* . . . . good

Eclipse Equity

P.O. Box 2196
Peachtree City, GA 30269
(800) 872-2710

total return	★★★★
risk reduction	★★★
management	★★★★
tax minimization	★★
expense control	★★★★
symbol EEQFX	17 points
up-market performance	good
down-market performance	good
predictability of returns	good

Total Return   ★★★★

Over the past five years (all periods ending 6/30/98), Eclipse Equity has taken $10,000 and turned it into $24,330 ($21,030 over three years and $41,490 over the past ten years). This translates into an average annual return of 19.5 percent over the past five years, 28.1 percent over the past three years, and 15.3 percent for the decade. Over the past five years, this fund has outperformed 75 percent of all mutual funds; within its general category it has done better than 60 percent of its peers. Aggressive growth funds have averaged 16 percent annually over these same five years.

Risk/Volatility   ★★★

Over the past five years, Eclipse Equity has been safer than 50 percent of all aggressive growth funds. Over the past decade, the fund has had two negative years, while the S&P 500 has had one (off 3 percent in 1990); the Russell 2000 fell twice (off 20 percent in 1990 and 2 percent in 1994). The fund has underperformed both the S&P 500 and the Russell 2000 six times in the last ten years.

	last 5 years		last 10 years	
worst year	–5%	1994	–14%	1990
best year	33%	1997	33%	1997

In the past, Equity has done better than 55 percent of its peer group in up markets and outperformed 60 percent of its competition in down markets. Consistency, or predictability, of returns for Eclipse Equity can be described as good.

Management   ★★★★

There are 335 stocks in this $210 million portfolio. The average aggressive growth fund today is $340 million in size. Close to 100 percent of the fund's holdings are in stocks. The stocks in this portfolio have an average price-earnings (p/e) ratio of

20 and a median market capitalization of $435 million. The portfolio's equity holdings can be categorized as small-cap and value-oriented issues.

Wesley G. McCain and Kathy O'Connor have managed this fund for the past 10 years. There are three funds besides Equity within the Eclipse Funds family. Overall, the fund family's risk-adjusted performance can be described as very good.

Tax Minimization   ★★
During the past five years, a $10,000 initial investment grew to $24,160 after taxes, assuming a 39.6 percent income tax bracket (state and federal combined) and a capital gains rate of 28 percent. This means that investors in this fund were able to preserve 79 percent of their total returns. Compared to other equity funds, this fund's tax savings are considered to be fair.

Expenses   ★★★★
Equity's expense ratio is 1.1 percent; it has also averaged 1.1 percent annually over the past three calendar years. The average expense ratio for the 800 funds in this category is 1.5 percent. This fund's turnover rate over the past year has been 55 percent, while its peer group average has been 100 percent.

Summary
Eclipse Equity, a small cap value fund, looks for stocks of companies that have improving profits as well solid cash flows. When proprietary valuations exceed their targets, management takes a disciplined step and sells, thereby keeping shareholder risk level at acceptable levels. Total return and expense control are the two strongest areas for this fund. Other funds within the Eclipse family are also recommended.

Profile
minimum initial investment $1,000	IRA accounts available . . . . yes
subsequent minimum investment $1	IRA minimum investment $1,000
available in all 50 states. . . . . yes	date of inception . . . . Jan. 1987
telephone exchanges. . . . . yes	dividend/income paid . . . . annually
number of funds in family 4	quality of annual reports . . . . . average

FAM Value

111 North Grand Street
P.O. Box 399
Cobleskill, NY 12043
(800) 932-3271

total return	★★★
risk reduction	★★★★★
management	★★★★
tax minimization	★★★★★
expense control	★★★★
symbol FAMVX	21 points
up-market performance	excellent
down-market performance	poor
predictability of returns	very good

Total Return   ★★★

Over the past five years (all periods ending 6/30/98), FAM Value has taken $10,000 and turned it into $22,090 ($18,620 over three years and $49,610 over the past ten years). This translates into an average annual return of 17.2 percent over the past five years, 23.0 percent over the past three years, and 17.4 percent for the decade. Over the past five years, this fund has outperformed 75 percent of all mutual funds; within its general category it has done better than 65 percent of its peers. Aggressive growth funds have averaged 16 percent annually over these same five years.

Risk/Volatility   ★★★★★

Over the past five years, FAM Value has been safer than 80 percent of all aggressive growth funds. Over the past decade, the fund has had one negative year, while the S&P 500 has also had one (off 3 percent in 1990); the Russell 2000 fell twice (off 20 percent in 1990 and 2 percent in 1994). The fund has underperformed the S&P 500 five times and the Russell 2000 three times in the last ten years.

	last 5 years		last 10 years	
worst year	.2%	1993	−5%	1990
best year	39%	1997	48%	1991

In the past, FAM Value has done better than 90 percent of its peer group in up markets and outperformed only 20 percent of its competition in down markets. Consistency, or predictability, of returns for FAM Value can be described as very good.

Management   ★★★★

There are 50 stocks in this $370 million portfolio. The average aggressive growth fund today is $340 million in size. Close to 97 percent of the fund's holdings are in stocks. The stocks in this portfolio have an average price-earnings (p/e) ratio of 20 and a median market capitalization of $1 billion. The portfolio's equity holdings can be categorized as mid-cap and value-oriented issues.

Thomas O. Putnam and Diane C. Van Buren have managed this fund for the past 11 years. There is one other fund besides Value within the FAM Funds family. Overall, the fund family's risk-adjusted performance can be described as very good.

Tax Minimization   ★★★★★
During the past five years, a $10,000 initial investment grew to $22,080 after taxes, assuming a 39.6 percent income tax bracket (state and federal combined) and a capital gains rate of 28 percent. This means that investors in this fund were able to preserve 94 percent of their total returns. Compared to other equity funds, this fund's tax savings are considered to be excellent.

Expenses   ★★★★
FAM Value's expense ratio is 1.2 percent; it has also averaged 1.2 percent annually over the past three calendar years. The average expense ratio for the 800 funds in this category is 1.5 percent. This fund's turnover rate over the past year has been 9 percent, while its peer group average has been 100 percent.

Summary
Management looks for for bargains based on a company's intrinsic value, superior management, and strong strategic marketing. The fund may hold onto the winners, even when they are no longer selling at a discount. FAM Value has an overall ranking of number two within the broad category of small cap and aggressive growth funds. The fund is sometimes categorized as a growth and income portfolio. However you categorize this fund, it is highly recommended.

Profile

minimum initial investment $2,000	*IRA accounts available* . . . . yes
subsequent minimum investment . . . $50	*IRA minimum investment* $100
available in all 50 states. . . . . yes	*date of inception* . . . . Jan. 1987
telephone exchanges . . . . no	*dividend/income paid* . . . . annually
number of funds in family 2	*quality of annual reports* . . . . good

Fasciano

190 South LaSalle Street, Suite 2800
Chicago, IL 60603
(800) 848-6050

total return	★★★★★
risk reduction	★★★
management	★★★★★
tax minimization	★★★★★
expense control	★★★★
symbol FASCX	22 points
up-market performance	good
down-market performance	excellent
predictability of returns	good

Total Return   ★★★★★

Over the past five years (all periods ending 6/30/98), Fasciano has taken $10,000
and turned it into $25,360 ($19,780 over three years and $47,010 over the past ten
years). This translates into an average annual return of 20.5 percent over the past
five years, 25.5 percent over the past three years, and 16.7 percent for the decade.
Over the past five years, this fund has outperformed 85 percent of all mutual funds;
within its general category it has done better than 75 percent of its peers.
Aggressive growth funds have averaged 16 percent annually over these same five
years.

Risk/Volatility   ★★★

Over the past five years, Fasciano has been safer than 95 percent of all aggressive
growth funds. Over the past decade, the fund has had one negative year, while the
S&P 500 has had one (off 3 percent in 1990); the Russell 2000 fell twice (off 20
percent in 1990 and 2 percent in 1994). The fund has underperformed the S&P 500
four times and the Russell 2000 five times in the last ten years.

	last 5 years		last 10 years	
worst year	4%	1994	−1%	1990
best year	31%	1995	35%	1991

In the past, Fasciano has done better than 45 percent of its peer group in up
markets and outperformed 95 percent of its competition in down markets.
Consistency, or predictability, of returns for Fasciano can be described as good.

Management   ★★★★★

There are 70 stocks in this $85 million portfolio. The average aggressive growth
fund today is $340 million in size. Close to 80 percent of the fund's holdings are
in stocks. The stocks in this portfolio have an average price-earnings (p/e) ratio of

31 and a median market capitalization of $1 billion. The portfolio's equity holdings can be categorized as small-cap and a blend of growth and value stocks.

Michael F. Fasciano has managed this fund for the past 11 years. This is the only fund within the Fasciano Fund family.

Tax Minimization   ★★★★★
During the past five years, a $10,000 initial investment grew to $25,290 after taxes, assuming a 39.6 percent income tax bracket (state and federal combined) and a capital gains rate of 28 percent. This means that investors in this fund were able to preserve 95 percent of their total returns. Compared to other equity funds, this fund's tax savings are considered to be excellent.

Expenses   ★★★★
Fasciano's expense ratio is 1.4 percent; it has averaged 1.5 percent annually over the past three calendar years. The average expense ratio for the 800 funds in this category is 1.5 percent. This fund's turnover rate over the past year has been 41 percent, while its peer group average has been 100 percent.

Summary
Management is willing to pay top dollar for stocks of companies it believes in, which often times results in owning corporations whose earnings are more predictable than their industry peers (e.g., strong balance sheets, little debt and high cash flows). Total return, tax minimization and management are excellent. This small cap fund that includes both growth and value issues has an overall score that is unsurpassed for its category. Unfortunately, management does not oversee any other portfolios.

Profile
minimum initial investment $1,000	*IRA accounts available* . . . . yes
subsequent minimum investment . . $100	*IRA minimum investment* $1,000
available in all 50 states . . . . no	*date of inception* . . . . Aug. 1987
telephone exchanges . . . . no	*dividend/income paid* . . . . annually
number of funds in family 1	*quality of annual reports* . . . . good

Galaxy Small Cap Value Return A

290 Donald Lynch Boulevard
Marlboro, MA 01752
(800) 628-0414

total return	★★★★★
risk reduction	★★★
management	★★★★
tax minimization	★★
expense control	★★★★
symbol SSCEX	18 points
up-market performance	n/a
down-market performance	n/a
predictability of returns	good

Total Return　　★★★★★

Over the past five years (all periods ending 6/30/98), Galaxy Small Cap Value Return A has taken $10,000 and turned it into $24,940 ($19,380 over three years). This translates into an average annual return of 20.1 percent over the past five years and 24.7 percent over the past three years. Over the past five years, this fund has outperformed 75 percent of all mutual funds; within its general category it has done better than 65 percent of its peers. Aggressive growth funds have averaged 16 percent annually over these same five years.

Risk/Volatility　　★★★

Over the past five years, Galaxy Small Cap Value Return A has been safer than 60 percent of all aggressive growth funds. Over the past decade, the fund has had no negative years, while the S&P 500 has had one (off 3 percent in 1990); the Russell 2000 fell twice (off 20 percent in 1990 and 2 percent in 1994). The fund has underperformed the S&P 500 three times and has outperformed the Russell 2000 every year since inception.

	last 5 years		since inception	
worst year	.3%	1994	.3%	1994
best year	31%	1997	31%	1997

Consistency, or predictability, of returns for Small Cap Value can be described as good.

Management　　★★★★

There are 250 stocks in this $100 million portfolio. The average aggressive growth fund today is $340 million in size. Close to 88 percent of the fund's holdings are in stocks. The stocks in this portfolio have an average price-earnings (p/e) ratio of 24 and a median market capitalization of $383 million. The portfolio's equity holdings can be categorized as small-cap and value-oriented issues.

Peter Larson has managed this fund for the past five years. There are 33 funds besides Small Cap Value within the Galaxy Funds family. Overall, the fund family's risk-adjusted performance can be described as good.

Tax Minimization   ★★
During the past five years, a $10,000 initial investment grew to $23,790 after taxes, assuming a 39.6 percent income tax bracket (state and federal combined) and a capital gains rate of 28 percent. This means that investors in this fund were able to preserve 80 percent of their total returns. Compared to other equity funds, this fund's tax savings are considered to be fair.

Expenses   ★★★★
Small Cap Value's expense ratio is 1.3 percent; it has averaged 1.4 percent annually over the past three calendar years. The average expense ratio for the 800 funds in this category is 1.5 percent. This fund's turnover rate over the past year has been 52 percent, while its peer group average has been 100 percent.

Summary
Galaxy Small Cap Value Return A is one of the more highly-rated small cap funds. Total return figures have been superb while management and control over expenses has been quite good. Only a very small percentage of all aggressive growth or small company growth funds appear in this book.

Profile

minimum initial investment $2,500	IRA accounts available . . . . yes
subsequent minimum investment . . $100	IRA minimum investment $500
available in all 50 states. . . . . yes	date of inception . . . . Feb. 1993
telephone exchanges. . . . . yes	dividend/income paid . . . . annually
number of funds in family 34	quality of annual reports . . . . n/a

Nicholas II

700 N. Water Street, Suite 1010
Milwaukee, WI 53202
(800) 227-5987

total return	★★★★★
risk reduction	★★★★
management	★★★★★
tax minimization	★★★
expense control	★★★★★
symbol NCTWX	22 points
up-market performance	good
down-market performance	fair
predictability of returns	good

Total Return   ★★★★★

Over the past five years (all periods ending 6/30/98), Nicholas II has taken $10,000 and turned it into $25,240 ($20,900 over three years and $42,320 over the past ten years). This translates into an average annual return of 20.3 percent over the past five years, 27.9 percent over the past three years, and 15.5 percent for the decade. Over the past five years, this fund has outperformed 85 percent of all mutual funds; within its general category it has done better than 65 percent of its peers. Aggressive growth funds have averaged 16 percent annually over these same five years.

Risk/Volatility   ★★★★

Over the past five years, Nicholas II has been safer than 70 percent of all aggressive growth funds. Over the past decade, the fund has had one negative year, while the S&P 500 has had one (off 3 percent in 1990); the Russell 2000 fell twice (off 20 percent in 1990 and 2 percent in 1994). The fund has underperformed the S&P 500 six times and the Russell 2000 four times in the last ten years.

	last 5 years		last 10 years	
worst year	1%	1994	–6%	1990
best year	37%	1997	39%	1991

In the past, Nicholas II has done better than 70 percent of its peer group in up markets and outperformed 30 percent of its competition in down markets. Consistency, or predictability, of returns for Nicholas II can be described as good.

Management   ★★★★★

There are 60 stocks in this $1.2 billion portfolio. The average aggressive growth fund today is $340 million in size. Close to 99 percent of fund's holdings are in stocks. The stocks in this portfolio have an average price-earnings (p/e) ratio of 30 and a median market capitalization of $2 billion. The portfolio's equity holdings can be categorized as mid-cap and value-oriented issues.

David O. Nicholas has managed this fund for the past five years. There are four funds besides Nicholas II within the Nicholas Group. Overall, the fund family's risk-adjusted performance can be described as very good.

Tax Minimization   ★★★

During the past five years, a $10,000 initial investment grew to $24,990 after taxes, assuming a 39.6 percent income tax bracket (state and federal combined) and a capital gains rate of 28 percent. This means that investors in this fund were able to preserve 85 percent of their total returns. Compared to other equity funds, this fund's tax savings are considered to be good.

Expenses   ★★★★★

Nicholas II's expense ratio is 0.6 percent; it has also averaged 0.6 percent annually over the past three calendar years. The average expense ratio for the 800 funds in this category is 1.5 percent. This fund's turnover rate over the past year has been 30 percent, while its peer group average has been 100 percent.

Summary

Management looks for companies that have strong prospects when it comes to competitiveness and growth. This Nicholas offering is viewed as being in the "middle" of the family's other fine offerings. Nicholas II is sometimes categorized as a growth fund. It has an overall ranking that is not surpassed by any of its small cap or aggressive growth peers. This fund is highly recommended.

Profile

minimum initial investment $500	*IRA accounts available* . . . . yes
subsequent minimum investment . . $100	*IRA minimum investment* $500
available in all 50 states . . . . yes	*date of inception* . . . . Oct. 1983
telephone exchanges . . . . yes	*dividend/income paid* . . . . annually
number of funds in family 5	*quality of annual reports* . . . . good

Stratton Small-Cap Yield

610 West Germantown Pike, Suite 300
Plymouth Meeting, PA 19462-1050
(800) 634-5726

total return	★★★
risk reduction	★★★★
management	★★★★
tax minimization	★★★★★
expense control	★★★
symbol STSCX	19 points
up-market performance	n/a
down-market performance	n/a
predictability of returns	very good

Total Return   ★★★

Over the past five years (all periods ending 6/30/98), Stratton Small-Cap Yield has taken $10,000 and turned it into $21,920 ($19,440 over three years). This translates into an average annual return of 17.0 percent over the past five years and 24.8 percent over the past three years. Over the past five years, this fund has outperformed 65 percent of all mutual funds; within its general category it has done better than 50 percent of its peers. Aggressive growth funds have averaged 16 percent annually over these same five years.

Risk/Volatility   ★★★★

Over the past five years, Stratton Small-Cap Yield has been safer than 75 percent of all aggressive growth funds. Over the past decade, the fund has had one negative year, while the S&P 500 has had one (off 3 percent in 1990); the Russell 2000 fell twice (off 20 percent in 1990 and 2 percent in 1994). The fund has underperformed the S&P 500 three times and the Russell 2000 three times in the last ten years.

	last 5 years		since inception	
worst year	–3%	1994	–3%	1994
best year	42%	1997	42%	1997

Consistency, or predictability, of returns for Small-Cap Yield can be described as very good.

Management   ★★★★

There are 55 stocks in this $60 million portfolio. The average aggressive growth fund today is $340 million in size. Close to 94 percent of the fund's holdings are in stocks. The stocks in this portfolio have an average price-earnings (p/e) ratio of 17 and a median market capitalization of $420 million. The portfolio's equity holdings can be categorized as small-cap and value-oriented issues.

Frank H. Reichel III has managed this fund for the past five years. There are two funds besides Small-Cap Yield within the Stratton Group. Overall, the fund family's risk-adjusted performance can be described as good.

Tax Minimization   ★★★★★
During the past five years, a $10,000 initial investment grew to $21,840 after taxes, assuming a 39.6 percent income tax bracket (state and federal combined) and a capital gains rate of 28 percent. This means that investors in this fund were able to preserve 94 percent of their total returns. Compared to other equity funds, this fund's tax savings are considered to be excellent.

Expenses   ★★★
Small-Cap Yield's expense ratio is 1.6 percent; it has averaged 1.7 percent annually over the past three calendar years. The average expense ratio for the 800 funds in this category is 1.5 percent. This fund's turnover rate over the past year has been 26 percent, while its peer group average has been 100 percent.

Summary
When it comes to ratings and rankings, Stratton Small-Cap Yield is one of the very best. Tax minimization is exceptional; management and risk reduction are also quite good. The fund's market-related risk is about 30% less than that of the S&P 500, which is quite a feat when you consider the usual volatility of this overall category. Having a low turnover rate keeps real operating costs much lower than might be suspected.

Profile
minimum initial investment $2,000	*IRA accounts available* . . . . no
subsequent minimum investment . . $100	*IRA minimum investment* . . . . n/a
available in all 50 states. . . . . yes	*date of inception*. . . . . Apr. 1993
telephone exchanges. . . . . yes	*dividend/income paid* . . . . annually
number of funds in family 3	*quality of annual reports* . . . . n/a

T. Rowe Price Small Cap Stock

100 East Pratt Street
Baltimore, MD 21202
(800) 638-5660

total return	★★★★★
risk reduction	★★★
management	★★★★
tax minimization	★★★
expense control	★★★★
symbol OTCFX	19 points
up-market performance	good
down-market performance	fair
predictability of returns	good

Total Return ★★★★★

Over the past five years (all periods ending 6/30/98), T. Rowe Price Small Cap Stock has taken $10,000 and turned it into $24,380 ($19,030 over three years and $39,240 over the past ten years). This translates into an average annual return of 19.5 percent over the past five years, 23.9 percent over the past three years, and 14.7 percent for the decade. Over the past five years, this fund has outperformed 80 percent of all mutual funds; within its general category it has done better than 60 percent of its peers. Aggressive growth funds have averaged 16 percent annually over these same five years.

Risk/Volatility ★★★

Over the past five years, T. Rowe Price Small Cap Stock has been safer than 95 percent of all aggressive growth funds. Over the past decade, the fund has had one negative year, while the S&P 500 has had one (off 3 percent in 1990); the Russell 2000 fell twice (off 20 percent in 1990 and 2 percent in 1994). The fund has underperformed the S&P 500 six times and the Russell 2000 four times in the last ten years.

	last 5 years		last 10 years	
worst year	1%	1994	−20%	1990
best year	34%	1995	39%	1991

Consistency, or predictability, of returns for T. Rowe Price Small Cap Stock can be described as good.

Management ★★★★

There are 215 stocks in this $1.1 billion portfolio. The average aggressive growth fund today is $340 million in size. Close to 90 percent of the fund's holdings are in stocks. The stocks in this portfolio have an average price-earnings (p/e) ratio of 26 and a median market capitalization of $560 million. The portfolio's equity holdings can be categorized as small-cap and value-oriented issues.

Gregory A. McCrickard has managed this fund for the past six years. There are 65 funds besides T. Rowe Price Small Cap Stock within the Price T. Rowe Funds family. Overall, the fund family's risk-adjusted performance can be described as very good.

Tax Minimization   ★★★
During the past five years, a $10,000 initial investment grew to $24,220 after taxes, assuming a 39.6 percent income tax bracket (state and federal combined) and a capital gains rate of 28 percent. This means that investors in this fund were able to preserve 85 percent of their total returns. Compared to other equity funds, this fund's tax savings are considered to be good.

Expenses   ★★★★
Small Cap Stock's expense ratio is 1 percent; it has also averaged 1.1 percent annually over the past three calendar years. The average expense ratio for the 800 funds in this category is 1.5 percent. This fund's turnover rate over the past year has been 23 percent, while its peer group average has been 100 percent.

Summary
T. Rowe Price Small Cap Stock invests at least 80% of its assets in OTC stocks; the fund may also invest up to 10% of the portfolio in foreign equities. Management looks for companies that are in the middle of some change that is expected to make their financials look more appealing. Although considered more value oriented than growth oriented, the fund is characterized as an aggressive growth portfolio by some sources. The overall score of this fund makes it one of the best, no matter how its stock selection is characterized.

Profile

minimum initial investment $2,500	*IRA accounts available* . . . . yes
subsequent minimum investment . . $100	*IRA minimum investment* $1,000
available in all 50 states. . . . . yes	*date of inception.* . . . . June 1956
telephone exchanges. . . . . yes	*dividend/income paid* . . . . annually
number of funds in family 66	*quality of annual reports* . . . . excellent

Balanced Funds

The objective of balanced funds, also referred to as *total return funds*, is to provide both growth and income. Fund management purchases common stocks, bonds, and convertible securities. Portfolio composition is almost always exclusively U.S. securities. The weighting of stocks compared to bonds depends upon the portfolio manager's perception of the stock market, interest rates, and risk levels. It is rare for less than 30 percent of the fund's holdings to be in stocks or bonds.

Balanced funds offer neither the best nor worst of both worlds. These funds will often outperform the different categories of bond funds during bull markets but suffer greater percentage losses during stock market declines. On the other hand, when interest rates are on the rise, balanced funds will typically decline less on a total-return basis (current yield plus or minus principal appreciation) than a bond fund. When rates are falling, balanced funds will also outperform bond funds if stocks are also doing well.

Over the past ten years, the average balanced fund had 79 percent of the return of growth funds with 53 percent less risk. Balanced funds are the perfect choice for the investor who cannot decide between stocks and bonds. This hybrid security is a middle-of-the-road approach, ideal for someone who wants a fund manager to determine the portfolio's weighting of stocks, bonds, and convertibles.

The price-earnings ratio for stocks in a typical balanced fund is 27, a figure which is about 11 percent lower than the S&P 500's p/e ratio. The average beta is 0.6, which means that this group has only 60 percent of the market-related risk of the S&P 500. During the past three years, balanced funds have lagged the performance of the S&P 500 by 13 percent annually. Over the past five years, this benchmark has outperformed balanced funds by an average of 10 percent per year. The figure falls to 6 percent annually for the past decade. Standard deviation for the past three years has been 8.9 percent. Average turnover during the last three years has been 99 percent per annum. Balanced funds throw off an income stream of less than 2.5 percent annually. The typical annual expense ratio for this group is 1.4 percent.

Over 420 funds make up the balanced category; market capitalization is $190 billion. Three other categories—asset allocation (270 funds, total market capitalization of $75 billion, 8.7 percent std. deviation), multi-asset global (105 funds, total market capitalization of $50 billion, 9.0 percent std. deviation), and convertible (55 funds, total market capitalization of $9 billion, 9.1 percent std. deviation)—have been combined with balanced. Thus, for this section, there were a total of 850 possible candidates. Total market capitalization of these four categories combined is $324 billion.

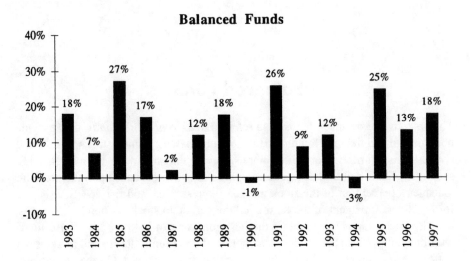

Balanced Funds

American Balanced

4 Embarcadero Center
P.O. Box 7650
San Francisco, CA 94120
(800) 421-4120

total return	★★★★
risk reduction	★★★★
management	★★★★
current income	★★
expense control	★★★★★
symbol ABALX	19 points
up-market performance	very good
down-market performance	fair
predictability of returns	very good

Total Return   ★★★★

Over the past five years (all periods ending 6/30/98), American Balanced has taken $10,000 and turned it into $19,360 ($16,260 over three years and $34,490 over the past ten years). This translates into an average annual return of 14.1 percent over the past five years, 17.6 percent over the past three years, and 13.2 percent for the decade. Over the past five years, this fund has outperformed 70 percent of all mutual funds; within its general category it has done better than 60 percent of its peers. Balanced funds have averaged 13 percent annually over these same five years.

During the past five years, a $10,000 initial investment grew to $18,210 after taxes, assuming a 39.6 percent income tax bracket (state and federal combined) and a capital gains rate of 28 percent. This means that investors in this fund were able to preserve 71 percent of their total returns. Compared to other fixed-income funds, this fund's tax savings are considered to be fair.

Risk/Volatility   ★★★★

Over the past five years, American Balanced has been safer than 90 percent of all balanced funds. Over the past decade, the fund has had one negative year, while the S&P 500 has had one (off 3 percent in 1990); the Lehman Brothers Aggregate Bond Index also fell once (off 3 percent in 1994). The fund has underperformed the S&P seven times and the Lehman Brothers Aggregate Bond Index one time in the last ten years.

	last 5 years		last 10 years	
worst year	.3%	1994	–2%	1990
best year	27%	1995	27%	1995

In the past, American Balanced has done better than 75 percent of its peer group in up markets and outperformed 30 percent of its competition in down markets. Consistency, or predictability, of returns for American Balanced can be described as very good.

Management   ★★★★

There are 130 stocks and 70 fixed-income securities in this $5.6 billion portfolio. The average balanced fund today is $365 million in size. Close to 55 percent of this fund's holdings are in stocks and 30 percent in bonds, the balance is in cash. The stocks in this portfolio have an average price-earnings (p/e) ratio of 24 and a median market capitalization of $16 billion. The average maturity of the bonds in this account is 8 years; the weighted coupon rate averages 7.4 percent. The portfolio's equity holdings can be categorized as large-cap and value-oriented issues. The portfolio's fixed-income holdings can be categorized as intermediate-term, high-quality debt.

A team has managed this fund for the past eight years. There are 24 funds besides Balanced within the American Funds Group. Overall, the fund family's risk-adjusted performance can be described as very good.

Current Income   ★★

Over the past year, American Balanced had a twelve-month yield of 3.2 percent. During this same twelve-month period, the typical balanced fund had a yield that averaged 2.5 percent.

Expenses   ★★★★★

Balanced's expense ratio is 0.7 percent; it has averaged 0.7 percent annually over the past three calendar years. The average expense ratio for the 730 funds in this category is 1.4 percent. This fund's turnover rate over the past year has been 44 percent, while its peer group average has been 105 percent.

Summary

Capital Research & Management, the portfolio managers for the American Funds Group have consistently been able to buy high-dividend-paying blue chip stocks at discounts; the holding period for the equity portion of the portfolio is quite long. The debt side of the portfolio is largely weighted with U.S. Government obligations. Over the past 20 years, the fund has had only one negative year (down less than 2% in 1990). Like numerous other offerings by this fund group, expenses are kept to a minimum. This is one company that truly has its shareholders' interests at the forefront.

Profile

minimum initial investment $500	*IRA accounts available* . . . . yes
subsequent minimum investment . . . $50	*IRA minimum investment* $250
available in all 50 states. . . . . yes	*date of inception* . . . . Jan. 1933
telephone exchanges. . . . . yes	*dividend/income paid*. . . . . monthly
number of funds in family 25	*quality of annual reports* . . . . excellent

Columbia Balanced

1301 SW Fifth Avenue
P.O. Box 1350
Portland, OR 97207-1350
(800) 547-1707

total return	★★★★
risk reduction	★★★★
management	★★★★
current income	★★★★★
expense control	★★★
symbol CBALX	20 points
up-market performance	n/a
down-market performance	n/a
predictability of returns	very good

Total Return   ★★★★

Over the past five years (all periods ending 6/30/98), Columbia Balanced has taken $10,000 and turned it into $19,470 ($16,450 over three years). This translates into an average annual return of 14.3 percent over the past five years and 18.0 percent over the past three years. Over the past five years, this fund has outperformed 70 percent of all mutual funds; within its general category it has done better than 65 percent of its peers. Balanced funds have averaged 13 percent annually over these same five years.

During the past five years, a $10,000 initial investment grew to $19,460 after taxes, assuming a 39.6 percent income tax bracket (state and federal combined) and a capital gains rate of 28 percent. This means that investors in this fund were able to preserve 86 percent of their total returns. Compared to other fixed-income funds, this fund's tax savings are considered to be excellent.

Risk/Volatility   ★★★★

Over the past five years, Columbia Balanced has been safer than 90 percent of all balanced funds. Over the past decade, the fund has had no negative years, while the S&P 500 has had one (off 3 percent in 1990); the Lehman Brothers Aggregate Bond Index also fell once (off 3 percent in 1994). The fund has underperformed the S&P 500 four times and has outperformed the Lehman Brothers Aggregate Bond Index every year for the last ten years.

	last 5 years		since inception	
worst year	.1%	1994	.1%	1994
best year	25%	1995	25%	1995

Consistency, or predictability, of returns for Columbia Balanced can be described as very good.

Management   ★★★★
There are 110 stocks and 100 fixed-income securities in this $920 million portfolio. The average balanced fund today is $365 million in size. Close to 51 percent of this fund's holdings are in stocks and 49 percent in bonds. The stocks in this portfolio have an average price-earnings (p/e) ratio of 34 and a median market capitalization of $35 billion. The average maturity of the bonds in this account is 5.4 years; the weighted coupon rate averages 7.2 percent. The portfolio's equity holdings can be categorized as large-cap and a blend of growth and value stocks. The portfolio's fixed-income holdings can be categorized as intermediate-term, high-quality debt.

A team has managed this fund for the past five years. There are 10 funds besides Balanced within the Columbia Funds family. Overall, the fund family's risk-adjusted performance can be described as very good.

Current Income   ★★★★★
Over the past year, Columbia Balanced had a twelve-month yield of 3.2 percent. During this same twelve-month period, the typical balanced fund had a yield that averaged 2.5 percent.

Expenses   ★★★
Columbia Balanced's expense ratio is 0.7 percent; it has also averaged 0.7 percent annually over the past three calendar years. The average expense ratio for the 730 funds in this category is 1.4 percent. This fund's turnover rate over the past year has been 150 percent, while its peer group average has been 105 percent.

Summary
Columbia Balanced has wide latitude in its investment strategy: up to a third of the portfolio may be in equities from developing countries, and there is no limit to the maturity of the bonds selected. Still, management favors domestic blue chip issues and high quality bonds with moderate maturities. The fund scores well in every category but does particularly well in the case of tax reduction and quality of management.

Profile
minimum initial investment $1,000	*IRA accounts available* .... yes
subsequent minimum investment .. $100	*IRA minimum investment* $1,000
available in all 50 states. .... yes	*date of inception* .... Sept. 1991
telephone exchanges. .... yes	*dividend/income paid*. .... monthly
number of funds in family 11	*quality of annual reports* .... good

Eclipse Balanced

P.O. Box 2196
Peachtree City, GA 30269
(800) 872-2710

total return	★★★★
risk reduction	★★★★
management	★★★★
current income	★★★
expense control	★★★★★
symbol EBALX	20 points
up-market performance	very good
down-market performance	very good
predictability of returns	good

Total Return   ★★★★

Over the past five years (all periods ending 6/30/98), Eclipse Balanced has taken $10,000 and turned it into $19,480 ($16,550 over three years). This translates into an average annual return of 14.3 percent over the past five years and 18.3 percent over the past three years. Over the past five years, this fund has outperformed 70 percent of all mutual funds; within its general category it has done better than 60 percent of its peers. Balanced funds have averaged 13 percent annually over these same five years.

During the past five years, a $10,000 initial investment grew to $19,440 after taxes, assuming a 39.6 percent income tax bracket (state and federal combined) and a capital gains rate of 28 percent. This means that investors in this fund were able to preserve 79 percent of their total returns. Compared to other fixed-income funds, this fund's tax savings are considered to be good.

Risk/Volatility   ★★★★

Over the past five years, Eclipse Balanced has been safer than 65 percent of all balanced funds. Over the past decade, the fund has had no negative years, while the S&P 500 has had one (off 3 percent in 1990); the Lehman Brothers Aggregate Bond Index also fell once (off 3 percent in 1994). The fund has underperformed the S&P 500 five times and the Lehman Brothers Aggregate Bond Index one time in the last ten years.

	last 5 years		since inception	
worst year	0%	1994	0%	1994
best year	23%	1997	23%	1997

In the past, Balanced has done better than 75 percent of its peer group in up markets and outperformed 85 percent of its competition in down markets. Consistency, or predictability, of returns for Eclipse Balanced can be described as good.

Management   ★★★★

There are 110 stocks and 60 fixed-income securities in this $95 million portfolio. The average balanced fund today is $365 million in size. Close to 65 percent of this fund's holdings are in stocks and 35 percent in bonds. The stocks in this portfolio have an average price-earnings (p/e) ratio of 22 and a median market capitalization of $3.7 billion. The average maturity of the bonds in this account is 7.9 years; the weighted coupon rate averages 6.9 percent. The portfolio's equity holdings can be categorized as mid-cap and value-oriented issues. The portfolio's fixed-income holdings can be categorized as intermediate-term, high-quality debt.

Joan Sabella and Wesley G. McCain have managed this fund for the past nine years. There are three funds besides Balanced within the Eclipse family. Overall, the fund family's risk-adjusted performance can be described as very good.

Current Income   ★★★

Over the past year, Eclipse Balanced had a twelve-month yield of 2.5 percent. During this same twelve-month period, the typical balanced fund also had a yield that averaged 2.5 percent.

Expenses   ★★★★★

Eclipse Balanced's expense ratio is 0.8 percent; it has also averaged 0.8 percent annually over the past three calendar years. The average expense ratio for the 730 funds in this category is 1.4 percent. This fund's turnover rate over the past year has been 47 percent, while its peer group average has been 105 percent.

Summary

Eclipse Balanced is very good when it comes to performance, safety and management; the fund's strongest suit is its ability to keep overhead to a bare minimum. This is a solid choice for any investor who wants a mix of stocks and bonds. This small fund family offers other gems besides this balanced portfolio.

Profile

minimum initial investment $1,000	*IRA accounts available* . . . . yes
subsequent minimum investment $1	*IRA minimum investment* $1,000
available in all 50 states. . . . . yes	*date of inception.* . . . . May 1989
telephone exchanges. . . . . yes	*dividend/income paid.* . . . . monthly
number of funds in family 4	*quality of annual reports* . . . . n/a

Gabelli ABC

One Corporate Center
Rye, NY 10580-1434
(800) 422-3554

total return	★
risk reduction	★★★★★
management	★★★
current income	★★★
expense control	★★★
symbol GABCX	15 points
up-market performance	n/a
down-market performance	n/a
predictability of returns	excellent

Total Return   ★

Over the past five years (all periods ending 6/30/98), Gabelli ABC has taken $10,000 and turned it into $15,930 ($13,310 over three years and $16,030). This translates into an average annual return of 9.8 percent over the past five years and 10.0 percent over the past three years. Over the past five years, this fund has outperformed 55 percent of all mutual funds; within its general category it has done better than 30 percent of its peers. Balanced funds have averaged 13 percent annually over these same five years.

During the past five years, a $10,000 initial investment grew to $15,920 after taxes, assuming a 39.6 percent income tax bracket (state and federal combined) and a capital gains rate of 28 percent. This means that investors in this fund were able to preserve 70 percent of their total returns. Compared to other fixed-income funds, this fund's tax savings are considered to be good.

Risk/Volatility   ★★★★★

Over the past five years, Gabelli ABC has been safer than 99 percent of all balanced funds. Over the past decade, the fund has had no negative years, while the S&P 500 has had one (off 3 percent in 1990); the Lehman Brothers Aggregate Bond Index also fell once (off 3 percent in 1994). The fund has underperformed the S&P three times and the Lehman Brothers Aggregate Bond Index two times in the last ten years.

	last 5 years		since inception	
worst year	5%	1994	5%	1994
best year	13%	1997	13%	1997

Consistency, or predictability, of returns for ABC can be described as excellent.

Management   ★★★

There are 76 stocks and no bonds in this $60 million portfolio. The average balanced fund today is $365 million in size. Close to 80 percent of this fund's holdings are in stocks and 20 percent in cash. The stocks in this portfolio have an average price-earnings (p/e) ratio of 24 and a median market capitalization of $685 million. The portfolio's equity holdings can be categorized as small-cap and value-oriented issues.

Mario J. Gabelli has managed this fund for the past five years. There are 10 funds besides ABC within the Gabelli family. Overall, the fund family's risk-adjusted performance can be described as very good.

Current Income   ★★★

Over the past year, Gabelli ABC had a twelve-month yield of 0.8 percent. During this same twelve-month period, the typical balanced fund had a yield that averaged 2.5 percent.

Expenses   ★★★

ABC's expense ratio is 2.3 percent; it has averaged 2.2 percent annually over the past three calendar years. The average expense ratio for the 730 funds in this category is 1.4 percent. This fund's turnover rate over the past year has been 495 percent, while its peer group average has been 105 percent.

Summary

Gabelli ABC's performance figures are offset by some amazing statistics: lowest standard deviation (meaning highest predictability of returns) and lower risk than any of its peers. The turnover rate for this portfolio is amazingly high, but tax minimization is still good. This fund is an excellent choice for the investor who is willing to trade off some returns for peace of mind.

Profile

minimum initial investment $1,000	*IRA accounts available* . . . . yes
subsequent minimum investment $1	*IRA minimum investment* $1,000
available in all 50 states. . . . . yes	*date of inception.* . . . . May 1993
telephone exchanges . . . . no	*dividend/income paid.* . . . . monthly
number of funds in family 11	*quality of annual reports* . . . . n/a

Gabelli Westwood Balanced Retail

One Corporate Center
Rye, NY 10580-1434
(800) 937-8966

total return	★★★★★
risk reduction	★★★★
management	★★★★★
current income	★★★
expense control	★★★
symbol WEBAX	20 points
up-market performance	n/a
down-market performance	n/a
predictability of returns	good

Total Return   ★★★★★

Over the past five years (all periods ending 6/30/98), Gabelli Westwood Balanced Retail has taken $10,000 and turned it into $22,750 ($17,560 over three years). This translates into an average annual return of 17.9 percent over the past five years and 20.6 percent over the past three years. Over the past five years, this fund has outperformed 75 percent of all mutual funds; within its general category it has also done better than 75 percent of its peers. Balanced funds have averaged 13 percent annually over these same five years.

During the past five years, a $10,000 initial investment grew to $22,710 after taxes, assuming a 39.6 percent income tax bracket (state and federal combined) and a capital gains rate of 28 percent. This means that investors in this fund were able to preserve 78 percent of their total returns. Compared to other fixed-income funds, this fund's tax savings are considered to be good.

Risk/Volatility   ★★★★

Over the past five years, Gabelli Westwood Balanced Retail has been safer than 80 percent of all balanced funds. Over the past decade, the fund has had no negative years, while the S&P 500 has had one (off 3 percent in 1990); the Lehman Brothers Aggregate Bond Index also fell once (off 3 percent in 1994). The fund has underperformed the S&P 500 five times and the Lehman Brothers Aggregate Bond Index one time in the last ten years.

	last 5 years		since inception	
worst year	1%	1994	1%	1994
best year	31%	1995	31%	1995

Consistency, or predictability, of returns for Westwood Balanced can be described as good.

Management   ★★★★★

There are 55 stocks and 40 fixed-income securities in this $130 million portfolio. The average balanced fund today is $365 million in size. Close to 58 percent of this fund's holdings are in stocks and 41 percent in bonds. The stocks in this portfolio have an average price-earnings (p/e) ratio of 25 and a median market capitalization of $13 billion. The average maturity of the bonds in this account is 5 years; the weighted coupon rate averages 7 percent. The portfolio's equity holdings can be categorized as large-cap and value-oriented issues. The portfolio's fixed-income holdings can be categorized as intermediate-term, very high-quality debt.

Susan M. Byrne and Patricia R. Fraze have managed this fund for the past seven years. There are five funds besides Westwood Balanced within the Gabelli-Westwood family. Overall, the fund family's risk-adjusted performance can be described as very good.

Current Income   ★★★

Over the past year, Westwood Balanced had a twelve-month yield of 2.2 percent. During this same twelve-month period, the typical balanced fund had a yield that averaged 2.5 percent.

Expenses   ★★★

Gabelli Westwood Balanced Retail's expense ratio is 1.3 percent; it has also averaged 1.3 percent annually over the past three calendar years. The average expense ratio for the 730 funds in this category is 1.4 percent. This fund's turnover rate over the past year has been 110 percent, while its peer group average has been 105 percent.

Summary

Gabelli Westwood Balanced Retail invests 30–70% of its assets in common stocks and convertibles issued by seasoned companies. The fund invests at least 20% of its assets in senior securities and may invest up to a quarter of its assets in foreign securities. Stock selection is initiated by first looking for companies that have posted earnings surprises that have been somewhat or largely overlooked by other analysts. Expectation of posting stock earnings growth is another equity criteria. The fund's performance has been exceptional, as has been its long-term management.

Profile

minimum initial investment $1,000	*IRA accounts available* . . . . yes
subsequent minimum investment $1	*IRA minimum investment* $1,000
available in all 50 states. . . . . yes	*date of inception* . . . . Oct. 1991
telephone exchanges. . . . . yes	*dividend/income paid.* . . . . monthly
number of funds in family 6	*quality of annual reports* . . . . good

Income Fund of America

4 Embarcadero Center
P.O. Box 94120
San Francisco, CA 94120
(800) 421-4120

total return	★★★★
risk reduction	★★★★
management	★★★★
current income	★
expense control	★★★★★
symbol AMECX	18 points
up-market performance	fair
down-market performance	good
predictability of returns	very good

Total Return ★★★★

Over the past five years (all periods ending 6/30/98), Income Fund of America has taken $10,000 and turned it into $19,740 ($16,830 over three years and $36,810 over the past ten years). This translates into an average annual return of 14.6 percent over the past five years, 19.0 percent over the past three years, and 13.9 percent for the decade. Over the past five years, this fund has outperformed 70 percent of all mutual funds; within its general category it has done better than 65 percent of its peers. Balanced funds have averaged 13 percent annually over these same five years.

During the past five years, a $10,000 initial investment grew to $18,600 after taxes, assuming a 39.6 percent income tax bracket (state and federal combined) and a capital gains rate of 28 percent. This means that investors in this fund were able to preserve 67 percent of their total returns. Compared to other fixed-income funds, this fund's tax savings are considered to be poor.

Risk/Volatility ★★★★

Over the past five years, Income Fund of America has been safer than 95 percent of all balanced funds. Over the past decade, the fund has had two negative years, while the S&P 500 has had one (off 3 percent in 1990); the Lehman Brothers Aggregate Bond Index also fell once (off 3 percent in 1994). The fund has underperformed the S&P seven times and the Lehman Brothers Aggregate Bond Index one time in the last ten years.

	last 5 years		last 10 years	
worst year	–2%	1994	–3%	1990
best year	29%	1995	29%	1995

In the past, Income Fund of America has done better than 40 percent of its peer group in up markets and outperformed 70 percent of its competition in down markets. Consistency, or predictability, of returns for Income can be described as very good.

Management   ★★★★

There are 390 stocks and 180 fixed-income securities in this $23 billion portfolio. The average balanced fund today is $365 million in size. Close to 52 percent of this fund's holdings are in stocks and 24 percent in bonds. The stocks in this portfolio have an average price-earnings (p/e) ratio of 21 and a median market capitalization of $16 billion. The average maturity of the bonds in this account is 6.5 years; the weighted coupon rate averages 7.9 percent. The portfolio's equity holdings can be categorized as large-cap and value-oriented issues. The portfolio's fixed-income holdings can be categorized as intermediate-term, medium-quality debt.

A team has managed this fund for the past 11 years. There are 24 funds besides Income Fund within the American Funds Group. Overall, the fund family's risk-adjusted performance can be described as very good.

Current Income   ★

Over the past year, Income Fund of America had a twelve-month yield of 4.1 percent. During this same twelve-month period, the typical balanced fund had a yield that averaged 2.5 percent.

Expenses   ★★★★★

Income Fund's expense ratio is 0.6 percent; it has averaged 0.8 percent annually over the past three calendar years. The average expense ratio for the 730 funds in this category is 1.4 percent. This fund's turnover rate over the past year has been 41 percent, while its peer group average has been 105 percent.

Summary

Income Fund of America is just one of several offerings from the folks at the American Funds Group to make this and all previous eight editions of this book. This balanced fund is particularly appealing for investors who are looking for preservation of capital as well as reasonable growth and current income. The equity side of the portfolio is conservatively invested, with a slant toward utilities and energy issues. The bond portion is divided between the highest of quality issues as well as issues with a single B rating—a strategy that continues to pay off handsomely. This is a no brainer that will be appreciated by the more sophisticated investor but should be strongly considered by all.

Profile

minimum initial investment $1,000	*IRA accounts available* . . . . yes
subsequent minimum investment . . . $50	*IRA minimum investment* $250
available in all 50 states. . . . . yes	*date of inception* . . . . Jan. 1971
telephone exchanges. . . . . yes	*dividend/income paid.* . . . . monthly
number of funds in family 25	*quality of annual reports* . . . . excellent

MFS World Total Return A

500 Boylston Street
Boston, MA 02116
(800) 637-2929

total return	★★★★
risk reduction	★★★★★
management	★★★★
current income	★★★
expense control	★
symbol MFWTX	17 points
up-market performance	good
down-market performance	n/a
predictability of returns	good

Total Return ★★★★

Over the past five years (all periods ending 6/30/98), MFS World Total Return A has taken $10,000 and turned it into $19,290 ($15,830 over three years). This translates into an average annual return of 14.0 percent over the past five years and 16.6 percent over the past three years. Over the past five years, this fund has outperformed 65 percent of all mutual funds; within its general category it has done better than 75 percent of its peers. Balanced funds have averaged 13 percent annually over these same five years.

During the past five years, a $10,000 initial investment grew to $18,350 after taxes, assuming a 39.6 percent income tax bracket (state and federal combined) and a capital gains rate of 28 percent. This means that investors in this fund were able to preserve 79 percent of their total returns. Compared to other fixed-income funds, this fund's tax savings are considered to be good.

Risk/Volatility ★★★★★

Over the past five years, Total Return has been safer than 75 percent of all balanced funds. Over the past decade, the fund has had one negative year, while the S&P 500 has also had one (off 3 percent in 1990); the Lehman Brothers Aggregate Bond Index also fell once (off 3 percent in 1994). The fund has underperformed the S&P 500 six times and the Lehman Brothers Aggregate Bond Index one time in the last ten years.

	last 5 years		since inception	
worst year	–3%	1994	–3%	1994
best year	22%	1993	22%	1993

In the past, MFS World Total Return A has done better than 50 percent of its peer group in up markets. Consistency, or predictability, of returns for MFS World Total Return A can be described as good.

Management   ★★★★

There are 75 stocks and 45 fixed-income securities in this $175 million portfolio. The average balanced fund today is $365 million in size. Close to 61 percent of this fund's holdings are in stocks and 36 percent in bonds. The stocks in this portfolio have an average price-earnings (p/e) ratio of 25 and a median market capitalization of $14 billion. The average maturity of the bonds in this account is 8 years; the weighted coupon rate averages 7 percent. The portfolio's equity holdings can be categorized as large-cap and value-oriented issues. The portfolio's fixed-income holdings can be categorized as intermediate-term, very high-quality debt.

Frederick J. Simmons has managed this fund for the past seven years. There are 138 funds besides Total Return A within the MFS Family of Funds family. Overall, the fund family's risk-adjusted performance can be described as good.

Current Income   ★★★

Over the past year, MFS World Total Return A had a twelve-month yield of 1.5 percent. During this same twelve-month period, the typical balanced fund had a yield that averaged 2.5 percent.

Expenses   ★

Total Return's expense ratio is 1.6 percent; it has averaged 1.7 percent annually over the past three calendar years. The average expense ratio for the 730 funds in this category is 1.4 percent. This fund's turnover rate over the past year has been 143 percent, while its peer group average has been 105 percent.

Summary

As the name implies, this multi-asset global balanced portfolio invests all around the world, with an emphasis on the U.S., Japan and Europe. Only 5% or less of the portfolio may be invested in debt instruments whose credit rating is below investment grade. Equities from companies with solid earnings potential that are expanding into global markets from a dominant domestic position are preferred. This is one of the most highly recommended funds for investors seeking foreign and domestic exposure.

Profile

minimum initial investment $1,000	*IRA accounts available* . . . . yes
subsequent minimum investment . . . $50	*IRA minimum investment* $250
available in all 50 states. . . . . yes	*date of inception* . . . . Aug. 1990
telephone exchanges. . . . . yes	*dividend/income paid.* . . . . monthly
number of funds in family 139	*quality of annual reports* . . . . excellent

Preferred Asset Allocation

P.O. Box 8320
Boston, MA 02266-8320
(800) 662-4769

total return	★★★★★
risk reduction	★★★★
management	★★★★
current income	★★★★
expense control	★★★★
symbol PFAAX	21 points
up-market performance	n/a
down-market performance	n/a
predictability of returns	fair

Total Return   ★★★★★

Over the past five years (all periods ending 6/30/98), Preferred Asset Allocation has taken $10,000 and turned it into $20,930 ($17,420 over three years). This translates into an average annual return of 15.9 percent over the past five years and 20.3 percent over the past three years. Over the past five years, this fund has outperformed 70 percent of all mutual funds; within its general category it has done better than 75 percent of its peers. Balanced funds have averaged 13 percent annually over these same five years.

During the past five years, a $10,000 initial investment grew to $20,940 after taxes, assuming a 39.6 percent income tax bracket (state and federal combined) and a capital gains rate of 28 percent. This means that investors in this fund were able to preserve 81 percent of their total returns. Compared to other fixed-income funds, this fund's tax savings are considered to be very good.

Risk/Volatility   ★★★★

Over the past five years, Preferred Asset Allocation has been safer than 55 percent of all balanced funds. Over the past decade, the fund has had one negative year, while the S&P 500 has also had one (off 3 percent in 1990); the Lehman Brothers Aggregate Bond Index also fell once (off 3 percent in 1994). The fund has underperformed the S&P 500 four times and has outperformed the Lehman Brothers Aggregate Bond Index every year for the last ten years.

	last 5 years		since inception	
worst year	–3%	1994	–3%	1994
best year	33%	1995	33%	1995

Consistency, or predictability, of returns for Asset Allocation can be described as fair.

Management   ★★★★

There are 225 stocks and 155 fixed-income securities in this $175 million portfolio. The average balanced fund today is $365 million in size. Close to 42 percent of this fund's holdings are in stocks and 29 percent in bonds. The stocks in this portfolio have an average price-earnings (p/e) ratio of 30 and a median market capitalization of $45 billion. The average maturity of the bonds in this account is 22 years; the weighted coupon rate averages 8.5 percent. The portfolio's equity holdings can be categorized as large-cap and a blend of growth and value stocks. The portfolio's fixed-income holdings can be categorized as long-term, very high-quality.

Thomas B. Hazuka has managed this fund for the past six years. There are six funds besides Asset Allocation within the Preferred Group. Overall, the fund family's risk-adjusted performance can be described as very good.

Current Income   ★★★★

Over the past year, Asset Allocation had a twelve-month yield of 2.8 percent. During this same twelve-month period, the typical balanced fund had a yield that averaged 2.5 percent.

Expenses   ★★★★

Asset Allocation's expense ratio is 1.0 percent; it has averaged 1.1 percent annually over the past three calendar years. The average expense ratio for the 730 funds in this category is 1.4 percent. This fund's turnover rate over the past year has been 28 percent, while its peer group average has been 105 percent.

Summary

Preferred Asset Allocation mostly consists of S&P 500 stocks plus U.S. government securities and other investment-grade bonds. Manager Tom Hazuka uses a quantitative model to forecast the risks and rewards of different asset categories; co-manager Ed Peters relies on economic factors and the relative yield of equities as well as debt instruments. Total return is where is fund really excels. Its overall point score plus individual rankings in every single category are quite impressive.

Profile

minimum initial investment $1,000	*IRA accounts available* . . . . yes
subsequent minimum investment . . . $50	*IRA minimum investment* $250
available in all 50 states. . . . . yes	*date of inception*. . . . . June 1992
telephone exchanges. . . . . yes	*dividend/income paid*. . . . . monthly
number of funds in family 7	*quality of annual reports* . . . . good

T. Rowe Price Balanced

100 East Pratt Steet
Baltimore, MD 21202
(800) 638-5660

total return	★★★★
risk reduction	★★★★
management	★★★★★
current income	★★★★★
expense control	★★★★★
symbol RPBAX	23 points
up-market performance	very good
down-market performance	excellent
predictability of returns	good

Total Return   ★★★★

Over the past five years (all periods ending 6/30/98), T. Rowe Price Balanced has taken $10,000 and turned it into $19,810 ($16,510 over three years and $36,270 over the past ten years). This translates into an average annual return of 14.7 percent over the past five years, 18.2 percent over the past three years, and 13.8 percent for the decade. Over the past five years, this fund has outperformed 70 percent of all mutual funds; within its general category it has done better than 60 percent of its peers. Balanced funds have averaged 13 percent annually over these same five years.

During the past five years, a $10,000 initial investment grew to $19,810 after taxes, assuming a 39.6 percent income tax bracket (state and federal combined) and a capital gains rate of 28 percent. This means that investors in this fund were able to preserve 87 percent of their total returns. Compared to other fixed-income funds, this fund's tax savings are considered to be excellent.

Risk/Volatility   ★★★★

Over the past five years, T. Rowe Price Balanced has been safer than 75 percent of all balanced funds. Over the past decade, the fund has had one negative year, while the S&P 500 has also had one (off 3 percent in 1990); the Lehman Brothers Aggregate Bond Index also fell once (off 3 percent in 1994). The fund has under-performed the S&P 500 eight times and the Lehman Brothers Aggregate Bond Index one time in the last ten years.

	last 5 years		last 10 years	
worst year	–2%	1994	–2%	1994
best year	25%	1995	25%	1995

In the past, T. Rowe Price Balanced has done better than 75 percent of its peer group in up markets and outperformed 95 percent of its competition in down markets. Consistency, or predictability, of returns for T. Rowe Price Balanced can be described as good.

Management   ★★★★★
There are 525 stocks and 335 fixed-income securities in this $1.4 billion portfolio. The average balanced fund today is $365 million in size. Close to 60 percent of this fund's holdings are in stocks and 38 percent in bonds. The stocks in this portfolio have an average price-earnings (p/e) ratio of 28 and a median market capitalization of $22 billion. The average maturity of the bonds in this account is 10 years; the weighted coupon rate averages 7.8 percent. The portfolio's equity holdings can be categorized as large-cap and a blend of growth and value stocks. The portfolio's fixed-income holdings can be categorized as intermediate-term, high-quality debt.

Richard T. Whitney has managed this fund for the past seven years. There are 65 funds besides Balanced within the T. Rowe Price family. Overall, the fund family's risk-adjusted performance can be described as very good.

Current Income   ★★★★★
Over the past year, Price Balanced had a twelve-month yield of 2.9 percent. During this same twelve-month period, the typical balanced fund had a yield that averaged 2.5 percent.

Expenses   ★★★★★
Price Balanced's expense ratio is 0.8 percent; it has averaged 0.9 percent annually over the past three calendar years. The average expense ratio for the 730 funds in this category is 1.4 percent. This fund's turnover rate over the past year has been 16 percent, while its peer group average has been 105 percent.

Summary
T. Rowe Price Balanced likes to keep about a fourth of its assets in foreign equities, with a strong bias toward European blue chips. About a fifth of the portfolio is in high-yield corporate bonds. This very broad-based fund is rated as the number one balanced portfolio—its overall score is close to perfect. Few funds in any category have received such a high ranking. This fund is highly recommended for the investor who wants a balanced approach.

Profile

minimum initial investment $2,500	*IRA accounts available* . . . . yes
subsequent minimum investment . . $100	*IRA minimum investment* $1,000
available in all 50 states. . . . . yes	*date of inception.* . . . . May 1938
telephone exchanges. . . . . yes	*dividend/income paid.* . . . . monthly
number of funds in family 66	*quality of annual reports* . . . . excellent

Vanguard STAR

Vanguard Financial Center
P.O. Box 2600
Valley Forge, PA 19482
(800) 662-7447

total return	★★★★★
risk reduction	★★★★
management	★★★★
current income	★★★★
expense control	★★★★★
symbol BGSTX	22 points
up-market performance	fair
down-market performance	good
predictability of returns	good

Total Return ★★★★★

Over the past five years (all periods ending 6/30/98), Vanguard STAR has taken $10,000 and turned it into $20,720 ($17,180 over three years and $35,980 over the past ten years). This translates into an average annual return of 15.7 percent over the past five years, 19.8 percent over the past three years, and 13.7 percent for the decade. Over the past five years, this fund has outperformed 75 percent of all mutual funds; within its general category it has done better than 80 percent of its peers. Balanced funds have averaged 13 percent annually over these same five years.

During the past five years, a $10,000 initial investment grew to $20,710 after taxes, assuming a 39.6 percent income tax bracket (state and federal combined) and a capital gains rate of 28 percent. This means that investors in this fund were able to preserve 81 percent of their total returns. Compared to other fixed-income funds, this fund's tax savings are considered to be very good.

Risk/Volatility ★★★★

Over the past five years, Vanguard STAR has been safer than 80 percent of all balanced funds. Over the past decade, the fund has had two negative years, while the S&P 500 has had one (off 3 percent in 1990); the Lehman Brothers Aggregate Bond Index also fell once (off 3 percent in 1994). The fund has underperformed the S&P 500 seven times and the Lehman Brothers Aggregate Bond Index one time in the last ten years.

	last 5 years		last 10 years	
worst year	−.2%	1994	−4%	1990
best year	29%	1995	29%	1995

In the past, STAR has done better than 25 percent of its peer group in up markets and outperformed 65 percent of its competition in down markets. Consistency, or predictability, of returns for Vanguard STAR can be described as good.

Management   ★★★★
This $8.5 billion "fund of funds" is typically invested in the following Vanguard funds: 50% in the Windsor and Windsor II funds (value funds), 25% in the GNMA and Long-Term Corporate bond funds (fixed-income funds), and 25% in Explorer, Primecap, U.S. growth, Morgan Growth, and Prime Portfolio (growth funds). The average balanced fund today is $365 million in size. The portfolio's fixed-income holdings can be categorized as high-quality, long-term. The average balanced fund today is $365 million in size.

A team has managed this fund for the past 13 years. There are 71 funds besides STAR within the Vanguard Group. Overall, the fund family's risk-adjusted performance can be described as very good.

Current Income   ★★★★
Over the past year, STAR had a twelve-month yield of 3 percent. During this same twelve-month period, the typical balanced fund had a yield that averaged 2.5 percent.

Expenses   ★★★★★
STAR's expense ratio is 0.3 percent; it has also averaged 0.3 percent annually over the past three calendar years. The average expense ratio for the 730 funds in this category is 1.4 percent. This fund's turnover rate over the past year has been 15 percent, while its peer group average has been 105 percent.

Summary
Vanguard STAR is the only "fund of funds" to appear in this book. One of the appeals of this particular fund, and approach, is that this is the only frugally run "fund of funds"—a concept or strategy that almost always entails extra layers of fees. Turnover is kept quite low, another anomoly for such a fund, thereby enhancing shareholder value. The equity portion of the portfolio is comprised of large cap, mid cap, and small cap growth and value stocks. The debt portion is made up of both intermediate- and long-term securities. This fund is highly recommended.

Profile

minimum initial investment $1,000	*IRA accounts available* . . . . yes
subsequent minimum investment . . $100	*IRA minimum investment* $1,000
available in all 50 states. . . . . yes	*date of inception*. . . . . Mar. 1985
telephone exchanges. . . . . yes	*dividend/income paid*. . . . . monthly
number of funds in family 72	*quality of annual reports* . . . . good

Corporate Bond Funds

Traditionally, bond funds are held by investors who require high current income and low risk. Interest income is normally paid on a monthly basis. Corporate bond funds are made up primarily of bonds issued by domestic corporations; government securities often represent a moderate part of these funds. Portfolio composition is almost always exclusively U.S. issues.

Bonds are normally purchased because of their income stream; one's principal in a bond fund fluctuates. The major influence on bond prices, and therefore the value of the fund's shares, is interest rates. There is an *inverse* relationship between interest rates and bond values; whatever one does, the other does the opposite. If interest rates rise, the price per share of a bond fund will fall, and vice versa.

The amount of appreciation or loss of a corporate bond fund primarily depends upon the average maturity of the bonds in the portfolio; the cumulative amount of interest rate movement and the typical yield of the bonds in the fund's portfolio are distant secondary concerns. *Short-term* bond funds, made up of debt instruments with an average maturity of five years or less, are subject to very little interest rate risk or reward. *Medium-term* bond funds, with maturities averaging between six and ten years, are subject to one-third to one-half the risk level of long-term funds. A long-term corporate bond fund will average an 8 percent increase or decrease in share price for every cumulative 1 percent change in interest rates.

Often investors can tell what kind of corporate bond fund they are purchasing by its name. Unless the fund includes the term "short" in its title, chances are that it is a medium- or long-term bond fund. Investors would be wise to contact the fund or counsel with an investment advisor to learn more about the portfolio's average maturity; most bond funds will dramatically reduce their portfolio's average maturity during periods of interest-rate uncertainty.

The average weighted maturity for the bonds in these funds is just over eight years, the average coupon rate is 7.2 percent, and the average weighted price is $1,020 (meaning that the bonds are worth $10 more than face value, on average). A price, or value, of par ($1,000 per bond) means that the bonds in a portfolio are worth face value and are not currently being traded at a discount (a price less than $1,000 per bond) or at a premium (some figure above $1,000). The portfolio of the "average" corporate bond fund is made up of securities purchased at a $20 per-bond premium ($1,020 vs. $1,000 for bonds bought at face value). A portfolio manager purchases bonds at a premium for one of two reasons: to increase the portfolio's current income, or to decrease the fund's volatility slightly (the higher the coupon rate, the less susceptible a bond is to the effects of interest-rate changes).

During the past five and ten years, corporate bond funds have underperformed the Lehman Brothers Aggregate Bond Index by 0.7 percent per year. Over the last three years the gap widens to 0.9 percent per year. Average turnover during the last three years has been 153 percent, a surprisingly high figure given the general belief that stocks are traded (turned over) much more frequently than bonds. (The typical growth fund has a turnover rate of 89 percent annually.) The average corporate bond fund throws off an annual income stream of about 5.5 percent. The typical annual expense ratio for this group is 0.9 percent.

Over the past fifteen years, *individual* corporate bonds have underperformed common stocks by over 5 percent per year. From 1983 to 1998, long-term corporate bonds averaged 11.9 percent compounded per year, compared to 17.5 percent for common stocks and 14.1 percent for small stocks. A $10,000 investment in corporate bonds grew to $44,070 over the past fifteen years; a similar initial investment in common stocks grew to $102,700 and $62,250 for small stocks.

Over the past half century, corporate bonds have only outpaced inflation on a pre-tax basis. A dollar invested in corporate bonds in 1948 grew to $17.64 by the end of 1997. This translates into an average compound return of 6.1 percent per year. During this same period, $1 inflated to $5.88; this translates into an average annual inflation rate of 3.9 percent. Over the past fifty years, the worst year for long-term corporate bonds, on a *total return* basis (yield plus or minus principal appreciation or loss), was 1969, when a loss of 8 percent was suffered. The best year so far has been 1982, when corporate bonds posted a gain of 43 percent.

Over 800 funds make up the corporate bonds category. Total market capitalization of this category is $190 billion. Over the past three and five years, corporate bond funds have had an average compound return of 7.0 and 6.1 percent per year, respectively. For the decade, corporate bond funds have averaged 8.4 percent per year and 9.7 percent per annum for the past fifteen years (all figures ending 6/30/98). All of these figures represent total returns. This means that bond appreciation (or depreciation) was added (or subtracted) from current yield.

The standard deviation for corporate bond funds has been 3.3 percent over the past three years. As you may recall, a low standard deviation means a greater predictability of returns (fewer surprises—for better or worse). If a fund, or fund category, such as corporate bonds, has an average annual return of 10 percent and a standard deviation of 3.3 percent, this means that returns for every two out of three years should be roughly 10 percent, plus or minus 3.3 percent (one standard deviation). If you want to increase certainty of returns, then you must look at *two* standard deviations. This means that returns, for about 95 percent of the time, would be 10 percent plus or minus 6.6 percent (or +3.4 percent to +16.6 percent). These funds have been less volatile than any equity fund and have shown similar return variances (volatility) as government bond funds.

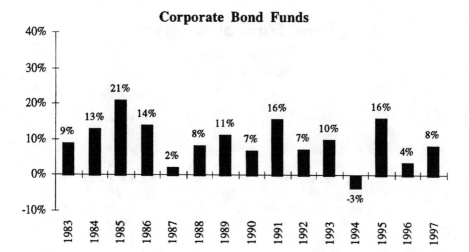

Bond Fund of America

333 South Hope Street
Los Angeles, CA 90071
(800) 421-4120

total return	★★★★★
risk reduction	★★★
management	★★★★
current income	★★★
expense control	★★★★★
symbol ABNDX	20 points
up-market performance	excellent
down-market performance	poor
predictability of returns	good

Total Return   ★★★★★

Over the past five years (all periods ending 6/30/98), Bond Fund of America has taken $10,000 and turned it into $14,180 ($12,930 over three years and $24,530 over the past ten years). This translates into an average annual return of 7.2 percent over the past five years, 9.0 percent over the past three years, and 9.4 percent for the decade. Over the past five years, this fund has outperformed 45 percent of all mutual funds; within its general category it has done better than 65 percent of its peers. Corporate bond funds have averaged 6 percent annually over these same five years.

During the past five years, a $10,000 initial investment grew to $13,530 after taxes, assuming a 39.6 percent income tax bracket (state and federal combined) and a capital gains rate of 28 percent. This means that investors in this fund were able to preserve 43 percent of their total returns. Compared to other fixed-income funds, this fund's tax savings are considered to be good.

Risk/Volatility   ★★★

Over the past five years, Bond Fund of America has been safer than 90 percent of all corporate bond funds. Over the past decade, the fund has had one negative year, while the Lehman Brothers Aggregate Bond Index has had one (off 3 percent in 1994); the Lehman Brothers Corporate Bond Index also fell once (off 4 percent in 1994). The fund has underperformed the Lehman Brothers Aggregate Bond Index five times and the Lehman Brothers Corporate Bond Index three times in the last ten years.

	last 5 years		last 10 years	
worst year	–5%	1994	–5%	1994
best year	18%	1995	21%	1991

In the past, Bond Fund of America has done better than 95 percent of its peer group in up markets but outperformed only 5 percent of its competition in down markets. Consistency, or predictability, of returns for Bond Fund of America can be described as good.

Management ★★★★

There are 850 fixed-income securities in this $9.0 billion portfolio. The average corporate bond fund today is $240 million in size. Close to 90 percent of the funds holdings are in bonds. The average maturity of the bonds in this account is 8 years; the weighted coupon rate averages 8 percent. The portfolio's fixed-income holdings can be categorized as intermediate-term, medium-quality debt.

A team has managed this fund for the past eight years. There are 24 funds besides Bond Fund of America within the American Funds Group. Overall, the fund family's risk-adjusted performance can be described as very good.

Current Income ★★★

Over the past year, Bond Fund of America had a twelve-month yield of 7.1 percent. During this same twelve-month period, the typical corporate bond fund had a yield that averaged 5.8 percent.

Expenses ★★★★★

Bond Fund of America's expense ratio is 0.7 percent; it has also averaged 0.7 percent annually over the past three calendar years. The average expense ratio for the 800 funds in this category is 1.0 percent. This fund's turnover rate over the past year has been 52 percent, while its peer group average has been 155 percent.

Summary

Bond Fund of America is yet another offering from the American Funds Group to appear in this and all previous editions of the book. Capital Guardian, the management division of this group does not get the credit it deserves for delivering long-term value and superlative returns for two reasons: (1) the names of their funds lack a consistent word or phrase that indicates which family it belongs to, and (2) the fund family does no advertising, yet continues to be one of the very biggest mutual fund families. Like the great majority of offerings from the American Funds Group, this one is also strongly recommended.

Profile

minimum initial investment $1,000	*IRA accounts available* . . . . yes
subsequent minimum investment . . . $50	*IRA minimum investment* $250
available in all 50 states. . . . . yes	*date of inception*. . . . . May 1974
telephone exchanges. . . . . yes	*dividend/income paid*. . . . . monthly
number of funds in family 25	*quality of annual reports* . . . . excellent

Forum Investors Bond

P.O. Box 446
Portland, ME 04112
(207) 879-8900

total return	★★★★★
risk reduction	★★★
management	★★★★
current income	★★★★★
expense control	★★★★★
symbol FOIBX	22 points
up-market performance	very good
down-market performance	very good
predictability of returns	very good

Total Return   ★★★★★

Over the past five years (all periods ending 6/30/98), Forum Investors Bond has taken $10,000 and turned it into $14,180 ($12,840 over three years). This translates into an average annual return of 7.2 percent over the past five years and 8.7 percent over the past three years. Over the past five years, this fund has outperformed 45 percent of all mutual funds; within its general category it has done better than 65 percent of its peers. Corporate bond funds have averaged 6 percent annually over these same five years.

During the past five years, a $10,000 initial investment grew to $13,650 after taxes, assuming a 39.6 percent income tax bracket (state and federal combined) and a capital gains rate of 28 percent. This means that investors in this fund were able to preserve 57 percent of their total returns. Compared to other fixed-income funds, this fund's tax savings are considered to be excellent.

Risk/Volatility   ★★★

Over the past five years, Forum Investors Bond has been safer than 70 percent of all corporate bond funds. Over the past decade, the fund has had one negative year, while the Lehman Brothers Aggregate Bond Index has had one (off 3 percent in 1994); the Lehman Brothers Corporate Bond Index also fell once (off 4 percent in 1994). The fund has underperformed the Lehman Brothers Aggregate Bond Index two times and the Lehman Brothers Corporate Bond Index three times in the last ten years.

	last 5 years		since inception	
worst year	–2%	1994	–2%	1994
best year	14%	1995	14%	1995

In the past, Investors Bond has done better than 75 percent of its peer group in up markets and outperformed 75 percent of its competition in down markets.

Consistency, or predictability, of returns for Forum Investors Bond can be described as very good.

Management   ★★★★
There are 15 fixed-income securities in this $85 million portfolio. The average corporate bond fund today is $240 million in size. Close to 70 percent of the funds holdings are in bonds. The average maturity of the bonds in this account is eight years; the weighted coupon rate averages 8 percent. The portfolio's fixed-income holdings can be categorized as intermediate-term, medium-quality debt.

Les Berthy has managed this fund for the past nine years. There are six funds besides Investors Bond within the Forum family. Overall, the fund family's risk-adjusted performance can be described as good.

Current Income   ★★★★★
Over the past year, Forum Investors Bond had a twelve-month yield of 6.4 percent. During this same twelve-month period, the typical corporate bond fund had a yield that averaged 5.8 percent.

Expenses   ★★★★★
Bond's expense ratio is 0.7 percent; it has averaged 0.6 percent annually over the past three calendar years. The average expense ratio for the 800 funds in this category is 1.0 percent. This fund's turnover rate over the past year has been 79 percent, while its peer group average has been 155 percent.

Summary
Forum Investors Bond ranks as the second best corporate bond fund, losing out to a peer by only a fraction. Management knows what is important and delivers—top returns, minimal tax exposure for a debt portfolio and a keen eye on controlling expenses. This somewhat small fund family also offers other portfolios worth considering. Forum Investors Bond is one of the few bond funds recommended.

Profile

minimum initial investment $5,000	*IRA accounts available* . . . . yes
subsequent minimum investment . . $500	*IRA minimum investment* $2,000
available in all 50 states . . . . no	*date of inception* . . . . Oct. 1989
telephone exchanges. . . . . yes	*dividend/income paid*. . . . . monthly
number of funds in family 7	*quality of annual reports* . . . . n/a

FPA New Income

11400 West Olympic Boulevard, Suite 1200
Los Angeles, CA 90064
(800) 982-4372

total return	★★★★★
risk reduction	★★★★
management	★★★★★
current income	★★★★★
expense control	★★★★★
symbol FPNIX	24 points
up-market performance	excellent
down-market performance	poor
predictability of returns	excellent

Total Return   ★★★★★

Over the past five years (all periods ending 6/30/98), FPA New Income has taken $10,000 and turned it into $14,270 ($12,150 over three years and $24,780 over the past ten years). This translates into an average annual return of 7.4 percent over the past five years, 7.7 percent over the past three years, and 9.5 percent for the decade. Over the past five years, this fund has outperformed 45 percent of all mutual funds; within its general category it has done better than 50 percent of its peers. Corporate bond funds have averaged 6 percent annually over these same five years.

During the past five years, a $10,000 initial investment grew to $13,590 after taxes, assuming a 39.6 percent income tax bracket (state and federal combined) and a capital gains rate of 28 percent. This means that investors in this fund were able to preserve 57 percent of their total returns. Compared to other fixed-income funds, this fund's tax savings are considered to be excellent.

Risk/Volatility   ★★★★

Over the past five years, FPA New Income has been safer than 99 percent of all corporate bond funds. Over the past decade, the fund has had no negative years, while the Lehman Brothers Aggregate Bond Index has had one (off 3 percent in 1994); the Lehman Brothers Corporate Bond Index also fell once (off 4 percent in 1994). The fund has underperformed the Lehman Brothers Aggregate Bond Index four times and the Lehman Brothers Corporate Bond Index three times in the last ten years.

	last 5 years		last 10 years	
worst year	1%	1994	1%	1994
best year	14%	1995	19%	1991

In the past, New Income has done better than 95 percent of its peer group in up markets and outperformed only 15 percent of its competition in down markets.

Consistency, or predictability, of returns for New Income can be described as excellent.

Management   ★★★★★
There are 65 fixed-income securities in this $630 million portfolio. The average corporate bond fund today is $240 million in size. Close to 78 percent of the funds holdings are in bonds. The average maturity of the bonds in this account is 4 years; the weighted coupon rate averages seven percent. The portfolio's fixed-income holdings can be categorized as short-term, high-quality debt.

Robert L. Rodriguez has managed this fund for the past 14 years. There are three funds besides New Income within the FPA family. Overall, the fund family's risk-adjusted performance can be described as very good.

Current Income   ★★★★★
Over the past year, FPA New Income had a twelve-month yield of 6 percent. During this same twelve-month period, the typical corporate bond fund had a yield that averaged 5.8 percent.

Expenses   ★★★★★
FPA New Income's expense ratio is 0.6 percent; it has also averaged 0.6 percent annually over the past three calendar years. The average expense ratio for the 800 funds in this category is 1.0 percent. This fund's turnover rate over the past year has been 69 percent, while its peer group average has been 155 percent.

Summary
FPA New Income comes as close to getting a perfect score across the board as you can get. Not only is this the number one overall rated corporate bond fund, its total point score (24 out of 25) pretty much puts it in a class by itself. Management seems to "get it"—go where the best risk-adjusted rewards are (now and in the future), short- and intermediate-term issues. FPA is a small fund family but one which is highly praised. Hopefully, the company will come out with more offerings.

Profile
minimum initial investment $1,500	*IRA accounts available* . . . . yes
subsequent minimum investment . . $100	*IRA minimum investment* $100
available in all 50 states. . . . . yes	*date of inception.* . . . . Apr. 1969
telephone exchanges. . . . . yes	*dividend/income paid.* . . . . monthly
number of funds in family 4	*quality of annual reports* . . . . good

Phoenix Multi-Sector Short-Term A

100 Bright Meadow Boulevard
P.O. Box 2200
Enfield, CT 06083-2200
(800) 243-4361

total return	★★★★★
risk reduction	★★★
management	★★★
current income	★★★★★
expense control	★
symbol NARAX	17 points
up-market performance	n/a
down-market performance	n/a
predictability of returns	very good

Total Return   ★★★★★

Over the past five years (all periods ending 6/30/98), Phoenix Multi-Sector Short-Term A has taken $10,000 and turned it into $14,430 ($13,140 over three years). This translates into an average annual return of 7.6 percent over the past five years and 9.5 percent over the past three years. Over the past five years, this fund has outperformed 45 percent of all mutual funds; within its general category it has done better than 60 percent of its peers. Corporate bond funds have averaged 6 percent annually over these same five years.

During the past five years, a $10,000 initial investment grew to $14,110 after taxes, assuming a 39.6 percent income tax bracket (state and federal combined) and a capital gains rate of 28 percent. This means that investors in this fund were able to preserve 57 percent of their total returns. Compared to other fixed-income funds, this fund's tax savings are considered to be excellent.

Risk/Volatility   ★★★

Over the past five years, Phoenix Multi-Sector Short-Term A has been safer than 90 percent of all corporate bond funds. Over the past decade, the fund has had one negative year, while the Lehman Brothers Aggregate Bond Index has had one (off 3 percent in 1994); the Lehman Brothers Corporate Bond Index also fell once (off 4 percent in 1994). The fund has underperformed the Lehman Brothers Aggregate Bond Index three times and the Lehman Brothers Corporate Bond Index three times in the last ten years.

	last 5 years		since inception	
worst year	–2%	1994	–2%	1994
best year	14%	1995	14%	1995

Consistency, or predictability, of returns for Short-Term A can be described as very good.

Management   ★★★
There are 75 fixed-income securities in this $36 million portfolio. The average corporate bond fund today is $240 million in size. Close to 94 percent of the funds holdings are in bonds. The average maturity of the bonds in this account is eight years; the weighted coupon rate averages 8 percent. The portfolio's fixed-income holdings can be categorized as short-term, medium-quality debt.

David Albrycht has managed this fund for the past six years. There are 92 funds besides Short-Term A within the Phoenix family. Overall, the fund family's risk-adjusted performance can be described as good.

Current Income   ★★★★★
Over the past year, Short-Term A had a twelve-month yield of 6.7 percent. During this same twelve-month period, the typical corporate bond fund had a yield that averaged 5.8 percent.

Expenses   ★
Short-Term A's expense ratio is 1.0 percent; it has also averaged 1.0 percent annually over the past three calendar years. The average expense ratio for the 800 funds in this category is 1.0 percent. This fund's turnover rate over the past year has been 232 percent, while its peer group average has been 155 percent.

Summary
Phoenix Multi-Sector Short-Term A is the perfect choice for the bond investor who wants the highest possible total return while taking on virtually no interest-rate risk. Tax minimization is also superb among its peer group. There are a couple of other worthy Phoenix offerings, but this particular member of the family is one of its shining lights.

Profile
minimum initial investment $500	*IRA accounts available* . . . . yes
subsequent minimum investment . . . $25	*IRA minimum investment* $25
available in all 50 states. . . . . yes	*date of inception* . . . . July 1992
telephone exchanges. . . . . yes	*dividend/income paid*. . . . . monthly
number of funds in family 93	*quality of annual reports* . . . . n/a

Pillar Short-Term Investment A

680 East Swedesford Road
Wayne, PA 19087-1658
(800) 932-7782

total return	★★
risk reduction	★★★★★
management	★★★★
current income	★★★★
expense control	★★★★
symbol PLSAX	19 points
up-market performance	n/a
down-market performance	n/a
predictability of returns	excellent

Total Return   ★★

Over the past five years (all periods ending 6/30/98), Pillar Short-Term Investment A has taken $10,000 and turned it into $12,370 ($11,460 over three years). This translates into an average annual return of 4.3 percent over the past five years and 4.6 percent over the past three years. Over the past five years, this fund has outperformed 35 percent of all mutual funds; within its general category it has done better than 35 percent of its peers. Corporate bond funds have averaged 6 percent annually over these same five years.

During the past five years, a $10,000 initial investment grew to $12,250 after taxes, assuming a 39.6 percent income tax bracket (state and federal combined) and a capital gains rate of 28 percent. This means that investors in this fund were able to preserve 50 percent of their total returns. Compared to other fixed-income funds, this fund's tax savings are considered to be very good.

Risk/Volatility   ★★★★★

Over the past five years, Pillar Short-Term Investment A has been safer than 98 percent of all corporate bond funds. Over the past decade, the fund has had no negative years, while the Lehman Brothers Aggregate Bond Index has had one (off 3 percent in 1994); the Lehman Brothers Corporate Bond Index also fell once (off 4 percent in 1994). The fund has underperformed the Lehman Brothers Aggregate Bond Index three times and the Lehman Brothers Corporate Bond Index three times in the last ten years.

	last 5 years		since inception	
worst year	3%	1994	3%	1994
best year	6%	1995	6%	1995

Consistency, or predictability, of returns for Pillar Short-Term Investment A can be described as excellent.

Management   ★★★★
There are 15 fixed-income securities in this $1 million portfolio. The average corporate bond fund today is $240 million in size. Close to 98 percent of the funds holdings are in bonds. The average maturity of the securities in this account is less than one year; the weighted coupon rate averages 7 percent. The portfolio's fixed-income holdings can be categorized as high quality and very short-term.

Robert B. Lowe, Jr. has managed this fund for the past six years. There are 22 funds besides Investment A within the Pillar family. Overall, the fund family's risk-adjusted performance can be described as good.

Current Income   ★★★★
Over the past year, Pillar Short-Term Investment A had a twelve-month yield of 5 percent. During this same twelve-month period, the typical corporate bond fund had a yield that averaged 5.8 percent.

Expenses   ★★★★
Investment A's expense ratio is 1.1 percent; it has also averaged 1.1 percent annually over the past three calendar years. The average expense ratio for the 800 funds in this category is 1.0 percent. This fund's turnover rate over the past year has been zero, while its peer group average has been 155 percent.

Summary
Pillar Short-Term Investment A's total return ranking suffers only because it keeps maturities quite short. This fund is not recommended for investors who believe interest rates are going to fall. It is strongly recommended for those who believe that rates are going to stay the same or increase. It is also a good choice for the bond investor who wants to keep tax consequences as low as possible, given the nature of the beast.

Profile
minimum initial investment $1,000	*IRA accounts available* . . . . no
subsequent minimum investment . . . $50	*IRA minimum investment* . . . . n/a
available in all 50 states . . . . no	*date of inception* . . . . Apr. 1992
telephone exchanges . . . . yes	*dividend/income paid* . . . . monthly
number of funds in family 23	*quality of annual reports* . . . . n/a

Global Equity Funds

International, also known as "foreign," funds invest only in stocks of foreign companies, while *global funds* invest in both foreign and U.S. stocks. For the purposes of this book, the universe of global equity funds shown encompasses both foreign (international) and world (global) portfolios.

The economic outlook of foreign countries is the major factor in mutual fund management's decision as to which nations and industries are to be favored. A secondary concern is the future anticipated value of the U.S. dollar relative to foreign currencies. A strong or weak dollar can detract or add to an international fund's overall performance. A strong dollar will lower a foreign portfolio's return; a weak dollar will enhance international performance. Trying to gauge the direction of any currency is as difficult as trying to figure out what the U.S. stock market will do tomorrow, next week, or the following year.

Investors who do not wish to be subjected to currency swings may wish to use a fund family that practices currency hedging for their foreign holdings. Currency hedging means that management is buying a kind of insurance policy that pays off in the event of a strong U.S. dollar. Basically, the foreign or international fund that is being hurt by the dollar is making a killing in currency futures contracts. When done properly, the gains in the futures contracts, the insurance policy, offset some, most, or all security losses attributable to a strong dollar. Some people may feel that buying currency contracts is risky business for the fund; it is not.

Like automobile insurance, currency hedging only pays off if there is an accident; that is, if the U.S. dollar increases in value against the currencies represented by the portfolio's securities. If the dollar remains level or decreases in value, so much the better; the foreign securities increase in value and the currency contracts become virtually worthless. The price of these contracts becomes a cost of doing business; as with car insurance, the protection is simply renewed. In the case of a currency contract, the contract expires and a new one is purchased, covering another period of time.

It is wise to consider investing abroad, since different economies experience prosperity and recession at different times. During the 1980s, foreign stocks were the number one performing investment, averaging a compound return of over 22 percent per year, compared to 18 percent for U.S. stocks and 5 percent for residential real estate. But during the past decade, U.S. stocks have outperformed foreign stocks (18.6% vs. 6.8%). Over the past fifteen years, U.S. stocks have had an average compound annual return of 17.2 percent versus 15.1 percent for foreign stocks (all periods ending 6/30/98).

To give you a broader perspective, take a look at how U.S. securities have fared against their foreign counterparts over each of the last twenty-six years.

Why Global Stocks and Bonds Deserve a Place
in Every Investor's Portfolio
(The following table shows the total return for each investment category in each of the past twenty-six years.)

Year	U.S. Stocks	U.S. Bonds	Non-U.S. Stocks	Non-U.S. Bonds
1972	+19.0	+5.7	+37.4	+ 4.4
1973	−14.6	−1.1	−14.2	+ 6.3
1974	−26.5	+4.4	−22.1	+ 5.3
1975	+37.2	+9.2	+37.0	+ 8.8
1976	+23.8	+16.8	+ 3.8	+10.5
1977	− 7.2	−0.7	+19.4	+38.9
1978	+ 6.6	−1.2	+34.3	+18.5
1979	+18.4	−1.2	+ 6.2	− 5.0
1980	+32.4	−4.0	+24.4	+13.7
1981	− 4.9	+1.9	− 1.0	− 4.6
1982	+22.5	+40.4	− 0.9	+11.9
1983	+22.6	+0.7	+24.6	+ 4.3
1984	+ 6.3	+15.5	+ 7.9	− 2.0
1985	+32.2	+31.0	+56.7	+37.2
1986	+18.5	+24.5	+67.9	+33.9
1987	+ 5.2	−2.7	+24.9	+36.1
1988	+16.8	+9.7	+28.6	+ 2.4
1989	+31.5	+18.1	+10.8	− 3.4
1990	− 3.2	+ 6.2	−14.9	+15.3
1991	+30.6	+19.3	+12.5	+16.2
1992	+ 7.7	+ 8.1	−12.2	+ 4.8
1993	+10.0	+18.2	+32.6	+15.1
1994	+ 1.3	− 7.8	+ 7.8	+ 6.0
1995	+37.4	+31.7	+11.2	+19.6
1996	+23.1	− 0.9	+6.1	+4.1
1997	+33.4	+15.9	+1.8	-4.3%

Number of years this category achieved the best results   9   4   8   5

Increasing your investment returns and reducing portfolio risk are two compelling reasons for investing worldwide. Global investing allows you to maximize your returns by investing in some of the world's best managed and most profitable companies. Japan, for example, is the world's leading producer of sophisticated electronics goods; Germany of heavy machinery; the United States of biotechnology; and Southeast Asia of commodity-manufactured goods.

World market dominance is constantly changing. Ten years ago the United States represented half of the world's stock market capital, while today it represents 42 percent of total world capitalization. Only three times in the past ten years has the U.S. stock market been among the five best performers in the world (1991, 1992, and 1995). The greatest potential for growth today lies in those countries that are industrializing, have the cheapest labor and the richest natural resources, and yet remain undervalued.

Diversification reduces investment risk: Recent studies have once again proven this most basic investment principle. A 1996 study showed that the least volatile investment portfolio over the past 25 years (1972–1996) would have been composed of 60 percent U.S. equities and 40 percent foreign equities. These results reflect the importance of balancing a portfolio between U.S. and foreign equities.

The newly industrialized countries are favored locations for the manufacture and assembly of consumer electronics products. Displaced from high-cost countries such as the United States and Japan, electronics factories in these developing countries significantly benefit from reduced labor costs. Today, in fact, Korea is the world's third-largest manufacturer of semiconductors.

The Pacific Region yields yet another country with strong economic growth: China. Opportunities to benefit from the industrialization of China come from firms listed on the Hong Kong Stock Exchange, in such basic areas as electricity, construction materials, public transportation, and fundamental telecommunications. Indeed, these low-tech and essential industries, once growth industries in the United States, are now the foundation of a natural growth progression occurring in the NICs of Southeast Asia.

Companies such as China Light and Power (Hong Kong), Siam Cement (Thailand), and Hyundai (Korea) offer much the same profit potential today as their northern European counterparts did one hundred years ago, their U.S. counterparts forty years ago, and their Japanese counterparts as recently as twenty years ago.

Investors have long been familiar with the names of many of Europe's major producers—Nestlé, Olivetti, Shell, Bayer, Volkswagen, and Perrier, to name just a few. Europe's impressive manufacturing capacity, diverse industrial base, quality labor pools, and many leading, multinational, blue-chip corporations can make it an environment for growth, accessible to you through foreign funds.

With economic deregulation and the elimination of internal trade barriers, many European companies are, for the first time in history, investing in and competing for exposure to the whole European market. Companies currently restricted to manufacturing and distributing within their national boundaries will soon be able to locate facilities anywhere in Europe, maximizing the efficient employment of labor, capital, and raw materials.

The global stock category is made up of 1,145 funds: 270 "World," 590 "Foreign," 100 "European" and 185 "Pacific." Total market capitalization of this entire category is $360 billion. These funds typically throw off a dividend of less than one percent and have an expense ratio of 1.8 percent. The price-earnings (p/e) ratio is 26, versus a p/e ratio of 30 for the typical stock in the S&P 500.

Over the past three years, global equity funds have had an average compound return of 9.9 percent per year. The annual return for the past five years has been 10.6 percent, 9.4 percent for the past ten years, and 12.8 percent for the last fifteen years. The standard deviation for global equity funds has been 15 percent over the past three years. This means that global equity funds have experienced about 10 percent less volatility than growth funds.

International, or foreign, funds should be part of most equity portfolios. They can provide superior returns and reduce overall portfolio risk. As with any other fund category, this one should not be looked at in a vacuum.

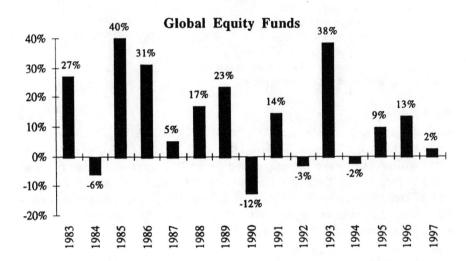

AIM Global Growth & Income A

11 Greenway Plaza, Suite 1919
Houston, TX 77046-1173
(800) 347-4246

total return	★★★
risk reduction	★★★★★
management	★★★★
tax minimization	★★★★
expense control	★★★★
symbol GAGIX	20 points
up-market performance	n/a
down-market performance	n/a
predictability of returns	excellent

Total Return   ★★★

Over the past five years (all periods ending 6/30/98), AIM Global Growth &
Income A has taken $10,000 and turned it into $20,470 ($17,560 over three years).
This translates into an average annual return of 15.4 percent over the past five years
and 20.6 percent over the past three years. Over the past five years, this fund has
outperformed 60 percent of all mutual funds; within its general category it has done
better than 75 percent of its peers. Global equity funds have averaged 11 percent
annually over these same five years.

Risk/Volatility   ★★★★★

Over the past five years, AIM Global Growth & Income A has been safer than 85
percent of all global equity funds. Over the past decade, the fund has had one negative year, while the S&P 500 has had one (off 3 percent in 1990); the EAFE fell
twice (off 23 percent in 1990 and 12 percent in 1992). The fund has underperformed the S&P 500 six times and the EAFE Index two times in the last ten years.

	last 5 years		since inception	
worst year	–4%	1994	–4%	1994
best year	27%	1993	27%	1993

In the past, Growth & Income A has done better than 65 percent of its peer
group in up markets. Consistency, or predictability, of returns for Growth &
Income A can be described as excellent.

Management   ★★★★

There are 95 stocks in this $330 million portfolio. The average global equity fund
today is $325 million in size. Close to 79 percent of the fund's holdings are in
stocks. The stocks in this portfolio have an average price-earnings (p/e) ratio of 26
and a median market capitalization of $23 billion. The portfolio's equity holdings
can be categorized as large-cap and a blend of growth and value stocks.

Paul Griffiths and Nicholas S. Train have managed this fund for the past five years. There are 117 funds besides Global Growth & Income A within the AIM Family of Funds. Overall, the fund family's risk-adjusted performance can be described as good.

Tax Minimization   ★★★★
During the past five years, a $10,000 initial investment grew to $16,490 after taxes, assuming a 39.6 percent income tax bracket (state and federal combined) and a capital gains rate of 28 percent. This means that investors in this fund were able to preserve 87 percent of their total returns. Compared to other equity funds, this fund's tax savings are considered to be very good.

Expenses   ★★★★
Growth & Income A's expense ratio is 1.5 percent; it has averaged 1.6 percent annually over the past three calendar years. The average expense ratio for the 1,100 funds in this category is 1.8 percent. This fund's turnover rate over the past year has been 50 percent, while its peer group average has been 75 percent.

Summary
AIM Global Growth & Income A offers the worldwide equity investor a high degree of safety while still delivering top-tier returns. The fund's overall ranking is quite high and it does not fall short in any category. The parent company, AIM, is well-regarded among the financial planning and brokerage communities. Look to AIM for additional offerings to help round out your portfolio.

Profile
minimum initial investment $500
subsequent minimum investment . . . $50
available in all 50 states. . . . . yes
telephone exchanges. . . . . yes
number of funds in family 118

IRA accounts available . . . . yes
IRA minimum investment $100
date of inception . . . . Sept. 1990
dividend/income paid . . . . annually
quality of annual reports . . . . excellent

Bartlett Europe A

36 East Fourth Street
Cincinnati, OH 45202
(800) 800-3609

total return	★★★★★
risk reduction	★★★★
management	★★★★
tax minimization	★★★
expense control	★
symbol BEPFX	17 points
up-market performance	very good
down-market performance	poor
predictability of returns	fair

Total Return   ★★★★★

Over the past five years (all periods ending 6/30/98), Bartlett Europe A has taken $10,000 and turned it into $27,950 ($22,090 over three years and $27,540 over the past ten years). This translates into an average annual return of 22.8 percent over the past five years, 30.2 percent over the past three years, and 10.7 percent for the decade. Over the past five years, this fund has outperformed 75 percent of all mutual funds; within its general category it has done better than 65 percent of its peers. Global equity funds have averaged 11 percent annually over these same five years.

Risk/Volatility   ★★★★

Over the past five years, Bartlett Europe A has been safer than 30 percent of all global equity funds. Over the past decade, the fund has had three negative years, while the S&P 500 has had one (off 3 percent in 1990); the EAFE fell twice (off 23 percent in 1990 and 12 percent in 1992). The fund has underperformed the S&P 500 seven times and the EAFE Index four times in the last ten years.

	last 5 years		last 10 years	
worst year	–4%	1994	–22%	1990
best year	30%	1996	30%	1996

In the past, Europe A has done better than 85 percent of its peer group in up markets but outperformed just 5 percent of its competition in down markets. Consistency, or predictability, of returns for Europe A can be described as fair.

Management   ★★★★

There are 50 stocks in this $60 million portfolio. The average global equity fund today is $325 million in size. Close to 98 percent of the fund's holdings are in stocks. The stocks in this portfolio have an average price-earnings (p/e) ratio of 30 and a median market capitalization of $29 billion. The portfolio's equity holdings can be categorized as large-cap and growth-oriented issues.

A team has managed this fund for the past five years. There are two funds besides Europe A within the Bartlett family. Overall, the fund family's risk-adjusted performance can be described as good.

Tax Minimization   ★★★
During the past five years, a $10,000 initial investment grew to $26,480 after taxes, assuming a 39.6 percent income tax bracket (state and federal combined) and a capital gains rate of 28 percent. This means that investors in this fund were able to preserve 83 percent of their total returns. Compared to other equity funds, this fund's tax savings are considered to be good.

Expenses   ★
Bartlett Europe A's expense ratio is 1.9 percent; it has averaged 2.0 percent annually over the past three calendar years. The average expense ratio for the 1,100 funds in this category is 1.8 percent. This fund's turnover rate over the past year has been 123 percent, while its peer group average has been 75 percent.

Summary
Bartlett Europe A went through a major change several years ago, abandoning a global approach and instead focusing on a pure European play that consists of a relatively small number of equities. Lead manager Armist's concentration and geographical shift have proven to be highly effective. Volatility at times can be quite high, but comparatively low for a specialized fund such as this one. Conceptually this fund makes a lot of sense, and in light of recent events in the Pacific Basin, having a foreign fund that totally avoids such chaos is comforting.

Profile

minimum initial investment $1,000	*IRA accounts available* . . . . yes
subsequent minimum investment . . $100	*IRA minimum investment* $1,000
available in all 50 states . . . . no	*date of inception* . . . . Aug. 1986
telephone exchanges . . . . no	*dividend/income paid* . . . . annually
number of funds in family 3	*quality of annual reports* . . . . n/a

Capital World Growth & Income

333 South Hope Street
Los Angeles, CA 90071
(800) 421-4120

total return	★★★★
risk reduction	★★★★★
management	★★★★★
tax minimization	★★
expense control	★★★★★
symbol CWGIX	21 points
up-market performance	n/a
down-market performance	n/a
predictability of returns	very good

Total Return   ★★★★

Over the past five years (all periods ending 6/30/98), Capital World Growth & Income has taken $10,000 and turned it into $23,590 ($17,710 over three years). This translates into an average annual return of 18.7 percent over the past five years and 21.0 percent over the past three years. Over the past five years, this fund has outperformed 75 percent of all mutual funds; within its general category it has done better than 70 percent of its peers. Global equity funds have averaged 11 percent annually over these same five years.

Risk/Volatility   ★★★★★

Over the past five years, Capital World Growth & Income has been safer than 98 percent of all global equity funds. Over the past decade, the fund has had no negative years, while the S&P 500 has had one (off 3 percent in 1990); the EAFE fell twice (off 23 percent in 1990 and 12 percent in 1992). The fund has underperformed the S&P 500 four times and has outperformed the EAFE every year for the last ten years.

	last 5 years		last 10 years	
worst year	1%	1994	1%	1994
best year	22%	1996	22%	1996

Consistency, or predictability, of returns for Capital World Growth & Income can be described as very good.

Management   ★★★★★

There are 305 stocks in this $9 billion portfolio. The average global equity fund today is $325 million in size. Close to 83 percent of the fund's holdings are in stocks. The stocks in this portfolio have an average price-earnings (p/e) ratio of 25 and a median market capitalization of $11 billion. The portfolio's equity holdings can be categorized as large-cap and a blend of growth and value stocks.

A team has managed this fund for the past five years. There are 24 funds besides Growth & Income within the American Funds Group. Overall, the fund family's risk-adjusted performance can be described as very good.

Tax Minimization   ★★

During the past five years, a $10,000 initial investment grew to $22,170 after taxes, assuming a 39.6 percent income tax bracket (state and federal combined) and a capital gains rate of 28 percent. This means that investors in this fund were able to preserve 79 percent of their total returns. Compared to other equity funds, this fund's tax savings are considered to be fair.

Expenses   ★★★★★

Growth & Income's expense ratio is 0.8 percent; it has also averaged 0.8 percent annually over the past three calendar years. The average expense ratio for the 1,100 funds in this category is 1.8 percent. This fund's turnover rate over the past year has been 32 percent, while its peer group average has been 75 percent.

Summary

Capital World Growth & Income, a member of the American Funds Group that is managed by Capital Guardian Trust Company, is one of a very few large fund families that has any business overseeing foreign securities. Management has extensive experience, manpower and resources that give it a significant edge over the competition. Like a large number of other offerings from this family, selecting this global equity fund is a no brainer.

Profile

minimum initial investment . . . . . $1,000   *IRA accounts available* . . . . yes
subsequent minimum investment . . . $50   *IRA minimum investment* $250
available in all 50 states. . . . . yes   *date of inception*. . . . . Mar. 1993
telephone exchanges. . . . . yes   *dividend/income paid* . . . . annually
number of funds in family 25   *quality of annual reports* . . . . excellent

Fidelity Europe

82 Devonshire Street
Boston, MA 02109
(800) 544-8888

total return	★★★★★
risk reduction	★★★★
management	★★★★★
tax minimization	★★★★
expense control	★★★★
symbol FIEUX	22 points
up-market performance	excellent
down-market performance	good
predictability of returns	good

Total Return   ★★★★★

Over the past five years (all periods ending 6/30/98), Fidelity Europe has taken $10,000 and turned it into $28,440 ($20,610 over three years and $41,960 over the past ten years). This translates into an average annual return of 23.3 percent over the past five years, 27.3 percent over the past three years, and 15.4 percent for the decade. Over the past five years, this fund has outperformed 85 percent of all mutual funds; within its general category it has done better than 65 percent of its peers. Global equity funds have averaged 11 percent annually over these same five years.

Risk/Volatility   ★★★★

Over the past five years, Fidelity Europe has been safer than 90 percent of all global equity funds. Over the past decade, the fund has had two negative years, while the S&P 500 has had one (off 3 percent in 1990); the EAFE fell twice (off 23 percent in 1990 and 12 percent in 1992). The fund has underperformed the S&P 500 six times and the EAFE Index four times in the last ten years.

	last 5 years		last 10 years	
worst year	6%	1994	–5%	1990
best year	27%	1993	32%	1989

In the past, Fidelity Europe has done better than 90 percent of its peer group in up markets and outperformed 50 percent of its competition in down markets. Consistency, or predictability, of returns for Fidelity Europe can be described as good.

Management   ★★★★★

There are 120 stocks in this $18 billion portfolio. The average global equity fund today is $325 million in size. Close to 97 percent of the fund's holdings are in stocks. The stocks in this portfolio have an average price-earnings (p/e) ratio of 28

and a median market capitalization of $20 billion. The portfolio's equity holdings can be categorized as large-cap and growth-oriented issues.

Sally E. Walden has managed this fund for the past six years. There are 144 funds besides Europe within the Fidelity Group. Overall, the fund family's risk-adjusted performance can be described as good.

Tax Minimization   ★★★★

During the past five years, a $10,000 initial investment grew to $27,450 after taxes, assuming a 39.6 percent income tax bracket (state and federal combined) and a capital gains rate of 28 percent. This means that investors in this fund were able to preserve 91 percent of their total returns. Compared to other equity funds, this fund's tax savings are considered to be very good.

Expenses   ★★★★

Fidelity Europe's expense ratio is 1.2 percent; it has also averaged 1.2 percent annually over the past three calendar years. The average expense ratio for the 1,100 funds in this category is 1.8 percent. This fund's turnover rate over the past year has been 57 percent, while its peer group average has been 75 percent.

Summary

Fidelity Europe has an overall ranking of number two in the broad-based category of foreign and global equity funds. Individual rankings in every category are either very good or excellent. Fidelity receives quite a bit of attention in the financial press as being the largest fund family in the country; sometimes some of their lesser known offerings such as this one are not given the positive publicity they deserve. Manager Walden sticks to her guns and only buys companies whose products or services she understands. This philosophy has paid off handsomely: the fund's risk-adjusted returns have been superb over the past three, five and ten years—an amazing accomplishment.

Profile

minimum initial investment $2,500	*IRA accounts available* . . . . yes
subsequent minimum investment . . $250	*IRA minimum investment* $500
available in all 50 states. . . . . yes	*date of inception* . . . . Oct. 1986
telephone exchanges. . . . . yes	*dividend/income paid* . . . . annually
number of funds in family 145	*quality of annual reports* . . . . excellent

# GAM Europe A

135 East 57th Street, 25th Floor
New York, NY 10022
(800) 426-4685

| | |
|---|---|
| total return | ★★★★ |
| risk reduction | ★★★★ |
| management | ★★★★ |
| tax minimization | ★★★ |
| expense control | ★★ |
| symbol GEURX | 17 points |
| up-market performance | good |
| down-market performance | poor |
| predictability of returns | good |

## Total Return ★★★★

Over the past five years (all periods ending 6/30/98), GAM Europe A has taken $10,000 and turned it into $24,520 ($19,630 over three years). This translates into an average annual return of 19.7 percent over the past five years and 25.2 percent over the past three years. Over the past five years, this fund has outperformed 75 percent of all mutual funds; within its general category it has done better than 45 percent of its peers. Global equity funds have averaged 11 percent annually over these same five years.

## Risk/Volatility ★★★★

Over the past five years, GAM Europe A has been safer than 65 percent of all global equity funds. Over the past decade, the fund has had four negative years, while the S&P 500 has had one (off 3 percent in 1990); the EAFE fell twice (off 23 percent in 1990 and 12 percent in 1992). The fund has underperformed the S&P 500 seven times and the EAFE Index two times in the last ten years.

| | last 5 years | | since inception | |
|---|---|---|---|---|
| worst year | –3% | 1994 | –16% | 1990 |
| best year | 28% | 1997 | 28% | 1997 |

In the past, Europe A has done better than 65 percent of its peer group in up markets and outperformed just 15 percent of its competition in down markets. Consistency, or predictability, of returns for GAM Europe A can be described as good.

## Management ★★★★

There are 50 stocks in this $60 million portfolio. The average global equity fund today is $325 million in size. Close to 100 percent of the fund's holdings are in stocks. The stocks in this portfolio have an average price-earnings (p/e) ratio of 28
```

and a median market capitalization of $30 billion. The portfolio's equity holdings can be categorized as large-cap and growth-oriented issues.

John Bennett has managed this fund for the past five years. There are 10 funds besides Europe A within the GAM family. Overall, the fund family's risk-adjusted performance can be described as good.

Tax Minimization ★★★

During the past five years, a $10,000 initial investment grew to $23,170 after taxes, assuming a 39.6 percent income tax bracket (state and federal combined) and a capital gains rate of 28 percent. This means that investors in this fund were able to preserve 85 percent of their total returns. Compared to other equity funds, this fund's tax savings are considered to be good.

Expenses ★★

GAM Europe A's expense ratio is 1.9 percent; it has averaged 2.0 percent annually over the past three calendar years. The average expense ratio for the 1,100 funds in this category is 1.8 percent. This fund's turnover rate over the past year has been 76 percent, while its peer group average has been 75 percent.

Summary

GAM Europe A is one of the few sector funds to make the grade. This foreign equity portfolio scores well in every important category. A solid choice for the investor who wants exposure outside of the U.S. but wants to avoid Asia.

Profile

minimum initial investment $5,000	*IRA accounts available* . . . . yes
subsequent minimum investment . . $500	*IRA minimum investment* $2,000
available in all 50 states. . . . . yes	*date of inception* . . . . Jan. 1990
telephone exchanges. . . . . yes	*dividend/income paid* . . . . annually
number of funds in family 11	*quality of annual reports* . . . . good

Idex Global A

201 Highland Avenue
Largo, FL 34640
(888) 233-4339

total return	★★★★★
risk reduction	★★★★
management	★★★★
tax minimization	★★★★
expense control	★★
symbol IGLBX	19 points
up-market performance	n/a
down-market performance	n/a
predictability of returns	good

Total Return   ★★★★★

Over the past five years (all periods ending 6/30/98), Idex Global A has taken $10,000 and turned it into $29,010 ($21,080 over three years). This translates into an average annual return of 23.7 percent over the past five years and 28.2 percent over the past three years. Over the past five years, this fund has outperformed 81 percent of all mutual funds; within its general category it has done better than 84 percent of its peers. Global equity funds have averaged 11 percent annually over these same five years.

Risk/Volatility   ★★★★

Over the past five years, Idex Global A has been safer than 75 percent of all global equity funds. Over the past decade, the fund has had no negative years, while the S&P 500 has had one (off 3 percent in 1990); the EAFE fell twice (off 23 percent in 1990 and 12 percent in 1992). The fund has underperformed the S&P 500 three times and the EAFE Index two times in the last ten years.

	last 5 years		since inception	
worst year	1%	1994	1%	1994
best year	31%	1993	31%	1993

Consistency, or predictability, of returns for Global A can be described as good.

Management   ★★★★

There are 210 stocks in this $320 million portfolio. The average global equity fund today is $325 million in size. Close to 97 percent of the fund's holdings are in stocks. The stocks in this portfolio have an average price-earnings (p/e) ratio of 36 and a median market capitalization of $20 billion. The portfolio's equity holdings can be categorized as large-cap and growth-oriented issues.

Helen Young Hayes has managed this fund for the past six years. There are 33 funds besides Global A within the Idex Group. Overall, the fund family's risk-adjusted performance can be described as good.

Tax Minimization   ★★★★

During the past five years, a $10,000 initial investment grew to $27,310 after taxes, assuming a 39.6 percent income tax bracket (state and federal combined) and a capital gains rate of 28 percent. This means that investors in this fund were able to preserve 88 percent of their total returns. Compared to other equity funds, this fund's tax savings are considered to be very good.

Expenses   ★★

Global A's expense ratio is 1.9 percent; it has averaged 2.0 percent annually over the past three calendar years. The average expense ratio for the 1,100 funds in this category is 1.8 percent. This fund's turnover rate over the past year has been 91 percent, while its peer group average has been 75 percent.

Summary

Idex Global A scores in the top quartile for each of the past several years; risk-adjusted returns over the past three and five years have been superb. The portfolio is mostly comprised of U.S. and foreign equities, but management also considers high-quality bonds from around the world. The two largest regional holdings are the U.S. and the U.K. Ony a small percentage of the fund is in Japan, Latin America, Asia and Japan. Total return has been exceptional, and risk management has been quite good.

Profile

minimum initial investment $500	IRA accounts available . . . . yes
subsequent minimum investment . . . $50	IRA minimum investment $50
available in all 50 states. . . . . yes	date of inception . . . . Oct. 1992
telephone exchanges. . . . . yes	dividend/income paid . . . . annually
number of funds in family 34	quality of annual reports . . . . excellent

Janus Worldwide

100 Fillmore Street, Suite 300
Denver, CO 80206-4923
(800) 525-8983

total return	★★★★★
risk reduction	★★★★
management	★★★★★
tax minimization	★★★★
expense control	★★★★
symbol JAWWX	22 points
up-market performance	n/a
down-market performance	n/a
predictability of returns	good

Total Return   ★★★★★

Over the past five years (all periods ending 6/30/98), Janus Worldwide has taken $10,000 and turned it into $28,850 ($21,400 over three years). This translates into an average annual return of 23.6 percent over the past five years and 28.9 percent over the past three years. Over the past five years, this fund has outperformed 85 percent of all mutual funds; within its general category it has done better than 90 percent of its peers. Global equity funds have averaged 11 percent annually over these same five years.

Risk/Volatility   ★★★★

Over the past five years, Janus Worldwide has been safer than 88 percent of all global equity funds. Over the past decade, the fund has had no negative years, while the S&P 500 has had one (off 3 percent in 1990); the EAFE fell twice (off 23 percent in 1990 and 12 percent in 1992). The fund has underperformed the S&P 500 two times and the EAFE Index two times in the last ten years.

	last 5 years		since inception	
worst year	3%	1994	3%	1994
best year	28%	1993	28%	1993

Consistency, or predictability, of returns for Worldwide can be described as good.

Management   ★★★★★

There are 190 stocks in this $16 billion portfolio. The average global equity fund today is $325 million in size. Close to 95 percent of the fund's holdings are in stocks. The stocks in this portfolio have an average price-earnings (p/e) ratio of 36 and a median market capitalization of $20 billion. The portfolio's equity holdings can be categorized as large-cap and growth-oriented issues.

Helen Young Hayes has managed this fund for the past six years. There are 15 funds besides Worldwide within the Janus family. Overall, the fund family's risk-adjusted performance can be described as very good.

Tax Minimization ★★★★
During the past five years, a $10,000 initial investment grew to $28,820 after taxes, assuming a 39.6 percent income tax bracket (state and federal combined) and a capital gains rate of 28 percent. This means that investors in this fund were able to preserve 92 percent of their total returns. Compared to other equity funds, this fund's tax savings are considered to be very good.

Expenses ★★★★
Janus Worldwide's expense ratio is 1.0 percent; it has averaged 1.1 percent annually over the past three calendar years. The average expense ratio for the 1,100 funds in this category is 1.8 percent. This fund's turnover rate over the past year has been 79 percent, while its peer group average has been 75 percent.

Summary
Janus Worldwide has had unsurpassed risk-adjusted returns for the past three and five years. On a pure total return basis, the fund has consistently ranked in the top quartile of its large peer group for each of the past several years. This fund ranks as one of the very best funds; its score in every category ranking is either very good or excellent. This, along with some other funds from Janus, is highly recommended.

Profile

minimum initial investment $2,500	*IRA accounts available* . . . . yes
subsequent minimum investment . . $100	*IRA minimum investment* $500
available in all 50 states. . . . . yes	*date of inception.* . . . . May 1991
telephone exchanges. . . . . yes	*dividend/income paid* . . . . annually
number of funds in family 16	*quality of annual reports* . . . . excellent

Merrill Lynch EuroFund B

Box 9011
Princeton, NJ 08543-901
(800) 637-3863

total return	★★★★★
risk reduction	★★★★
management	★★★★
tax minimization	★★★
expense control	★★
symbol MBEFX	18 points
up-market performance	excellent
down-market performance	good
predictability of returns	good

Total Return   ★★★★★

Over the past five years (all periods ending 6/30/98), Merrill Lynch EuroFund B has taken $10,000 and turned it into $26,590 ($19,460 over three years and $39,210 over the past ten years). This translates into an average annual return of 21.6 percent over the past five years, 24.8 percent over the past three years, and 14.6 percent for the decade. Over the past five years, this fund has outperformed 75 percent of all mutual funds; within its general category it has done better than 45 percent of its peers. Global equity funds have averaged 11 percent annually over these same five years.

Risk/Volatility   ★★★★

Over the past five years, Merrill Lynch EuroFund B has been safer than 55 percent of all global equity funds. Over the past decade, the fund has had two negative years, while the S&P 500 has had one (off 3 percent in 1990); the EAFE fell twice (off 23 percent in 1990 and 12 percent in 1992). The fund has underperformed the S&P 500 seven times and the EAFE Index three times in the last ten years.

	last 5 years		last 10 years	
worst year	3%	1994	–6%	1992
best year	31%	1993	31%	1993

In the past, EuroFund B has done better than 90 percent of its peer group in up markets and outperformed 50 percent of its competition in down markets. Consistency, or predictability, of returns for EuroFund B can be described as good.

Management   ★★★★

There are 105 stocks in this $975 million portfolio. The average global equity fund today is $325 million in size. Close to 80 percent of the fund's holdings are in stocks. The stocks in this portfolio have an average price-earnings (p/e) ratio of 25 and a median market capitalization of $11 billion. The portfolio's equity holdings can be categorized as large-cap and value-oriented issues.

Adrian Holmes has managed this fund for the past five years. There are 284 funds besides EuroFund B within the Merrill Lynch family. Overall, the fund family's risk-adjusted performance can be described as good.

Tax Minimization ★★★

During the past five years, a $10,000 initial investment grew to $26,240 after taxes, assuming a 39.6 percent income tax bracket (state and federal combined) and a capital gains rate of 28 percent. This means that investors in this fund were able to preserve 82 percent of their total returns. Compared to other equity funds, this fund's tax savings are considered to be good.

Expenses ★★

Merrill Lynch EuroFund B's expense ratio is 2.1 percent; it has also averaged 2.1 percent annually over the past three calendar years. The average expense ratio for the 1,100 funds in this category is 1.8 percent. This fund's turnover rate over the past year has been 93 percent, while its peer group average has been 75 percent.

Summary

Merrill Lynch EuroFund B invests at least four-fifths of its holdings in European equities. By sticking with large cap value stocks, the fund has been able to maintain a superb risk-adjusted return ranking for the past three, five and ten years. Portfolio manager Holmes first looks for industry sectors that have been taking a beating, then narrows the selection process to those equities of companies he believes have strong growth prospects. Although management is quite active in its approach, the fund is not afraid to sometimes hold a rather high percentage in cash equivalents.

Profile

minimum initial investment $1,000	*IRA accounts available* . . . . yes
subsequent minimum investment . . . $50	*IRA minimum investment* $100
available in all 50 states. . . . . yes	*date of inception* . . . . Jan. 1987
telephone exchanges . . . . no	*dividend/income paid* . . . . annually
number of funds in family 285	*quality of annual reports* . . . . good

Oppenheimer Quest Global Value Fund, Inc. A

Oppenheimer Funds, Inc.
Two World Trade Center, 34th Floor
New York, NY 10048
(800) 525-7048

total return	★★★
risk reduction	★★★★★
management	★★★★
tax minimization	★★★
expense control	★★★
symbol OVGLX	20 points
up-market performance	good
down-market performance	n/a
predictability of returns	excellent

Total Return   ★★★

Over the past five years (all periods ending 6/30/98), Oppenheimer Quest Global Value A has taken $10,000 and turned it into $21,050 ($16,460 over three years). This translates into an average annual return of 16.1 percent over the past five years and 18.1 percent over the past three years. Over the past five years, this fund has outperformed 75 percent of all mutual funds; within its general category it has done better than 70 percent of its peers. Global equity funds have averaged 11 percent annually over these same five years.

Risk/Volatility   ★★★★★

Over the past five years, Oppenheimer Quest Global Value A has been safer than 96 percent of all global equity funds. Over the past eight years, the fund has had no negative years, while the S&P 500 has had one (off 3 percent in 1990); the EAFE fell twice (off 23 percent in 1990 and 12 percent in 1992). The fund has underperformed the S&P 500 five times and the EAFE Index two times in the last ten years.

	last 5 years		since inception	
worst year	3%	1994	2%	1992
best year	25%	1993	25%	1993

In the past, Global Value has done better than 60 percent of its peer group in up markets. Consistency, or predictability, of returns for Global Value can be described as excellent.

Management   ★★★★

There are 130 stocks in this $320 million portfolio. The average global equity fund today is $325 million in size. Close to 94 percent of the fund's holdings are in stocks. The stocks in this portfolio have an average price-earnings (p/e) ratio of 26 and a median market capitalization of $27 billion. The portfolio's equity holdings can be categorized as large-cap and a blend of growth and value stocks.

James Sheldon and Richard Glasebrook II have managed this fund for the past six years. There are over 65 funds besides Global Value A within the Oppenheimer family. Overall, the fund family's risk-adjusted performance can be described as good.

Tax Minimization   ★★★

During the past five years, a $10,000 initial investment grew to $19,810 after taxes, assuming a 39.6 percent income tax bracket (state and federal combined) and a capital gains rate of 28 percent. This means that investors in this fund were able to preserve 81 percent of their total returns. Compared to other equity funds, this fund's tax savings are considered to be good.

Expenses   ★★★

Global Value A's expense ratio is 1.7 percent; it has averaged 1.8 percent annually over the past three calendar years. The average expense ratio for the 1,100 funds in this category is 1.8 percent. This fund's turnover rate over the past year has been 32 percent, while its peer group average has been 75 percent.

Summary

Oppenheimer Quest Global Value A's risk reduction methods have been so successful as to attract even the most skeptical overseas investor. Approximately a third or more of the portfolio is in domestic equities, with Europe as a close second. The fund has very little exposure to Latin America or Asian economies. Managers Sheldon and Glasebrook love companies with large returns on equity and plenty of cash flow. The approach has resulted in very good returns with very low risk.

Profile

minimum initial investment $1,000	*IRA accounts available* . . . . yes
subsequent minimum investment . . . $25	*IRA minimum investment* $250
available in all 50 states. . . . . yes	*date of inception* . . . . Jul. 1990
telephone exchanges. . . . . yes	*dividend/income paid* . . . . annually
number of funds in family . . . . . over 65	*quality of annual reports* . . . . good

Scout Worldwide

P.O. Box 410498
Kansas City, MO 64141-0498
(800) 422-2766

total return	★★★
risk reduction	★★★★★
managemen	★★★★★
tax minimization	★★★★★
expense control	★★★★★
symbol UMBWX	23 points
up-market performance	n/a
down-market performance	n/a
predictability of returns	excellent

Total Return   ★★★

Over the past five years (all periods ending 6/30/98), Scout Worldwide has taken $10,000 and turned it into $20,860 ($17,430 over three years). This translates into an average annual return of 15.8 percent over the past five years and 20.4 percent over the past three years. Over the past five years, this fund has outperformed 70 percent of all mutual funds; within its general category it has done better than 85 percent of its peers. Global equity funds have averaged 11 percent annually over these same five years.

Risk/Volatility   ★★★★★

Over the past five years, Scout Worldwide has been safer than 99 percent of all global equity funds. Over the past decade, the fund has had no negative years, while the S&P 500 has had one (off 3 percent in 1990); the EAFE fell twice (off 23 percent in 1990 and 12 percent in 1992). The fund has underperformed the S&P 500 three times and the EAFE Index one time in the last ten years.

	last 5 years		since inception	
worst year	4%	1994	4%	1994
best year	18%	1996	18%	1996

Consistency, or predictability, of returns for Worldwide can be described as excellent.

Management   ★★★★★

There are 65 stocks in this $80 million portfolio. The average global equity fund today is $325 million in size. Close to 85 percent of the fund's holdings are in stocks. The stocks in this portfolio have an average price-earnings (p/e) ratio of 29 and a median market capitalization of $17 billion. The portfolio's equity holdings can be categorized as large-cap and growth-oriented issues.

James L. Moffett has managed this fund for the past five years. There are four funds besides Worldwide within the Scout family. Overall, the fund family's risk-adjusted performance can be described as good.

Tax Minimization ★★★★★
During the past five years, a $10,000 initial investment grew to $20,840 after taxes, assuming a 39.6 percent income tax bracket (state and federal combined) and a capital gains rate of 28 percent. This means that investors in this fund were able to preserve 94 percent of their total returns. Compared to other equity funds, this fund's tax savings are considered to be excellent.

Expenses ★★★★★
Worldwide's expense ratio is 0.9 percent; it has also averaged 0.9 percent annually over the past three calendar years. The average expense ratio for the 1,100 funds in this category is 1.8 percent. This fund's turnover rate over the past year has been 18 percent, while its peer group average has been 75 percent.

Summary
Scout Worldwide has ranked in the top quartile among its peers for each of the past several years; risk-adjusted returns have been just great. Manager Moffett has successfully avoided emerging markets and instead looks to blue chip issues that are well-followed by the brokerage industry. This cautious approach, along with fantastic management that is in control of overhead and tax efficiency, has resulted in this fund obtaining an almost-perfect score. This is the most highly ranked foreign or global fund in the book.

Profile
minimum initial investment $1,000	*IRA accounts available* . . . . yes
subsequent minimum investment . . $100	*IRA minimum investment* $250
available in all 50 states . . . . no	*date of inception.* . . . . Mar. 1993
telephone exchanges. . . . . yes	*dividend/income paid* . . . . annually
number of funds in family 5	*quality of annual reports* . . . . good

T. Rowe Price European Stock

100 East Pratt Street
Baltimore, MD 21202
(800) 638-5660

total return	★★★★★
risk reduction	★★★★
management	★★★★★
tax minimization	★★★★★
expense control	★★★★
symbol PRESX	23 points
up-market performance	excellent
down-market performance	good
predictability of returns	good

Total Return   ★★★★★
Over the past five years (all periods ending 6/30/98), T. Rowe Price European Stock has taken $10,000 and turned it into $27,740 ($19,880 over three years). This translates into an average annual return of 22.6 percent over the past five years and 25.7 percent over the past three years. Over the past five years, this fund has outperformed 85 percent of all mutual funds; within its general category it has done better than 60 percent of its peers. Global equity funds have averaged 11 percent annually over these same five years.

Risk/Volatility   ★★★★
Over the past five years, T. Rowe Price European Stock has been safer than 80 percent of all global equity funds. Over the past decade, the fund has had one negative year, while the S&P 500 has had one (off 3 percent in 1990); the EAFE fell twice (off 23 percent in 1990 and 12 percent in 1992). The fund has underperformed the S&P 500 four times and the EAFE Index three times in the last ten years.

	last 5 years		since inception	
worst year	4%	1994	–6%	1992
best year	27%	1993	27%	1993

In the past, European Stock has done better than 85 percent of its peer group in up markets and outperformed 70 percent of its competition in down markets. Consistency, or predictability, of returns for European Stock can be described as good.

Management   ★★★★★
There are 235 stocks in this $1.5 billion portfolio. The average global equity fund today is $325 million in size. Close to 93 percent of the fund's holdings are in stocks. The stocks in this portfolio have an average price-earnings (p/e) ratio of 31

and a median market capitalization of $19 billion. The portfolio's equity holdings can be categorized as large-cap and growth-oriented issues.

A team has managed this fund for the past five years. There are 65 funds besides European Stock within the T. Rowe Price family. Overall, the fund family's risk-adjusted performance can be described as very good.

Tax Minimization   ★★★★★
During the past five years, a $10,000 initial investment grew to $27,730 after taxes, assuming a 39.6 percent income tax bracket (state and federal combined) and a capital gains rate of 28 percent. This means that investors in this fund were able to preserve 96 percent of their total returns. Compared to other equity funds, this fund's tax savings are considered to be excellent.

Expenses   ★★★★
T. Rowe Price European Stock's expense ratio is 1.1 percent; it has also averaged 1.1 percent annually over the past three calendar years. The average expense ratio for the 1,100 funds in this category is 1.8 percent. This fund's turnover rate over the past year has been 18 percent, while its peer group average has been 75 percent.

Summary
T. Rowe Price European Stock ranks as one of the very best foreign or global funds but beats out the other contenders with a superior total return. The fund tracks the MSCI Europe Index more closely than almost any other international portfolio. Part of the reason management has been able to keep the fund's risk level well below its peer group average is by sticking to large multinational companies. Tax minimization has also been great.

Profile
minimum initial investment . . . . . $2,500   *IRA accounts available* . . . . yes
subsequent minimum investment . . $100   *IRA minimum investment* $1,000
available in all 50 states. . . . . yes   *date of inception* . . . . Feb. 1990
telephone exchanges. . . . . yes   *dividend/income paid* . . . . annually
number of funds in family 66   *quality of annual reports* . . . . excellent

Tweedy, Browne Global Value

52 Vanderbilt Avenue
New York, NY 10017
(800) 432-4789

total return	★★★★
risk reduction	★★★★★
management	★★★★★
tax minimization	★★★★★
expense control	★★★★
symbol TBGVX	23 points
up-market performance	n/a
down-market performance	n/a
predictability of returns	very good

Total Return   ★★★★

Over the past five years (all periods ending 6/30/98), Tweedy, Browne Global Value has taken $10,000 and turned it into $22,960 ($18,580 over three years). This translates into an average annual return of 18.1 percent over the past five years and 22.9 percent over the past three years. Over the past five years, this fund has outperformed 70 percent of all mutual funds; within its general category it has done better than 75 percent of its peers. Global equity funds have averaged 11 percent annually over these same five years.

Risk/Volatility   ★★★★★

Over the past five years, Tweedy, Browne Global Value has been safer than 99 percent of all global equity funds. Over the past decade, the fund has had no negative years, while the S&P 500 has had one (off 3 percent in 1990); the EAFE fell twice (off 23 percent in 1990 and 12 percent in 1992). The fund has underperformed the S&P 500 three times and the EAFE Index two times in the last ten years.

	last 5 years		since inception	
worst year	4%	1994	4%	1994
best year	23%	1997	23%	1997

Consistency, or predictability, of returns for Global Value can be described as very good.

Management   ★★★★★

There are 265 stocks in this $2.8 billion portfolio. The average global equity fund today is $325 million in size. Close to 91 percent of the fund's holdings are in stocks. The stocks in this portfolio have an average price-earnings (p/e) ratio of 27 and a median market capitalization of $3 billion. The portfolio's equity holdings can be categorized as mid-cap and value-oriented issues.

A team has managed this fund for the past five years. There is one other fund besides Global Value within the Tweedy Browne family. Overall, the fund family's risk-adjusted performance can be described as excellent.

Tax Minimization   ★★★★★
During the past five years, a $10,000 initial investment grew to $22,940 after taxes, assuming a 39.6 percent income tax bracket (state and federal combined) and a capital gains rate of 28 percent. This means that investors in this fund were able to preserve 94 percent of their total returns. Compared to other equity funds, this fund's tax savings are considered to be excellent.

Expenses   ★★★★
Tweedy, Browne Global Value's expense ratio is 1.4 percent; it has also averaged 1.4 percent annually over the past three calendar years. The average expense ratio for the 1,100 funds in this category is 1.8 percent. This fund's turnover rate over the past year has been 16 percent, while its peer group average has been 75 percent.

Summary
Tweedy, Browne Global Value rates overall as one of the very best foreign and global equity funds. The edge this portfolio has over the other two top-rankings is even lower risk. This fund is the perfect choice for the investor who wants some overseas exposure but with the highest amount of safety. Risk reduction has been partially accomplished by currency hedging plus a value approach to equity selection. Managers Browne and Spears look for companies selling at inexpensive p/e multiples across the board; the fund holds small, medium and large cap issues.

Profile
minimum initial investment $2,500	*IRA accounts available* . . . . yes
subsequent minimum investment . . $250	*IRA minimum investment* $500
available in all 50 states. . . . . yes	*date of inception.* . . . . June 1993
telephone exchanges. . . . . yes	*dividend/income paid* . . . . annually
number of funds in family 2	*quality of annual reports* . . . . excellent

Vanguard International Equity European

Vanguard Financial Center
P.O. Box 2600
Valley Forge, PA 19482
(800) 662-7447

total return	★★★★★
risk reduction	★★★★
management	★★★★★
tax minimization	★★★★★
expense control	★★★★★
symbol VEURX	24 points
up-market performance	excellent
down-market performance	n/a
predictability of returns	good

Total Return   ★★★★★

Over the past five years (all periods ending 6/30/98), Vanguard International Equity European has taken $10,000 and turned it into $28,410 ($20,550 over three years). This translates into an average annual return of 23.2 percent over the past five years and 27.1 percent over the past three years. Over the past five years, this fund has outperformed 85 percent of all mutual funds; within its general category it has done better than 65 percent of its peers. Global equity funds have averaged 11 percent annually over these same five years.

Risk/Volatility   ★★★★

Over the past five years, Vanguard International Equity European has been safer than 75 percent of all global equity funds. Over the past decade, the fund has had one negative year, while the S&P 500 has had one (off 3 percent in 1990); the EAFE fell twice (off 23 percent in 1990 and 12 percent in 1992). The fund has underperformed the S&P 500 five times and the EAFE Index two times in the last ten years.

	last 5 years		since inception	
worst year	2%	1994	–3%	1992
best year	24%	1997	29%	1993

In the past, Equity European has done better than 95 percent of its peer group in up markets. Consistency, or predictability, of returns for Equity European can be described as good.

Management   ★★★★★

There are 560 stocks in this $3.8 billion portfolio. The average global equity fund today is $325 million in size. Close to 98 percent of the fund's holdings are in stocks. The stocks in this portfolio have an average price-earnings (p/e) ratio of 29 and a median market capitalization of $29 billion. The portfolio's equity holdings can be categorized as large-cap and a blend of growth and value stocks.

George U. Sauter has managed this fund for the past eight years. There are 71 funds besides Equity European within the Vanguard Group. Overall, the fund family's risk-adjusted performance can be described as very good.

Tax Minimization   ★★★★★

During the past five years, a $10,000 initial investment grew to $28,390 after taxes, assuming a 39.6 percent income tax bracket (state and federal combined) and a capital gains rate of 28 percent. This means that investors in this fund were able to preserve 96 percent of their total returns. Compared to other equity funds, this fund's tax savings are considered to be excellent.

Expenses   ★★★★★

Equity European's expense ratio is 0.3 percent; it has averaged 0.4 percent annually over the past three calendar years. The average expense ratio for the 1,100 funds in this category is 1.8 percent. This fund's turnover rate over the past year has been 3 percent, while its peer group average has been 75 percent.

Summary

Vanguard International Equity European not only ranks as the number one foreign or global equity fund in the book, it is also unsurpassed by any fund in any category. The fund's objective is to match the MSCI Europe Index. It scores a perfect or near perfect score in every single category. Part of the portfolio's success lies in management's determination to keep expenses to a bare minimum. Risk-adjusted returns have been excellent over both the past three and five years. This fund is highly recommended.

Profile

minimum initial investment $3,000	*IRA accounts available* . . . . yes
subsequent minimum investment . . $100	*IRA minimum investment* $1,000
available in all 50 states . . . . yes	*date of inception* . . . . June 1990
telephone exchanges . . . . no	*dividend/income paid* . . . . annually
number of funds in family 72	*quality of annual reports* . . . . good

Government Bond Funds

These funds invest in direct and indirect U.S. government obligations. Government bond funds are made up of one or more of the following: T-bills, T-notes, T-bonds, GNMAs, and FNMAs. Treasury bills, notes, and bonds make up the entire *marketable* debt of the U.S. government. Such instruments are exempt from state income taxes.

Although GNMAs are considered an *indirect obligation* of the government, they are still backed by the full faith and credit of the United States. FNMAs are not issued by the government but are considered virtually identical in safety to GNMAs. FNMAs and GNMAs are both subject to state and local income taxes. *All* of the securities in a government bond fund are subject to federal income taxes.

The average maturity of securities found in government bond funds varies broadly, depending upon the type of fund, as well as on management's perception of risk and the future direction of interest rates. A more thorough discussion of interest rates and the volatility of bond fund prices can be found in the introductory pages of the corporate bond section.

Over the past fifteen years, government bonds have returned an average compound return of 11.9 percent—the same as long-term corporate bonds. This means that government bonds were a better investment since their interest is exempt from state income taxes plus there is no chance of default or a reduction in quality rating. During this same period, government bond funds have underperformed corporate bond funds, returning 8.8 percent, compared to 9.7 percent for corporate bond funds. A $10,000 investment in U.S. government bonds grew to $65,300 over the past fifteen years; a similar initial investment in corporate bonds grew to $68,200.

Looking at a longer time frame, government bonds have only slightly outperformed inflation. A dollar invested in governments in 1948 grew to $15.98 by the end of 1997. This translates into an average compound return of 5.7 percent per year. Adjusted for inflation, the figure falls to $2.32. Over the past fifty years, the worst year for government bonds was 1967, when a loss of 9 percent was suffered. The best year so far has been 1982, when government bonds posted a gain of 40 percent. All of these figures are based on total return (current yield plus or minus any appreciation or loss of principal).

Over the past half century, there have been forty-six five-year periods (1948–1952, 1949–1953, etc.). On a pre-tax basis, government bonds have outperformed inflation during twenty-four of the forty-six five-year periods. Over the past fifty years, there have been forty-one ten-year periods (1948–1957, 1949–1958, etc.). On a pre-tax basis, government bonds have outperformed inflation during only nineteen of the forty-one ten-year periods. Over the past half century, there have been thirty-one twenty-year periods (1948–1967, 1949–1968, etc.). On a pre-tax basis, government bonds have outperformed inflation during only twelve of these thirty-one periods. All twelve of those twenty-year periods were the most recent in time (1966–1985, 1967–1986, etc.).

Six hundred funds make up the government bonds category. Total market capitalization of this category is $125 billion.

Over the past three and five years, government funds have had an average compound annual return of 6.6 and 5.6 percent, respectively. For the decade, these funds have averaged 7.9 percent a year; over the last fifteen years, 8.8 percent a year. The standard deviation for government bond funds has been 3.3 percent over the past three years. This means that these funds have been less volatile than any other category except corporate bonds and money market funds.

Government bond funds are the perfect choice for the conservative investor who wants to avoid any possibility of defaults. These securities should be avoided by even conservative investors who are in a high tax bracket or unable to shelter such an investment in a retirement plan or annuity. Such investors should first look at the advantages of municipal bond funds.

The prospective investor should always remember that government and corporate bonds are generally not a good investment once inflation and taxes are factored in. The investor who appreciates the cumulative effects of even low levels of inflation should probably avoid government and corporate bonds except as part of a retirement plan.

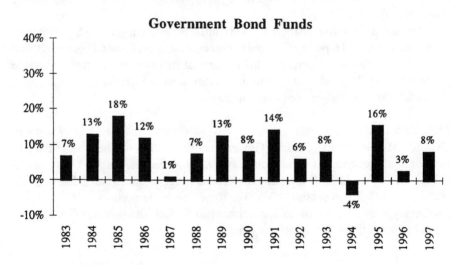

Government Bond Funds

Cardinal Government Obligation

155 East Broad Street
Columbus, OH 43215
(800) 848-7734

total return	★★★★
risk reduction	★★★★★
management	★★★★★
current income	★
expense control	★★★★
symbol CGOGX	20 points
up-market performance	fair
down-market performance	excellent
predictability of returns	very good

Total Return   ★★★★

Over the past five years (all periods ending 6/30/98), Cardinal Government Obligation has taken $10,000 and turned it into $13,600 ($12,500 over three years and $21,210 over the past ten years). This translates into an average annual return of 6.3 percent over the past five years, 7.7 percent over the past three years, and 7.8 percent for the decade. Over the past five years, this fund has outperformed 45 percent of all mutual funds; within its general category it has done better than 60 percent of its peers. Government bond funds have averaged 6 percent annually over these same five years.

During the past five years, a $10,000 initial investment grew to $12,990 after taxes, assuming a 39.6 percent income tax bracket (state and federal combined) and a capital gains rate of 28 percent. This means that investors in this fund were able to preserve 33 percent of their total returns. Compared to other fixed-income funds, this fund's tax savings are considered to be poor.

Risk/Volatility   ★★★★★

Over the past five years, Cardinal Government Obligation has been safer than 75 percent of all government bond funds. Over the past decade, the fund has had one negative year, while both the Lehman Brothers Aggregate Bond Index had one (both were off 3 percent in 1994). The fund has underperformed the Lehman Brothers Aggregate Bond Index seven times and the Lehman Brothers Government Bond Index six times in the last ten years.

	last 5 years		last 10 years	
worst year	−1%	1994	−1%	1994
best year	14%	1995	14%	1995

In the past, Cardinal Government Obligation has done better than 30 percent of its peer group in up markets and outperformed 90 percent of its competition in down markets. Consistency, or predictability, of returns for Government Obligation can be described as very good.

Management ★★★★★

There are 165 fixed-income securities in this $120 million portfolio. The average government bond fund today is $205 million in size. Close to 95 percent of the funds holdings are in bonds. The average maturity of the bonds in this account is 24 years; the weighted coupon rate averages 8 percent. The portfolio's fixed-income holdings can be categorized as long-term, high-quality debt.

John R. Carle has managed this fund for the past 12 years. There are three funds besides Government Obligation within the Cardinal Group. Overall, the fund family's risk-adjusted performance can be described as good.

Current Income ★

Over the past year, Government Obligation had a twelve-month yield of 6.9 percent. During this same twelve-month period, the typical government bond fund had a yield that averaged 5.6 percent.

Expenses ★★★★

Government Obligation's expense ratio is 0.8 percent; it has averaged 0.8 percent annually over the past three calendar years. The average expense ratio for the 625 funds in this category is 1.1 percent. This fund's turnover rate over the past year has been 34 percent, while its peer group average has been 180 percent.

Summary

Cardinal Government Obligation is a small fund that has not received the attention it deserves. By loading up heavily on long-term GNMAs, management has taken advantage of falling interest rates, resulting in superior returns and current income. However, the fund's real strength has been in keeping risk at a very low level—a surprising accomplishment when you consider the lengthy maturity of its largest holdings. This is only one of a handful of government bond funds to make the book.

Profile

minimum initial investment $1,000
subsequent minimum investment . . . $50
available in all 50 states . . . . no
telephone exchanges . . . . no
number of funds in family 4

IRA accounts available . . . . yes
IRA minimum investment $1,000
date of inception . . . . Feb. 1986
dividend/income paid . . . . monthly
quality of annual reports . . . . . average

Franklin Strategic Mortgage

777 Mariners Island Boulevard
San Mateo, CA 94403-7777
(800) 342-5236

total return	★★★★★
risk reduction	★★★★
management	★★★★★
current income	★★
expense control	★★★★★
symbol FSMIX	21 points
up-market performance	n/a
down-market performance	n/a
predictability of returns	good

Total Return   ★★★★★

Over the past five years (all periods ending 6/30/98), Franklin Strategic Mortgage
has taken $10,000 and turned it into $13,840 ($12,510 over three years). This trans-
lates into an average annual return of 6.7 percent over the past five years and 7.8
percent over the past three years. Over the past five years, this fund has outperformed 45 percent of all mutual funds; within its general category it has done better
than 75 percent of its peers. Government bond funds have averaged 6 percent annually over these same five years.

During the past five years, a $10,000 initial investment grew to $13,260 after
taxes, assuming a 39.6 percent income tax bracket (state and federal combined) and
a capital gains rate of 28 percent. This means that investors in this fund were able
to preserve 43 percent of their total returns. Compared to other fixed-income funds,
this fund's tax savings are considered to be fair.

Risk/Volatility   ★★★★

Over the past five years, Franklin Strategic Mortgage has been safer than 70 percent of all government bond funds. Over the past decade, the fund has had one negative year, while both the Lehman Brothers Aggregate Bond Index had one (both
were off 3 percent in 1994). The fund has underperformed the Lehman Brothers
Aggregate Bond Index two times and the Lehman Brothers Government Bond
Index two times in the last ten years.

	last 5 years		since inception	
worst year	–2%	1994	–2%	1994
best year	17%	1995	17%	1995

Consistency, or predictability, of returns for Strategic Mortgage can be
described as good.

Management ★★★★★
There are 60 fixed-income securities in this $14 million portfolio. The average government bond fund today is $205 million in size. Close to 80 percent of the funds holdings are in bonds. The average maturity of the bonds in this account is 18 years; the weighted coupon rate averages 7 percent. The portfolio's fixed-income holdings can be categorized as long-term, very high-qaulity debt.

A team has managed this fund for the past five years. There are 154 funds besides Strategic Mortgage within the Franklin family. Overall, the fund family's risk-adjusted performance can be described as very good.

Current Income ★★
Over the past year, Strategic Mortgage had a twelve-month yield of 6.7 percent. During this same twelve-month period, the typical government bond fund had a yield that averaged 5.6 percent.

Expenses ★★★★★
Strategic Mortgage's expense ratio is 0.8 percent; it has averaged 0.8 percent annually over the past three calendar years. The average expense ratio for the 625 funds in this category is 1.1 percent. This fund's turnover rate over the past year has been 14 percent, while its peer group average has been 180 percent.

Summary
Franklin Strategic Mortgage is not a well-known fund, but its parent company Franklin Templeton is one of the very largest fund families in the world. This little gem turns in ultra-high returns and current income. Part of the fund's success lies in its ability to keep an eye on expenses and turnover—something most of the hundreds of other funds in this category have lost sight of. There are a large number of other funds in the Franklin Templeton group that are also highly recommended. Known best as a fixed-income group, this management company also offers a number of superb equity funds.

Profile

minimum initial investment $100	*IRA accounts available* . . . . yes
subsequent minimum investment . . . $25	*IRA minimum investment* $100
available in all 50 states. . . . . yes	*date of inception* . . . . Feb. 1993
telephone exchanges. . . . . yes	*dividend/income paid.* . . . . monthly
number of funds in family 155	*quality of annual reports* . . . . n/a

Lexington GNMA Income

Park 80 West Plaza Two
P.O. Box 1515
Saddle Brook, NJ 07662
(800) 526-0056

total return	★★★★★
risk reduction	★★★★
management	★★★★★
current income	★★★★
expense control	★★★
symbol LEXNX	21 points
up-market performance	excellent
down-market performance	poor
predictability of returns	good

Total Return   ★★★★★

Over the past five years (all periods ending 6/30/98), Lexington GNMA Income has taken $10,000 and turned it into $13,980 ($12,700 over three years and $23,180 over the past ten years). This translates into an average annual return of 6.9 percent over the past five years, 8.3 percent over the past three years, and 8.8 percent for the decade. Over the past five years, this fund has outperformed 45 percent of all mutual funds; within its general category it has done better than 75 percent of its peers. Government bond funds have averaged 6 percent annually over these same five years.

During the past five years, a $10,000 initial investment grew to $13,990 after taxes, assuming a 39.6 percent income tax bracket (state and federal combined) and a capital gains rate of 28 percent. This means that investors in this fund were able to preserve 57 percent of their total returns. Compared to other fixed-income funds, this fund's tax savings are considered to be very good.

Risk/Volatility   ★★★★

Over the past five years, Lexington GNMA Income has been safer than 97 percent of all government bond funds. Over the past decade, the fund has had one negative year, while both the Lehman Brothers Aggregate Bond Index had one (both were off 3 percent in 1994). The fund has underperformed the Lehman Brothers Aggregate Bond Index five times and the Lehman Brothers Government Bond Index four times in the last ten years.

	last 5 years		last 10 years	
worst year	–2%	1994	–2%	1994
best year	16%	1995	16%	1995

In the past, GNMA Income has done better than 95 percent of its peer group in up markets and outperformed 20 percent of its competition in down markets.

Consistency, or predictability, of returns for Lexington GNMA Income can be described as good.

Management   ★★★★★
There are 85 fixed-income securities in this $210 million portfolio. The average government bond fund today is $205 million in size. Close to 88 percent of the funds holdings are in bonds. The average maturity of the bonds in this account is 4 years; the weighted coupon rate averages 8 percent. The portfolio's fixed-income holdings can be categorized as short-term, high-quality debt.

Denis P. Jamison has managed this fund for the past 17 years. There are 13 funds besides GNMA Income within the Lexington family. Overall, the fund family's risk-adjusted performance can be described as good.

Current Income   ★★★★
Over the past year, GNMA Income had a twelve-month yield of 5.9 percent. During this same twelve-month period, the typical government bond fund had a yield that averaged 5.6 percent.

Expenses   ★★★
GNMA Income's expense ratio is 1.0 percent; it has averaged 1.0 percent annually over the past three calendar years. The average expense ratio for the 625 funds in this category is 1.1 percent. This fund's turnover rate over the past year has been 134 percent, while its peer group average has been 180 percent.

Summary
Lexington GNMA Income has averaged very good risk-adjusted returns over the past three, five and ten years. Manager Jamison has found a niche that few of his competitors have discovered: GNMA project loans. These securities are structured so that they throw off high current income but with less prepayment risk than traditional GNMAs. This fund remains highly recommended for the investor seeking maximum conservative monthly income.

Profile
minimum initial investment $1,000	*IRA accounts available* . . . . yes
subsequent minimum investment . . . $50	*IRA minimum investment* $250
available in all 50 states. . . . . yes	*date of inception* . . . . Oct. 1973
telephone exchanges. . . . . yes	*dividend/income paid.* . . . . monthly
number of funds in family 14	*quality of annual reports* . . . . . average

Sit U.S. Government Securities

4600 Norwest Center
90 South 7th Street
Minneapolis, MN 55402-4130
(800) 332-5580

total return	★★★★
risk reduction	★★★★★
management	★★★★★
current income	★★★★★
expense control	★★★★
symbol SNGVX	23 points
up-market performance	good
down-market performance	good
predictability of returns	excellent

Total Return   ★★★★

Over the past five years (all periods ending 6/30/98), Sit U.S. Government Securities has taken $10,000 and turned it into $13,610 ($12,280 over three years and $21,390 over the past ten years). This translates into an average annual return of 6.4 percent over the past five years, 7.1 percent over the past three years, and 7.9 percent for the decade. Over the past five years, this fund has outperformed 45 percent of all mutual funds; within its general category it has done better than 85 percent of its peers. Government bond funds have averaged 6 percent annually over these same five years.

During the past five years, a $10,000 initial investment grew to $13,610 after taxes, assuming a 39.6 percent income tax bracket (state and federal combined) and a capital gains rate of 28 percent. This means that investors in this fund were able to preserve 67 percent of their total returns. Compared to other fixed-income funds, this fund's tax savings are considered to be excellent.

Risk/Volatility   ★★★★★

Over the past five years, Sit U.S. Government Securities has been safer than 85 percent of all government bond funds. Over the past decade, the fund has had no negative years, while both the Lehman Brothers Aggregate Bond Index had one (both were off 3 percent in 1994). The fund has underperformed the Lehman Brothers Aggregate Bond Index seven times and the Lehman Brothers Government Bond Index three times in the last ten years.

	last 5 years		last 10 years	
worst year	2%	1994	2%	1994
best year	12%	1995	13%	1991

In the past, Government Securities has done better than 50 percent of its peer group in up markets and outperformed 50 percent of its competition in down markets. Consistency, or predictability, of returns for Government Securities can be described as excellent.

Management   ★★★★★

There are 300 fixed-income securities in this $120 million portfolio. The average government bond fund today is $205 million in size. Close to 99 percent of the funds holdings are in bonds. The average maturity of the bonds in this account is 7 years; the weighted coupon rate averages 8 percent. The portfolio's fixed-income holdings can be categorized as intermediate-term, high-quality debt.

Bryce Doty and Michael C. Brilley have managed this fund for the past seven years. There are 9 funds besides Government Securities within the Sit Group. Overall, the fund family's risk-adjusted performance can be described as good.

Current Income   ★★★★★

Over the past year, Government Securities had a twelve-month yield of 5.6 percent. During this same twelve-month period, the typical government bond fund had a yield that averaged 5.6 percent.

Expenses   ★★★★

Sit U.S. Government Securities's expense ratio is 0.8 percent; it has averaged 0.9 percent annually over the past three calendar years. The average expense ratio for the 625 funds in this category is 1.1 percent. This fund's turnover rate over the past year has been 51 percent, while its peer group average has been 180 percent.

Summary

Sit U.S. Government Securities ties for number one as the best overall government bond fund. Fund managers Brilley and Doty are especially attracted to mobile home mortgage-backed securities for two reasons: (1) low loan balances on the mobile homes and (2) lower borrow creditworthiness which results in lower pre-payment risk. Risk-adjusted returns over the past three, five and ten years have been very good. Tax minimization is superb.

Profile

minimum initial investment $2,000	*IRA accounts available*. . . . . no
subsequent minimum investment . . $100	*IRA minimum investment* . . . . n/a
available in all 50 states. . . . . yes	*date of inception* 1987
telephone exchanges. . . . . yes	*dividend/income paid*. . . . . monthly
number of funds in family 10	*quality of annual reports* . . . . excellent

Smith Breeden Short Duration U.S. Government

100 Europa Drive, Suite 200
Chapel Hill, NC 27514
(800) 221-3138

total return	★★★★
risk reduction	★★★★★
management	★★★★★
current income	★★★★★
expense control	★★★★
symbol SBSHX	23 points
up-market performance	n/a
down-market performance	n/a
predictability of returns	excellent

Total Return   ★★★★

Over the past five years (all periods ending 6/30/98), Smith Breeden Short
Duration U.S. Government has taken $10,000 and turned it into $13,090 ($11,910
over three years). This translates into an average annual return of 5.5 percent over
the past five years and 6.0 percent over the past three years. Over the past five
years, this fund has outperformed 40 percent of all mutual funds; within its general
category it has done better than 70 percent of its peers. Government bond funds
have averaged 6 percent annually over these same five years.

During the past five years, a $10,000 initial investment grew to $13,080 after
taxes, assuming a 39.6 percent income tax bracket (state and federal combined) and
a capital gains rate of 28 percent. This means that investors in this fund were able
to preserve 50 percent of their total returns. Compared to other fixed-income funds,
this fund's tax savings are considered to be excellent.

Risk/Volatility   ★★★★★

Over the past five years, Smith Breeden Short Duration U.S. Government has been
safer than 40 percent of all government bond funds. Over the past decade, the fund
has had no negative years, while both the Lehman Brothers Aggregate Bond Index
had one (both were off 3 percent in 1994). The fund has underperformed the
Lehman Brothers Aggregate Bond Index three times and the Lehman Brothers
Government Bond Index one time in the last ten years.

	last 5 years		since inception	
worst year	4%	1994	4%	1994
best year	6%	1997	6%	1997

Consistency, or predictability, of returns for Short Duration can be described
as excellent.

Management   ★★★★★
There are 35 fixed-income securities in this $80 million portfolio. The average government bond fund today is $205 million in size. Close to 100 percent of the funds holdings are in bonds. The average maturity of the bonds in this account is 0.5 year; the weighted coupon rate averages 8 percent. The portfolio's fixed-income holdings can be categorized as very short-term, high-quality debt.

Daniel C. Dektar has managed this fund for the past six years. There are three funds besides Short Duration within the Smith Breeden family. Overall, the fund family's risk-adjusted performance can be described as very good.

Current Income   ★★★★★
Over the past year, Short Duration had a twelve-month yield of 5.0 percent. During this same twelve-month period, the typical government bond fund had a yield that averaged 5.6 percent.

Expenses   ★★★★
Short Duration's expense ratio is 0.8 percent; it has averaged 0.6 percent annually over the past three calendar years. The average expense ratio for the 625 funds in this category is 1.1 percent. This fund's turnover rate over the past year has been 550 percent, while its peer group average has been 180 percent.

Summary
Smith Breeden Short Duration U.S. Government ties for number one as the best overall government securities fund. Fund manager Dektar keeps the portfolio's average maturity very short but is able to get a high total return by leveraging the portfolio. This fund is recommended as a conservative alternative to a money market account.

Profile

minimum initial investment $1,000	*IRA accounts available* . . . . yes
subsequent minimum investment . . . $50	*IRA minimum investment* $250
available in all 50 states. . . . . yes	*date of inception.* . . . . Mar. 1992
telephone exchanges. . . . . yes	*dividend/income paid.* . . . . monthly
number of funds in family 4	*quality of annual reports* . . . . good

Growth Funds

These funds generally seek capital appreciation, with current income as a distant secondary concern. Growth funds typically invest in U.S. common stocks, while avoiding speculative issues and aggressive trading techniques. The goal of most of these funds is *long-term growth*. The approaches used to attain this appreciation can vary significantly among growth funds.

Over the past fifteen years, U.S. stocks have outperformed both corporate and government bonds. From 1983 through 1997, common stocks have averaged 17.5 percent compounded per year, compared to 11.9 percent for both corporate and government bonds. A $10,000 investment in stocks, as measured by the S&P 500, grew to over $102,700 over the past fifteen years; a similar initial investment in corporate bonds grew to $44,070.

Looking at a longer time frame, common stocks have also fared quite well. A dollar invested in stocks in 1948 grew to $473 by the end of 1997. This translates into an average compound return of 13.1 percent per year. Over the past fifty years, the worst year for common stocks was 1974, when a loss of 26 percent was suffered. One year later, these same stocks posted a gain of 37 percent. The best year so far has been 1954, when growth stocks posted a gain of 53 percent.

Growth stocks have outperformed bonds in every single decade. If President George Washington had invested $1 in common stocks with an average return of 12 percent, his investment would be worth over $261 billion today. If George had been a bit lucky and averaged 14 percent on his stock portfolio, his portfolio would be large enough to pay our national debt four times over!

To give you an idea as to the likelihood of making money in common stocks, look at the table below. It covers more than 120 years and shows the odds of making money (a positive return) over each of several different time periods.

Standard & Poor's Composite 500 Stock Index
Various periods, 1871–1997 (dividends not included)

Length of Period	Total Number of Periods	Number of Periods in which Stock Prices			Percentage Opportunity for Profit (not including dividends)
		Rose	Declined	Unchanged	
1 year	127	81	45	1	64%
5 years	123	97	25	1	79%
10 years	118	106	12	0	90%
15 years	113	104	9	0	92%
20 years	108	105	3	0	97%
25 years	103	102	1	0	99%
30 years	98	98	0	0	100%

Fifteen hundred funds make up the growth category. Total market capitalization of this category is $800 billion. The standard deviation for this group is 16.6 percent; beta (stock market-related risk) is 0.9, 10% less than that of the overall market, as measured by the S&P 500. The typical portfolio of a growth fund is divided up as follows: 90 percent U.S. stocks, 5 percent foreign stocks and the balance in money market instruments. Turnover rate is 89 percent per year. The yield on growth funds averages about 0.3 percent annually. Fund expenses for this group average 1.4 percent per year.

Over the past three years, growth funds have had an average compound return of 23.6 percent per year; the *annual* return for the past five years has been 18.8 percent. For the past decade, growth funds have averaged 16.2 percent annually and 14.1 percent per year for the past fifteen years.

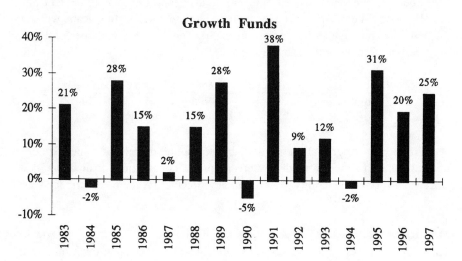

Growth Funds

Ariel Appreciation

307 North Michigan Avenue, Suite 500
Chicago, IL 60601
(800) 292-7435

total return	★★★
risk reduction	★★★★
management	★★★★
tax minimization	★★★★
expense control	★★★★
symbol CAAPX	19 points
up-market performance	good
down-market performance	good
predictability of returns	very good

Total Return   ★★★

Over the past five years (all periods ending 6/30/98), Ariel Appreciation has taken $10,000 and turned it into $24,380 ($21,580 over three years). This translates into an average annual return of 19.5 percent over the past five years and 29.2 percent over the past three years. Over the past five years, this fund has outperformed 70 percent of all mutual funds; within its general category it has done better than 60 percent of its peers. Growth funds have averaged 19 percent annually over these same five years.

Risk/Volatility   ★★★★

Over the past five years, Ariel Appreciation has been safer than 40 percent of all growth funds. Over the past decade, the fund has had two negative years, while the S&P 500 has had one (off 3 percent in 1990). The fund has underperformed the S&P 500 three times in the last ten years.

	last 5 years		since inception	
worst year	–8%	1994	–8%	1994
best year	38%	1997	38%	1997

In the past, Appreciation has done better than 60 percent of its peer group in up markets and outperformed 60 percent of its competition in down markets. Consistency, or predictability, of returns for Appreciation can be described as very good.

Management   ★★★★

There are 40 stocks in this $250 million portfolio. The average growth fund today is $560 million in size. Close to 96 percent of the fund's holdings are in stocks. The stocks in this portfolio have an average price-earnings (p/e) ratio of 25 and a median market capitalization of $2.6 billion. The portfolio's equity holdings can be categorized as mid-cap and value-oriented issues.

Eric T. McKissack has managed this fund for the past nine years. There are three funds besides Appreciation within the Ariel family. Overall, the fund family's risk-adjusted performance can be described as very good.

Tax Minimization   ★★★★
During the past five years, a $10,000 initial investment grew to $24,350 after taxes, assuming a 39.6 percent income tax bracket (state and federal combined) and a capital gains rate of 28 percent. This means that investors in this fund were able to preserve 90 percent of their total returns. Compared to other equity funds, this fund's tax savings are considered to be very good.

Expenses   ★★★★
Appreciation's expense ratio is 1.3 percent; it has also averaged 1.3 percent annually over the past three calendar years. The average expense ratio for the 1,500 funds in this category is 1.4 percent. This fund's turnover rate over the past year has been 19 percent, while its peer group average has been 90 percent.

Summary
Ariel Appreciation's philosophy is that boring can be exciting. Manager McKissack seeks out companies with niche positions within mundane industry groups. The selected stocks are often selling at large discounts to their real worth; the typical holding period is several years. Risk is reduced by selling off those securities whose price has been climbing.

Profile

minimum initial investment . . . . . $1,000   *IRA accounts available* . . . . yes
subsequent minimum investment . . . $50   *IRA minimum investment* $250
available in all 50 states. . . . . yes   *date of inception*. . . . . Dec. 1989
telephone exchanges. . . . . yes   *dividend/income paid* . . . . annually
number of funds in family 4   *quality of annual reports* . . . . excellent

Clipper

9601 Wilshire Boulevard, Suite 828
Beverly Hills, CA 90210
(800) 776-5033

total return	★★★
risk reduction	★★★★
management	★★★
tax minimization	
expense control	★★★★★
symbol CFIMX	19 points
up-market performance	very good
down-market performance	good
predictability of returns	very good

Total Return   ★★★

Over the past five years (all periods ending 6/30/98), Clipper has taken $10,000 and turned it into $24,530 ($19,340 over three years and $48,190 over the past ten years). This translates into an average annual return of 20.6 percent over the past five years, 24.6 percent over the past three years, and 17.0 percent for the decade. Over the past five years, this fund has outperformed 80 percent of all mutual funds; within its general category it has done better than 55 percent of its peers. Growth funds have averaged 19 percent annually over these same five years.

Risk/Volatility   ★★★★

Over the past five years, Clipper has been safer than 35 percent of all growth funds. Over the past decade, the fund has had two negative years, while the S&P 500 has had one (off 3 percent in 1990). The fund has underperformed the S&P 500 four times in the last ten years.

	last 5 years		last 10 years	
worst year	–3%	1994	–8%	1990
best year	45%	1995	45%	1995

In the past, Clipper has done better than 80 percent of its peer group in up markets and outperformed 50 percent of its competition in down markets. Consistency, or predictability, of returns for Clipper can be described as very good.

Management   ★★★

There are 20 stocks in this $975 million portfolio. The average growth fund today is $560 million in size. Close to 55 percent of the fund's holdings are in stocks. The stocks in this portfolio have an average price-earnings (p/e) ratio of 23 and a median market capitalization of $47 billion. The portfolio's equity holdings can be categorized as large-cap and value-oriented issues.

A team has managed this fund for the past 13 years. Clipper is the only fund in the "family." Overall, the fund family's risk-adjusted performance can be described as very good.

Tax Minimization
During the past five years, a $10,000 initial investment grew to $25,540 after taxes, assuming a 39.6 percent income tax bracket (state and federal combined) and a capital gains rate of 28 percent. This means that investors in this fund were able to preserve 81 percent of their total returns. Compared to other equity funds, this fund's tax savings are considered to be good.

Expenses   ★★★★★
Clipper's expense ratio is 1.1 percent; it has also averaged 1.1 percent annually over the past three calendar years. The average expense ratio for the 1,500 funds in this category is 1.4 percent. This fund's turnover rate over the past year has been 31 percent, while its peer group average has been 90 percent.

Summary
Clipper likes to hold a large percentage of its assets in cash; the number of stocks in the portfolio is quite small. Managers Gipson and Sandler are drawn to world-class companies whose stock price is 70% of its intrinsic value—if they can't find what they like, they are content with cash equivalents. This growth fund has been able to keep risk low and overhead costs even lower. Risk-adjusted returns for the past three, five and ten years have been very good.

Profile
minimum initial investment $5,000

subsequent minimum investment . $1,000

available in all 50 states. . . . . yes

telephone exchanges . . . . no

number of funds in family 1

IRA accounts available . . . . yes

IRA minimum investment $2,000

date of inception . . . . Feb. 1984

dividend/income paid . . . . annually

quality of annual reports . . . . excellent

Dreyfus Appreciation

One Exchange Place
Boston, MA 02109
(800) 373-9387

total return	★★★★
risk reduction	★★★
management	★★★★
tax minimization	★★★★★
expense control	★★★★★
symbol DGAGX	21 points
up-market performance	good
down-market performance	good
predictability of returns	good

Total Return ★★★★

Over the past five years (all periods ending 6/30/98), Dreyfus Appreciation has taken $10,000 and turned it into $29,490 ($22,520 over three years and $49,060 over the past ten years). This translates into an average annual return of 24.2 percent over the past five years, 31.1 percent over the past three years, and 17.2 percent for the decade. Over the past five years, this fund has outperformed 95 percent of all mutual funds; within its general category it has done better than 80 percent of its peers. Growth funds have averaged 19 percent annually over these same five years.

Risk/Volatility ★★★

Over the past five years, Dreyfus Appreciation has been safer than 95 percent of all growth funds. Over the past decade, the fund has had one negative year, while the S&P 500 has had one (off 3 percent in 1990). The fund has underperformed the S&P 500 four times in the last ten years.

	last 5 years		last 10 years	
worst year	.7%	1993	–2%	1990
best year	37%	1995	38%	1991

In the past, Appreciation has done better than 70 percent of its peer group in up markets and outperformed 75 percent of its competition in down markets. Consistency, or predictability, of returns for Appreciation can be described as good.

Management ★★★★

There are 70 stocks in this $3 billion portfolio. The average growth fund today is $560 million in size. Close to 98 percent of the fund's holdings are in stocks. The stocks in this portfolio have an average price-earnings (p/e) ratio of 30 and a median market capitalization of $68 billion. The portfolio's equity holdings can be categorized as large-cap and a blend of growth and value stocks.

Fayez Sarofim and Russell Hawkins have managed this fund for the past eight years. There are 79 funds besides Appreciation within the Dreyfus family. Overall, the fund family's risk-adjusted performance can be described as good.

Tax Minimization   ★★★★★
During the past five years, a $10,000 initial investment grew to $29,480 after taxes, assuming a 39.6 percent income tax bracket (state and federal combined) and a capital gains rate of 28 percent. This means that investors in this fund were able to preserve 100 percent of their total returns. Compared to other equity funds, this fund's tax savings are considered to be excellent.

Expenses   ★★★★★
Appreciation's expense ratio is 0.9 percent; it has also averaged 0.9 percent annually over the past three calendar years. The average expense ratio for the 1,500 funds in this category is 1.4 percent. This fund's turnover rate over the past year has been 5 percent, while its peer group average has been 90 percent.

Summary
Dreyfus Appreciation is one of the most overall highly rated growth funds in the book; tax minimization and expense control have been exceptional while total return figures have been quite good. Managers Sarofim and Hawkins concentrate on huge multinational companies that produce consistent long-term growth. The turnover rate of this fund is extremely low. Holding onto winning securities for a number of years has paid off. The overall change in investment philosophy that the fund experienced a handful of years ago has certainly paid off.

Profile
minimum initial investment $2,500
subsequent minimum investment . . $100
available in all 50 states. . . . . yes
telephone exchanges. . . . . yes
number of funds in family 80

IRA accounts available . . . . yes
IRA minimum investment $750
date of inception . . . . Jan. 1984
dividend/income paid . . . . annually
quality of annual reports . . . . . average

First Eagle Fund of America Y

1345 Avenue of the Americas
New York, NY 10105-4300
(800) 451-3623

total return	★★★★
risk reduction	★★★
management	★★★★
tax minimization	★★★★
expense control	★★
symbol FEAFX	17 points
up-market performance	excellent
down-market performance	good
predictability of returns	fair

Total Return   ★★★★

Over the past five years (all periods ending 6/30/98), First Eagle Fund of America Y has taken $10,000 and turned it into $29,400 ($23,650 over three years and $53,960 over the past ten years). This translates into an average annual return of 24.1 percent over the past five years, 33.2 percent over the past three years, and 18.4 percent for the decade. Over the past five years, this fund has outperformed 90 percent of all mutual funds; within its general category it has done better than 80 percent of its peers. Growth funds have averaged 19 percent annually over these same five years.

Risk/Volatility   ★★★

Over the past five years, First Eagle Fund of America Y has been safer than 30 percent of all growth funds. Over the past decade, the fund has had two negative years, while the S&P 500 has had one (off 3 percent in 1990). The fund has underperformed the S&P 500 six times in the last ten years.

	last 5 years		last 10 years	
worst year	–3%	1994	–18%	1990
best year	36%	1995	36%	1995

In the past, Fund of America has done better than 85 percent of its peer group in up markets and outperformed 60 percent of its competition in down markets. Consistency, or predictability, of returns for Fund of America can be described as fair.

Management   ★★★★

There are 60 stocks in this $360 million portfolio. The average growth fund today is $560 million in size. Close to 95 percent of the fund's holdings are in stocks. The stocks in this portfolio have an average price-earnings (p/e) ratio of 26 and a median market capitalization of $5 billion. The portfolio's equity holdings can be categorized as large-cap and value-oriented issues.

David L. Cohen and Harold J. Levy have managed this fund for the past 10 years. There is one other fund besides Fund of America within the First Eagle family. Overall, the fund family's risk-adjusted performance can be described as excellent.

Tax Minimization   ★★★★
During the past five years, a $10,000 initial investment grew to $29,480 after taxes, assuming a 39.6 percent income tax bracket (state and federal combined) and a capital gains rate of 28 percent. This means that investors in this fund were able to preserve 88 percent of their total returns. Compared to other equity funds, this fund's tax savings are considered to be very good.

Expenses   ★★
Fund of America's expense ratio is 1.7 percent; it has averaged 1.8 percent annually over the past three calendar years. The average expense ratio for the 1,500 funds in this category is 1.4 percent. This fund's turnover rate over the past year has been 98 percent, while its peer group average has been 90 percent.

Summary
First Eagle Fund of America Y takes a different approach to equity selection. Managers Levy and Cohen start their selection process by searching for news stories about companies that are "exciting," often because of changes in management, new products or a corporate restructuring. Companies then selected are researched from the bottom up, a departure from the more commonly used "top down" approach to security selection. Management is particularly concerned with cash flow and forward-earnings projections.

Profile
minimum initial investment $2,500	*IRA accounts available* . . . . yes
subsequent minimum investment . . $100	*IRA minimum investment* $500
available in all 50 states . . . . no	*date of inception* . . . . Apr. 1987
telephone exchanges . . . . no	*dividend/income paid* . . . . annually
number of funds in family 2	*quality of annual reports* . . . . n/a

GAM North America A

135 East 57th Street, 25th Floor
New York, NY 10022
(800) 426-4685

total return	★★★★
risk reduction	★★★
management	★★
tax minimization	★★★
expense control	
symbol GNAAX	12 points
up-market performance	fair
down-market performance	excellent
predictability of returns	good

Total Return   ★★★★

Over the past five years (all periods ending 6/30/98), GAM North America A has taken $10,000 and turned it into $21,190 ($21,030 over three years). This translates into an average annual return of 22 percent over the past five years and 31 percent over the past three years. Over the past five years, this fund has outperformed 90 percent of all mutual funds; within its general category it has done better than 70 percent of its peers. Growth funds have averaged 19 percent annually over these same five years.

Risk/Volatility   ★★★

Over the past five years, GAM North America A has been safer than 70 percent of all growth funds. Over the past decade, the fund has had one negative year, while the S&P 500 has had one (off 3 percent in 1990). The fund has underperformed the S&P 500 four times in the last ten years.

	last 5 years		since inception	
worst year	–2%	1993	–2%	1993
best year	31%	1995	31%	1995

In the past, America A has done better than 30 percent of its peer group in up markets and outperformed 99 percent of its competition in down markets. Consistency, or predictability, of returns for America A can be described as good.

Management   ★★

There are 55 stocks in this $18 million portfolio. The average growth fund today is $560 million in size. Close to 99 percent of the fund's holdings are in stocks. The stocks in this portfolio have an average price-earnings (p/e) ratio of 31 and a median market capitalization of $72 billion. The portfolio's equity holdings can be categorized as large-cap and a blend of growth and value stocks.

Fayez Sarofim has managed this fund for the past eight years. There are 10 funds besides America A within the GAM family. Overall, the fund family's risk-adjusted performance can be described as good.

Tax Minimization   ★★★

During the past five years, a $10,000 initial investment grew to $25,900 after taxes, assuming a 39.6 percent income tax bracket (state and federal combined) and a capital gains rate of 28 percent. This means that investors in this fund were able to preserve 86 percent of their total returns. Compared to other equity funds, this fund's tax savings are considered to be good.

Expenses

America A's expense ratio is 2.6 percent; it has averaged 2.7 percent annually over the past three calendar years. The average expense ratio for the 1,500 funds in this category is 1.4 percent. This fund's turnover rate over the past year has been 9 percent, while its peer group average has been 90 percent.

Summary

GAM North America A is a domestic equity fund that has racked up an impressive track record over the past three and five years. This portfolio is a fine choice for the equity investor who wants protection during those periods when the market is headed downward. The turnover rate of this fund is incredibly low which helps compensate for a high expense ratio.

Profile

minimum initial investment $5,000
subsequent minimum investment . . $500
available in all 50 states. . . . . yes
telephone exchanges. . . . . yes
number of funds in family 11

IRA accounts available . . . . yes
IRA minimum investment $2,000
date of inception . . . . Jan. 1990
dividend/income paid . . . . annually
quality of annual reports . . . . n/a

Hilliard Lyons Growth A

Hilliard Lyons Center
Louisville, KY 40202
(800) 444-1854

total return	★★★
risk reduction	★★★★★
management	★★★★
tax minimization	★★★★
expense control	★★★★
symbol HLGRX	20 points
up-market performance	n/a
down-market performance	n/a
predictability of returns	excellent

Total Return   ★★★

Over the past five years (all periods ending 6/30/98), Hilliard Lyons Growth A has taken $10,000 and turned it into $24,180 ($19,810 over three years). This translates into an average annual return of 19.3 percent over the past five years and 25.6 percent over the past three years. Over the past five years, this fund has outperformed 80 percent of all mutual funds; within its general category it has done better than 55 percent of its peers. Growth funds have averaged 19 percent annually over these same five years.

Risk/Volatility   ★★★★★

Over the past five years, Hilliard Lyons Growth A has been safer than 75 percent of all growth funds. Over the past decade, the fund has had no negative years, while the S&P 500 has had one (off 3 percent in 1990). The fund has underperformed the S&P 500 three times in the last ten years.

	last 5 years		since inception	
worst year	3%	1994	3%	1994
best year	40%	1997	40%	1997

Consistency, or predictability, of returns for Hilliard Lyons Growth A can be described as excellent.

Management   ★★★★

There are 25 stocks in this $85 million portfolio. The average growth fund today is $560 million in size. Close to 76 percent of the fund's holdings are in stocks. The stocks in this portfolio have an average price-earnings (p/e) ratio of 26 and a median market capitalization of $6 billion. The portfolio's equity holdings can be categorized as large-cap and value-oriented issues.

Samuel C. Harvey has managed this fund for the past six years. Growth A is the only fund within the Hilliard Lyons "family." Overall, the fund family's risk-adjusted performance can be described as very good.

Tax Minimization ★★★★

During the past five years, a $10,000 initial investment grew to $23,000 after taxes, assuming a 39.6 percent income tax bracket (state and federal combined) and a capital gains rate of 28 percent. This means that investors in this fund were able to preserve 89 percent of their total returns. Compared to other equity funds, this fund's tax savings are considered to be very good.

Expenses ★★★★

Growth A's expense ratio is 1.3 percent; it has averaged 1.6 percent annually over the past three calendar years. The average expense ratio for the 1,500 funds in this category is 1.4 percent. This fund's turnover rate over the past year has been 22 percent, while its peer group average has been 90 percent.

Summary

Hilliard Lyons Growth A is not a well-known equity fund, but it is certainly one of the very best. This rather small portfolio has demonstrated exceptional risk control; it is also one of the more consistent funds within its broad category. Hopefully, management will add other funds. It is a shame that this is an "orphan" fund and has no other family members.

Profile

minimum initial investment $1,000	*IRA accounts available* . . . . yes
subsequent minimum investment . . $100	*IRA minimum investment* $1,000
available in all 50 states . . . . no	*date of inception* . . . . Jan. 1992
telephone exchanges . . . . no	*dividend/income paid* . . . . annually
number of funds in family 1	*quality of annual reports* . . . . n/a

MAP Equity

520 Broad Street
Newark, NJ 07102-3111
(800) 559-5535

total return	★★★
risk reduction	★★★★★
management	★★★★
tax minimization	★
expense control	★★★★★
symbol MUBFX	18 points
up-market performance	good
down-market performance	very good
predictability of returns	excellent

Total Return   ★★★

Over the past five years (all periods ending 6/30/98), MAP Equity has taken $10,000 and turned it into $25,660 ($21,210 over three years and $48,730 over the past ten years). This translates into an average annual return of 20.7 percent over the past five years, 28.5 percent over the past three years, and 17.2 percent for the decade. Over the past five years, this fund has outperformed 90 percent of all mutual funds; within its general category it has done better than 75 percent of its peers. Growth funds have averaged 19 percent annually over these same five years.

Risk/Volatility   ★★★★★

Over the past five years, MAP Equity has been safer than 98 percent of all growth funds. Over the past decade, the fund has had one negative year, while the S&P 500 has had one (off 3 percent in 1990). The fund has underperformed the S&P 500 six times in the last ten years.

	last 5 years		last 10 years	
worst year	3%	1994	–5%	1990
best year	33%	1995	33%	1995

In the past, Equity has done better than 60 percent of its peer group in up markets and outperformed 70 percent of its competition in down markets. Consistency, or predictability, of returns for Equity can be described as excellent.

Management   ★★★★

There are 100 stocks in this $110 million portfolio. The average growth fund today is $560 million in size. Close to 94 percent of the fund's holdings are in stocks. The stocks in this portfolio have an average price-earnings (p/e) ratio of 29 and a median market capitalization of $4 billion. The portfolio's equity holdings can be categorized as mid-cap and value-oriented issues.

A team has managed this fund for the past 15 years. Equity is the only fund within the MAP "family." Overall, the fund family's risk-adjusted performance can be described as excellent.

Tax Minimization ★

During the past five years, a $10,000 initial investment grew to $24,270 after taxes, assuming a 39.6 percent income tax bracket (state and federal combined) and a capital gains rate of 28 percent. This means that investors in this fund were able to preserve 71 percent of their total returns. Compared to other equity funds, this fund's tax savings are considered to be poor.

Expenses

Equity's expense ratio is 0.8 percent; it has also averaged 0.8 percent annually over the past three calendar years. The average expense ratio for the 1,500 funds in this category is 1.4 percent. This fund's turnover rate over the past year has been 58 percent, while its peer group average has been 90 percent.

Summary

MAP Equity is atypical from most funds in that it has three managers who each run their own "sub-portfolio." Managers Lob, Mullarkey and Stone all look for value plays, but that is where the similarity ends. Lob favors revenue growth, Mullarkey looks for growth catalysts, while Stone likes strong cash flows. The cash portion of the portfolio can be quite high—a major ingredient for making this one of the lowest risk growth funds.

Profile

minimum initial investment $250	*IRA accounts available*........... no
subsequent minimum investment ... $50	*IRA minimum investment*......... n/a
available in all 50 states......... yes	*date of inception* .... Jan. 1971
telephone exchanges............. yes	*dividend/income paid* .... annually
number of funds in family 1	*quality of annual reports* .... good

MFS Capital Opportunities A

500 Boylston Street
Boston, MA 02216
(800) 637-2929

total return	★★★★
risk reduction	★★★★
management	★★★★
tax minimization	★★★
expense control	★★
symbol MCOFX	17 points
up-market performance	excellent
down-market performance	fair
predictability of returns	good

Total Return ★★★★

Over the past five years (all periods ending 6/30/98), MFS Capital Opportunities A has taken $10,000 and turned it into $27,140 ($21,260 over three years and $50,940 over the past ten years). This translates into an average annual return of 22.1 percent over the past five years, 28.6 percent over the past three years, and 17.7 percent for the decade. Over the past five years, this fund has outperformed 85 percent of all mutual funds; within its general category it has done better than 65 percent of its peers. Growth funds have averaged 19 percent annually over these same five years.

Risk/Volatility ★★★★

Over the past five years, MFS Capital Opportunities A has been safer than 75 percent of all growth funds. Over the past decade, the fund has had two negative years, while the S&P 500 has had one (off 3 percent in 1990). The fund has underperformed the S&P 500 six times in the last ten years.

	last 5 years		last 10 years	
worst year	–2%	1994	–12%	1990
best year	44%	1995	44%	1995

In the past, Opportunities A has done better than 85 percent of its peer group in up markets and outperformed 45 percent of its competition in down markets. Consistency, or predictability, of returns for Opportunities A can be described as good.

Management ★★★★

There are 90 stocks in this $800 million portfolio. The average growth fund today is $560 million in size. Close to 95 percent of the fund's holdings are in stocks. The stocks in this portfolio have an average price-earnings (p/e) ratio of 30 and a median market capitalization of $10 billion. The portfolio's equity holdings can be categorized as large-cap and value-oriented issues.

John F. Brennan Jr. has managed this fund for the past seven years. There are 138 funds besides Opportunities A within the MFS family. Overall, the fund family's risk-adjusted performance can be described as good.

Tax Minimization   ★★★
During the past five years, a $10,000 initial investment grew to $25,420 after taxes, assuming a 39.6 percent income tax bracket (state and federal combined) and a capital gains rate of 28 percent. This means that investors in this fund were able to preserve 82 percent of their total returns. Compared to other equity funds, this fund's tax savings are considered to be good.

Expenses   ★★
MFS Capital Opportunities A's expense ratio is 1.3 percent; it has also averaged 1.3 percent annually over the past three calendar years. The average expense ratio for the 1,500 funds in this category is 1.4 percent. This fund's turnover rate over the past year has been 144 percent, while its peer group average has been 90 percent.

Summary
MFS Capital Opportunities A has a safety record that puts it in the top quartile; the fund has also outperformed over 80% of all other mutual funds. The portfolio scores very well in every important category: total return, risk reduction and quality of management. This growth fund is part of a huge fund family (which actually offers the oldest mutual fund in the U.S.—dating back to the 1920s) that includes some other very worthy candidates.

Profile
minimum initial investment $1,000	*IRA accounts available* . . . . yes
subsequent minimum investment . . . $50	*IRA minimum investment* $250
available in all 50 states. . . . . yes	*date of inception*. . . . . June 1983
telephone exchanges. . . . . yes	*dividend/income paid* . . . . annually
number of funds in family 139	*quality of annual reports* . . . . excellent

Oak Value

312 Walnut Street
P.O. Box 5354
Cincinnati, OH 45201-5354
(800) 622-2474

total return	★★★★★
risk reduction	★★★★
management	★★★★
tax minimization	★★★★
expense control	★★
symbol OAKVX	19 points
up-market performance	n/a
down-market performance	n/a
predictability of returns	good

Total Return   ★★★★★

Over the past five years (all periods ending 6/30/98), Oak Value has taken $10,000 and turned it into $31,190 ($24,240 over three years). This translates into an average annual return of 25.6 percent over the past five years and 34.3 percent over the past three years. Over the past five years, this fund has outperformed 90 percent of all mutual funds; within its general category it has done better than 70 percent of its peers. Growth funds have averaged 19 percent annually over these same five years.

Risk/Volatility   ★★★★

Over the past five years, Oak Value has been safer than 70 percent of all growth funds. Over the past decade, the fund has had one negative year, while the S&P 500 has had one (off 3 percent in 1990). The fund has underperformed the S&P 500 two times in the last ten years.

	last 5 years		since inception	
worst year	–2%	1994	–2%	1994
best year	38%	1997	38%	1997

Consistency, or predictability, of returns for Oak Value can be described as good.

Management   ★★★★

There are 25 stocks in this $355 million portfolio. The average growth fund today is $560 million in size. Close to 79 percent of the fund's holdings are in stocks. The stocks in this portfolio have an average price-earnings (p/e) ratio of 27 and a median market capitalization of $6 billion. The portfolio's equity holdings can be categorized as large-cap and value-oriented issues.

David R. Carr Jr. and George W. Brumley have managed this fund for the past five years. Oak Value is the only fund within the Tuscarora Investment Trust family. Overall, the fund "family's" risk-adjusted performance can be described as excellent.

Tax Minimization   ★★★★

During the past five years, a $10,000 initial investment grew to $31,170 after taxes, assuming a 39.6 percent income tax bracket (state and federal combined) and a capital gains rate of 28 percent. This means that investors in this fund were able to preserve 92 percent of their total returns. Compared to other equity funds, this fund's tax savings are considered to be very good.

Expenses   ★★

Oak Value's expense ratio is 1.6 percent; it has averaged 1.8 percent annually over the past three calendar years. The average expense ratio for the 1,500 funds in this category is 1.4 percent. This fund's turnover rate over the past year has been 22 percent, while its peer group average has been 90 percent.

Summary

Oak Value has appeared in previous editions of this book. It is a highly favored fund that excels when it comes to performance, but it also has a very low risk level. The fund has been highly recommended in the past and such kudos are equally valid today. Hopefully, the parent company, Tuscarora Investment Trust, will offer other funds in the future.

Profile

minimum initial investment $2,500	*IRA accounts available* . . . . yes
subsequent minimum investment . . $100	*IRA minimum investment* $1,000
available in all 50 states. . . . . yes	*date of inception* . . . . Jan. 1993
telephone exchanges . . . . no	*dividend/income paid* . . . . annually
number of funds in family 1	*quality of annual reports* . . . . n/a

Oppenheimer Quest Value Fund, Inc. A

Oppenheimer Funds, Inc.
Two World Trade Center, 34th Floor
New York, NY 10048-0203
(800) 525-7048

total return	★★★
risk reduction	★★★★★
management	★★★★
tax minimization	★★★
expense control	★★
symbol QFVFX	17 points
up-market performance	very good
down-market performance	fair
predictability of returns	very good

Total Return   ★★★

Over the past five years (all periods ending 6/30/98), Oppenheimer Quest Value A has taken $10,000 and turned it into $25,150 ($19,880 over three years and $46,010 over the past ten years). This translates into an average annual return of 20.3 percent over the past five years, 25.7 percent over the past three years, and 16.5 percent for the decade. Over the past five years, this fund has outperformed 85 percent of all mutual funds; within its general category it has done better than 75 percent of its peers. Growth funds have averaged 19 percent annually over these same five years.

Risk/Volatility   ★★★★★

Over the past five years, Oppenheimer Quest Value A has been safer than 60 percent of all growth funds. Over the past decade, the fund has had one negative year, while the S&P 500 has had one (off 3 percent in 1990). The fund has underperformed the S&P 500 six times in the last ten years.

	last 5 years		last 10 years	
worst year	1%	1994	−7%	1990
best year	37%	1995	37%	1995

In the past, Quest Value has done better than 70 percent of its peer group in up markets and outperformed 40 percent of its competition in down markets. Consistency, or predictability, of returns for Quest Value can be described as very good.

Management   ★★★★

There are 45 stocks in this $975 million portfolio. The average growth fund today is $560 million in size. Close to 85 percent of the fund's holdings are in stocks. The stocks in this portfolio have an average price-earnings (p/e) ratio of 22 and a median market capitalization of $10 billion. The portfolio's equity holdings can be categorized as large-cap and value-oriented issues.

Eileen P. Rominger has managed this fund for the past nine years. There are over 65 funds besides Quest Value within the Oppenheimer family. Overall, the fund family's risk-adjusted performance can be described as good.

Tax Minimization   ★★★
During the past five years, a $10,000 initial investment grew to $23,640 after taxes, assuming a 39.6 percent income tax bracket (state and federal combined) and a capital gains rate of 28 percent. This means that investors in this fund were able to preserve 85 percent of their total returns. Compared to other equity funds, this fund's tax savings are considered to be good.

Expenses   ★★
Quest Value's expense ratio is 1.6 percent; it has averaged 1.7 percent annually over the past three calendar years. The average expense ratio for the 1,500 funds in this category is 1.4 percent. This fund's turnover rate over the past year has been 20 percent, while its peer group average has been 90 percent.

Summary
Oppenheimer Quest Value A has had very good risk-adjusted returns for the past three, five and ten years. Portfolio manager Rominger looks for stocks whose valuation is moderately or significantly below market averages. She is not afraid to load up heavily on just a handful of stocks or commit a significant portion of the fund to cash when there are few buying opportunities.

Profile
minimum initial investment $1,000
subsequent minimum investment . . $250
available in all 50 states. . . . . yes
telephone exchanges. . . . . yes
number of funds in family . . . . . over 65

IRA accounts available . . . . yes
IRA minimum investment $250
date of inception. . . . . May 1980
dividend/income paid . . . . annually
quality of annual reports . . . . good

Performance Large Cap Equity

230 Park Avenue
New York, NY 10169
(800) 737-3676

total return	★★★★
risk reduction	★★★
management	★★★★
tax minimization	★★★★★
expense control	★★★★★
symbol PFECX	21 points
up-market performance	n/a
down-market performance	n/a
predictability of returns	very good

Total Return   ★★★★

Over the past five years (all periods ending 6/30/98), Performance Large Cap Equity has taken $10,000 and turned it into $26,580 ($22,460 over three years). This translates into an average annual return of 21.6 percent over the past five years and 31.0 percent over the past three years. Over the past five years, this fund has outperformed 85 percent of all mutual funds; within its general category it has done better than 70 percent of its peers. Growth funds have averaged 19 percent annually over these same five years.

Risk/Volatility   ★★★

Over the past five years, Performance Large Cap Equity has been safer than 65 percent of all growth funds. Over the past decade, the fund has had one negative year, while the S&P 500 has had one (off 3 percent in 1990). The fund has underperformed the S&P 500 three times in the last ten years.

	last 5 years		since inception	
worst year	–4%	1994	–4%	1994
best year	36%	1995	36%	1995

Consistency, or predictability, of returns for Large Cap Equity can be described as very good.

Management   ★★★★

There are 130 stocks in this $45 million portfolio. The average growth fund today is $560 million in size. Close to 97 percent of the fund's holdings are in stocks. The stocks in this portfolio have an average price-earnings (p/e) ratio of 30 and a median market capitalization of $62 billion. The portfolio's equity holdings can be categorized as large-cap and a blend of growth and value stocks.

Charles H. Windham has managed this fund for the past six years. There are 7 funds besides Large Cap Equity within the Performance Trust family. Overall, the fund family's risk-adjusted performance can be described as very good.

Tax Minimization   ★★★★★
During the past five years, a $10,000 initial investment grew to $26,580 after taxes, assuming a 39.6 percent income tax bracket (state and federal combined) and a capital gains rate of 28 percent. This means that investors in this fund were able to preserve 95 percent of their total returns. Compared to other equity funds, this fund's tax savings are considered to be excellent.

Expenses   ★★★★★
Performance Large Cap Equity's expense ratio is 1.1 percent; it has also averaged 1.1 percent annually over the past three calendar years. The average expense ratio for the 1,500 funds in this category is 1.4 percent. This fund's turnover rate over the past year has been 6 percent, while its peer group average has been 90 percent.

Summary
Performance Large Cap Equity has been safer than two-thirds of its growth fund peers while still outperforming about 70% of the competition. This small fund has received little publicity and that is unfortunate. It is strongly recommended for anyone who wants to participate in U.S. stocks. The Performance Funds Trust family includes a number of other highly rated portfolios.

Profile
minimum initial investment $1,000	*IRA accounts available* . . . . yes
subsequent minimum investment . . $100	*IRA minimum investment* $250
available in all 50 states . . . . no	*date of inception* . . . . June 1992
telephone exchanges . . . . yes	*dividend/income paid* . . . . annually
number of funds in family 8	*quality of annual reports* . . . . n/a

T. Rowe Price Blue Chip Growth

100 East Pratt Street
Baltimore, MD 21202
(800) 638-5660

total return	★★★★
risk reduction	★★★★
management	★★★★★
tax minimization	★★★★★
expense control	★★★★★
symbol TRBCX	23 points
up-market performance	n/a
down-market performance	n/a
predictability of returns	very good

Total Return   ★★★★

Over the past five years (all periods ending 6/30/98), T. Rowe Price Blue Chip Growth has taken $10,000 and turned it into $30,420 ($22,000 over three years). This translates into an average annual return of 24.9 percent over the past five years and 30.1 percent over the past three years. Over the past five years, this fund has outperformed 90 percent of all mutual funds; within its general category it has done better than 80 percent of its peers. Growth funds have averaged 19 percent annually over these same five years.

Risk/Volatility   ★★★★

Over the past five years, T. Rowe Price Blue Chip Growth has been safer than 95 percent of all growth funds. Over the past decade, the fund has had no negative years, while the S&P 500 has had one (off 3 percent in 1990). The fund has underperformed the S&P 500 two times in the last ten years.

	last 5 years		since inception	
worst year	1%	1994	1%	1994
best year	38%	1995	38%	1995

Consistency, or predictability, of returns for Blue Chip Growth can be described as very good.

Management   ★★★★★

There are 155 stocks in this $3.2 billion portfolio. The average growth fund today is $560 million in size. Close to 93 percent of the fund's holdings are in stocks. The stocks in this portfolio have an average price-earnings (p/e) ratio of 33 and a median market capitalization of $24 billion. The portfolio's equity holdings can be categorized as large-cap and a blend of growth and value stocks.

Larry Puglia has managed this fund for the past five years. There are 65 funds besides Blue Chip Growth within the T. Rowe Price family. Overall, the fund family's risk-adjusted performance can be described as very good.

Tax Minimization ★★★★★

During the past five years, a $10,000 initial investment grew to $30,410 after taxes, assuming a 39.6 percent income tax bracket (state and federal combined) and a capital gains rate of 28 percent. This means that investors in this fund were able to preserve 96 percent of their total returns. Compared to other equity funds, this fund's tax savings are considered to be excellent.

Expenses ★★★★★

Blue Chip Growth's expense ratio is 1.0 percent; it has averaged 1.1 percent annually over the past three calendar years. The average expense ratio for the 1,500 funds in this category is 1.4 percent. This fund's turnover rate over the past year has been 24 percent, while its peer group average has been 90 percent.

Summary

T. Rowe Price Blue Chip Growth takes its name very seriously. Manager Puglia likes those companies that represent industry leadership. Volatility has been quite a bit below average while tax minimization and expense control have been exceptional. Management is also superb; this is the second most highly ranked growth fund and like other T. Rowe Price equity funds mentioned in this book, it is strongly recommended.

Profile

minimum initial investment $2,500	*IRA accounts available* . . . . yes
subsequent minimum investment . . $100	*IRA minimum investment* $1,000
available in all 50 states. . . . . yes	*date of inception.* . . . . June 1993
telephone exchanges. . . . . yes	*dividend/income paid* . . . . annually
number of funds in family 66	*quality of annual reports* . . . . excellent

Torray

6610 Rockledge Drive
Bethesda, MD 20817
(800) 443-3036

total return	★★★★★
risk reduction	★★★★
management	★★★★★
tax minimization	★★★★★
expense control	★★★★★
symbol TORYX	24 points
up-market performance	n/a
down-market performance	n/a
predictability of returns	good

Total Return   ★★★★★

Over the past five years (all periods ending 6/30/98), Torray has taken $10,000 and turned it into $32,350 ($24,820 over three years). This translates into an average annual return of 26.5 percent over the past five years and 35.4 percent over the past three years. Over the past five years, this fund has outperformed 95 percent of all mutual funds; within its general category it has done better than 85 percent of its peers. Growth funds have averaged 19 percent annually over these same five years.

Risk/Volatility   ★★★★

Over the past five years, Torray has been safer than 95 percent of all growth funds. Over the past decade, the fund has had no negative years, while the S&P 500 has had one (off 3 percent in 1990). The fund has underperformed the S&P 500 two times in the last ten years.

	last 5 years		since inception	
worst year	2%	1994	2%	1994
best year	50%	1995	50%	1995

Consistency, or predictability, of returns for Torray can be described as good.

Management   ★★★★★

There are 45 stocks in this $1.7 billion portfolio. The average growth fund today is $560 million in size. Close to 99 percent of the fund's holdings are in stocks. The stocks in this portfolio have an average price-earnings (p/e) ratio of 27 and a median market capitalization of $20 billion. The portfolio's equity holdings can be categorized as large-cap and value-oriented issues.

Douglas C. Eby and Robert E. Torray have managed this fund for the past seven years. Torray is the only fund within the Torray "family." Overall, the fund family's risk-adjusted performance can be described as excellent.

Tax Minimization   ★★★★★

During the past five years, a $10,000 initial investment grew to $32,350 after taxes, assuming a 39.6 percent income tax bracket (state and federal combined) and a capital gains rate of 28 percent. This means that investors in this fund were able to preserve 96 percent of their total returns. Compared to other equity funds, this fund's tax savings are considered to be excellent.

Expenses   ★★★★★

Torray's expense ratio is 1.1 percent; it has averaged 1.2 percent annually over the past three calendar years. The average expense ratio for the 1,500 funds in this category is 1.4 percent. This fund's turnover rate over the past year has been 12 percent, while its peer group average has been 90 percent.

Summary

Torray has been on a winning streak now for a number of years. It has consistently ranking in the top quartile of all growth funds for each of the past several years; risk-adjusted returns for the most recent three and five years have been excellent. This fund is also the most highly ranked equity fund in the book. Its near-perfect score (24 out of 25 possible points) makes this fund a smart choice for any investor.

Profile

minimum initial investment $10,000	*IRA accounts available* . . . . yes
subsequent minimum investment . $2,000	*IRA minimum investment* $10,000
available in all 50 states . . . . no	*date of inception* . . . . Dec. 1990
telephone exchanges . . . . no	*dividend/income paid* . . . . annually
number of funds in family 1	*quality of annual reports* . . . . good

Weitz Value

One Pacific Place
1125 South 103 Street
Omaha, NE 68124-6008
(800) 232-4161

total return	★★★★
risk reduction	★★★★
management	★★★★★
tax minimization	★★★★
expense control	★★★★
symbol WVALX	21 points
up-market performance	excellent
down-market performance	very good
predictability of returns	good

Total Return   ★★★★

Over the past five years (all periods ending 6/30/98), Weitz Value has taken $10,000 and turned it into $28,190 ($23,550 over three years and $52,740 over the past ten years). This translates into an average annual return of 23.0 percent over the past five years, 33.0 percent over the past three years, and 18.1 percent for the decade. Over the past five years, this fund has outperformed 75 percent of all mutual funds; within its general category it has done better than 65 percent of its peers. Growth funds have averaged 19 percent annually over these same five years.

Risk/Volatility   ★★★★

Over the past five years, Weitz Value has been safer than 70 percent of all growth funds. Over the past decade, the fund has had two negative years, while the S&P 500 has had one (off 3 percent in 1990). The fund has underperformed the S&P 500 six times in the last ten years.

	last 5 years		last 10 years	
worst year	−10%	1994	−10%	1994
best year	39%	1997	39%	1997

In the past, Value has done better than 85 percent of its peer group in up-markets and outperformed 75 percent of its competition in down markets. Consistency, or predictability, of returns for Value can be described as good.

Management   ★★★★★

There are 65 stocks in this $500 million portfolio. The average growth fund today is $560 million in size. Close to 73 percent of the fund's holdings are in stocks. The stocks in this portfolio have an average price-earnings (p/e) ratio of 26 and a median market capitalization of $4 billion. The portfolio's equity holdings can be categorized as mid-cap and value-oriented issues.

Wallace R. Weitz has managed this fund for the past 12 years. There are three funds besides Value within the Weitz family. Overall, the fund family's risk-adjusted performance can be described as excellent.

Tax Minimization   ★★★★

During the past five years, a $10,000 initial investment grew to $27,080 after taxes, assuming a 39.6 percent income tax bracket (state and federal combined) and a capital gains rate of 28 percent. This means that investors in this fund were able to preserve 91 percent of their total returns. Compared to other equity funds, this fund's tax savings are considered to be very good.

Expenses   ★★★★

Value's expense ratio is 1.3 percent; it has averaged 1.4 percent annually over the past three calendar years. The average expense ratio for the 1,500 funds in this category is 1.4 percent. This fund's turnover rate over the past year has been 39 percent, while its peer group average has been 90 percent.

Summary

Weitz Value targets stocks that are believed to be undervalued; once the market-place recognizes the true value and the stock price has been run up, the security is sold. The portfolio holds only a modest number of stocks, and management is not hesitant to hold a rather large cash position when warranted. At times, REITs are also a modest part of the portfolio. This is one of the better ranked growth funds whose investment philosophy has successfully shifted over the years.

Profile

minimum initial investment $25,000	*IRA accounts available* .... yes
subsequent minimum investment . $5,000	*IRA minimum investment* $2,000
available in all 50 states .... no	*date of inception* .... May 1986
telephone exchanges .... yes	*dividend/income paid* .... annually
number of funds in family 4	*quality of annual reports* .... good

Growth and Income Funds

These funds attempt to produce both capital appreciation and current income, with priority given to appreciation potential in the stocks purchased. Growth and income fund portfolios include seasoned, well-established firms that pay relatively high cash dividends. The goal of these funds is to provide long-term growth without excessive volatility in share price. Portfolio composition is almost always exclusively U.S. stocks, with an emphasis on financial, industrial cyclical, service, health, technology and energy common stocks.

Over the past fifty years (ending 12/31/97), common stocks have outperformed inflation, on average, 80 percent of the time over one-year periods, 83 percent of the time over five- and ten-year periods, 86 percent of the time over fifteen-year periods and 100 percent of the time over any given twenty-year period of time. Over the same period, high-quality, long-term corporate bonds have outperformed inflation, on average, 60 percent of the time over one-year periods, 59 percent of the time over five-year periods, 56 percent of the time over ten-year periods, 67 percent of the time over fifteen-year periods and 68 percent over any given twenty-year period of time.

As you can see by the table below, crossing a 1,000 point barrier has become easier and easier for the Dow Jones Industrial Average (DJIA). As of March 12, 1997 (the most recent changes in the composition of the Dow), the 30 stocks that comprise the DJIA were/are: Allied Signal, Alcoa, American Express, AT&T, Boeing, Caterpillar, Chevron, Coca-Cola, Walt Disney, DuPont, Eastman Kodak, Exxon, GE, GM, Goodyear, Hewlett-Packard, IBM, International Paper, Johnson & Johnson, McDonald's, Merck, 3M, J.P. Morgan, Philip Morris, Proctor & Gamble, Sears, Travelers Group, Union Carbide, United Technology, and WalMart.

Dow Milestones

Level of the Dow & Date Reached	Description
100 (1/12/06)	Not until 10 years after the DJIA is created does it hit 100.
1,000 (11/14/72)	Flirts with the 1,000 mark many times during the previous 6 yrs.
2,000 (1/8/87)	Four years of a bull market.
3,000 (4/17/91)	Rally after Gulf War.
5,000 (11/21/95)	Nine months earlier the Dow breaks 3,000.
6,000 (10/14/96)	Inflationary concerns are subdued.
7,000 (2/13/97)	The quickest 1,000 point ever for the Dow.
8,000 (7/16/97)	Market recovers after 9.8% March and April drop.

Seven hundred funds make up the growth and income category. Another category, "equity-income" funds, has been combined with growth and income. Thus, for this section, there were a total of 920 possible candidates. Total market capitalization of these two categories combined is $870 billion.

Over the past three and five years, growth and income funds have had an average compound return of 25.2 percent per year and 19.3 percent during the last five years (vs. 23.1 and 17.6 percent for equity-income funds). These funds have averaged 15.3 percent annually over the last ten years and 13.8 percent annually for the past fifteen years (vs. 15.0 and 15.1 percent for equity-income). The standard deviation for growth and income funds has been 13.9 percent over the past three years (compared to 11.8 for equity-income and 16.6 percent for growth funds). This means that growth and income funds have had the same volatility as "world stock" and "European" funds but have been about 17 percent less predictable than pure equity-income funds.

Growth & Income Funds

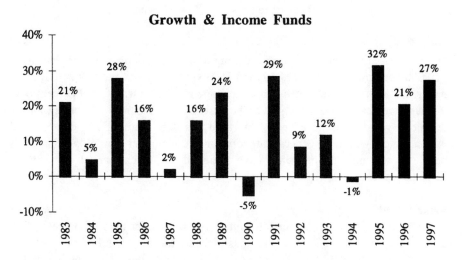

American Mutual

333 South Hope Street
Los Angeles, CA 90071
(800) 421-4120

total return	★★
risk reduction	★★★★★
management	★★★★
tax minimization	★★
expense control	★★★★★
symbol AMRMX	18 points
up-market performance	fair
down-market performance	very good
predictability of returns	very good

Total Return   ★★
Over the past five years (all periods ending 6/30/98), American Mutual has taken $10,000 and turned it into $21,860 ($18,160 over three years and $39,210 over the past ten years). This translates into an average annual return of 16.9 percent over the past five years, 22.0 percent over the past three years, and 14.6 percent for the decade. Over the past five years, this fund has outperformed 75 percent of all mutual funds; within its general category it has done better than 40 percent of its peers. Growth and income funds have averaged 19 percent annually over these same five years.

Risk/Volatility   ★★★★★
Over the past five years, American Mutual has been safer than 95 percent of all growth and income funds. Over the past decade, the fund has had one negative year, while the S&P 500 has had one (off 3 percent in 1990). The fund has under-performed the S&P 500 seven times in the last ten years.

	last 5 years		last 10 years	
worst year	.3%	1994	−2%	1990
best year	31%	1995	31%	1995

In the past, American Mutual has done better than 50 percent of its peer group in up markets and outperformed 75 percent of its competition in down markets. Consistency, or predictability, of returns for American Mutual can be described as very good.

Management   ★★★★
There are 130 stocks in this $11 billion portfolio. The average growth and income fund today is $970 million in size. Close to 75 percent of the fund's holdings are in stocks. The stocks in this portfolio have an average price-earnings (p/e) ratio of

25 and a median market capitalization of $21 billion. The portfolio's equity holdings can be categorized as large-cap and value-oriented issues.

A team has managed this fund for the past 22 years. There are 24 funds besides American Mutual within the American Funds Group. Overall, the fund family's risk-adjusted performance can be described as very good.

Tax Minimization ★★

During the past five years, a $10,000 initial investment grew to $20,540 after taxes, assuming a 39.6 percent income tax bracket (state and federal combined) and a capital gains rate of 28 percent. This means that investors in this fund were able to preserve 76 percent of their total returns. Compared to other equity funds, this fund's tax savings are considered to be fair.

Expenses ★★★★★

American Mutual's expense ratio is 0.6 percent; it has also averaged 0.6 percent annually over the past three calendar years. The average expense ratio for the 900 funds in this category is 1.3 percent. This fund's turnover rate over the past year has been 19 percent, while its peer group average has been 65 percent.

Summary

American Mutual is yet another member of the American Funds Group to make this as well as all previous editions of the book. The five managers who run this fund, Dunton, Lovelace Jr., O'Donnell, Shanahan and Armour, each independently oversee a chuck of the portfolio. The guiding light of management is to produce income and conserve principal while hopefully increasing total return. Risk is extremely low due to a heavy dose of dividend-paying blue chips plus a sizeable position in cash equivalents.

Profile

minimum initial investment $250	IRA accounts available . . . . yes
subsequent minimum investment . . . $50	IRA minimum investment $250
available in all 50 states. . . . . yes	date of inception . . . . Feb. 1950
telephone exchanges. . . . . yes	dividend/income paid . . . . annually
number of funds in family 25	quality of annual reports . . . . excellent

Capital Income Builder

333 South Hope Street
Los Angeles, CA 90071
(800) 421-4120

total return	★
risk reduction	★★★★★
management	★★★★
tax minimization	★★
expense control	★★★★★
symbol CAIBX	17 points
up-market performance	very good
down-market performance	excellent
predictability of returns	excellent

Total Return   ★

Over the past five years (all periods ending 6/30/98), Capital Income Builder has taken $10,000 and turned it into $20,840 ($17,730 over three years and $39,380 over the past ten years). This translates into an average annual return of 15.8 percent over the past five years, 21.0 percent over the past three years, and 14.7 percent for the decade. Over the past five years, this fund has outperformed 70 percent of all mutual funds; within its general category it has done better than 65 percent of its peers. Growth and income funds have averaged 19 percent annually over these same five years.

Risk/Volatility   ★★★★★

Over the past five years, Capital Income Builder has been safer than 60 percent of all growth and income funds. Over the past decade, the fund has had one negative year, while the S&P 500 has had one (off 3 percent in 1990). The fund has underperformed the S&P 500 seven times in the last ten years.

	last 5 years		last 10 years	
worst year	–2%	1994	–2%	1994
best year	25%	1995	26%	1991

In the past, Income Builder has done better than 65 percent of its peer group in up markets and outperformed 90 percent of its competition in down markets. Consistency, or predictability, of returns for Income Builder can be described as excellent.

Management   ★★★★

There are 225 stocks in this $9 billion portfolio. The average growth and income fund today is $970 million in size. Close to 66 percent of the fund's holdings are in stocks. The stocks in this portfolio have an average price-earnings (p/e) ratio of

23 and a median market capitalization of $13 billion. The portfolio's equity hold-ings can be categorized as large-cap and value-oriented issues.

A team has managed this fund for the past 11 years. There are 24 funds besides Income Builder within the American Funds Group. Overall, the fund family's risk-adjusted performance can be described as very good.

Tax Minimization ★★
During the past five years, a $10,000 initial investment grew to $19,610 after taxes, assuming a 39.6 percent income tax bracket (state and federal combined) and a capital gains rate of 28 percent. This means that investors in this fund were able to preserve 75 percent of their total returns. Compared to other equity funds, this fund's tax savings are considered to be fair.

Expenses ★★★★★
Income Builder's expense ratio is 0.7 percent; it has also averaged 0.7 percent annually over the past three calendar years. The average expense ratio for the 900 funds in this category is 1.3 percent. This fund's turnover rate over the past year has been 28 percent, while its peer group average has been 65 percent.

Summary
Capital Income Builder, managed by Capital Guardian Trust Company (American Funds Group) is a growth and income fund that emphasizes current income much more than the vast majority of its peers. A fifth of the fund is in bonds and close to a third is in foreign equities. Management has been able to turn in decent returns with extremely low risk. This fund is recommended for investors who are willing to give up some of the upside potential in return for a good night's sleep.

Profile

minimum initial investment $1,000	*IRA accounts available* . . . . yes
subsequent minimum investment . . . $50	*IRA minimum investment* $250
available in all 50 states. . . . . yes	*date of inception* . . . . July 1987
telephone exchanges. . . . . yes	*dividend/income paid* . . . . annually
number of funds in family 25	*quality of annual reports* . . . . excellent

Mairs & Power Balanced

W-2062 First National Bank Buiilding
St. Paul, MN 55101
(612) 222-8478

total return	★★
risk reduction	★★★★★
management	★★★★
tax minimization	★★★★★
expense control	★★★★★
symbol MAPOX	21 points
up-market performance	excellent
down-market performance	very good
predictability of returns	excellent

Total Return   ★★

Over the past five years (all periods ending 6/30/98), Mairs & Power Balanced has taken $10,000 and turned it into $21,500 ($18,190 over three years and $37,460 over the past ten years). This translates into an average annual return of 16.5 percent over the past five years, 22.1 percent over the past three years, and 14.1 percent for the decade. Over the past five years, this fund has outperformed 75 percent of all mutual funds; within its general category it has done better than 80 percent of its peers. Growth and income funds have averaged 19 percent annually over these same five years.

Risk/Volatility   ★★★★★

Over the past five years, Mairs & Power Balanced has been safer than 35 percent of all growth and income funds. Over the past decade, the fund has had one negative year, while the S&P 500 has had one (off 3 percent in 1990). The fund has underperformed the S&P 500 eight times in the last ten years.

	last 5 years		last 10 years	
worst year	–2%	1994	–2%	1994
best year	30%	1995	30%	1995

In the past, Balanced has done better than 90 percent of its peer group in up markets and outperformed 65 percent of its competition in down markets. Consistency, or predictability, of returns for Balanced can be described as excellent.

Management   ★★★★

There are 85 stocks in this $35 million portfolio. The average growth and income fund today is $970 million in size. Close to 64 percent of the fund's holdings are in stocks. The stocks in this portfolio have an average price-earnings (p/e) ratio of 25 and a median market capitalization of $21 billion. The portfolio's equity holdings can be categorized as large-cap and value-oriented issues.

William B. Frels has managed this fund for the past six years. There is one other fund besides Balanced within the Mairs & Power family. Overall, the fund family's risk-adjusted performance can be described as excellent.

Tax Minimization   ★★★★★
During the past five years, a $10,000 initial investment grew to $21,500 after taxes, assuming a 39.6 percent income tax bracket (state and federal combined) and a capital gains rate of 28 percent. This means that investors in this fund were able to preserve 88 percent of their total returns. Compared to other equity funds, this fund's tax savings are considered to be excellent.

Expenses   ★★★★★
Balanced's expense ratio is 0.9 percent; it has averaged 1.0 percent annually over the past three calendar years. The average expense ratio for the 900 funds in this category is 1.3 percent. This fund's turnover rate over the past year has been 5 percent, while its peer group average has been 65 percent.

Summary
Mairs & Power Balanced, considered by other sources as a balanced fund, as noted in its name, is actually more like a growth and income fund with the safety of a balanced portfolio. This tiny fund boasts some of the best and highest rankings in its category (however you want to classify it) and certainly is one of the best funds in the entire book. Mairs & Power Funds is a very small family that deserves more of the spotlight.

Profile
minimum initial investment . . . . . $2,500   *IRA accounts available* . . . . yes
subsequent minimum investment . . $100   *IRA minimum investment* $1,000
available in all 50 states . . . . no   *date of inception.* . . . . Mar. 1961
telephone exchanges . . . . no   *dividend/income paid* . . . . annually
number of funds in family 2   *quality of annual reports* . . . . n/a

MFS Massachusetts Investors A

500 Boylston Street
Boston, MA 02116
(800) 637-2929

total return	★★★★★
risk reduction	★★★
management	★★★★★
tax minimization	★★★
expense control	★★★★★
symbol MITTX	21 points
up-market performance	excellent
down-market performance	good
predictability of returns	fair

Total Return   ★★★★★
Over the past five years (all periods ending 6/30/98), MFS Massachusetts Investors A has taken $10,000 and turned it into $28,060 ($22,630 over three years and $55,710 over the past ten years). This translates into an average annual return of 22.9 percent over the past five years, 31.3 percent over the past three years, and 18.7 percent for the decade. Over the past five years, this fund has outperformed 90 percent of all mutual funds; within its general category it has done better than 75 percent of its peers. Growth and income funds have averaged 19 percent annually over these same five years.

Risk/Volatility   ★★★
Over the past five years, MFS Massachusetts Investors A has been safer than 80 percent of all growth and income funds. Over the past decade, the fund has had two negative years, while the S&P 500 has had one (off 3 percent in 1990). The fund has underperformed the S&P 500 six times in the last ten years.

	last 5 years		last 10 years	
worst year	−1%	1994	−1%	1994
best year	39%	1995	39%	1995

In the past, Investors A has done better than 85 percent of its peer group in up markets and outperformed 65 percent of its competition in down markets. Consistency, or predictability, of returns for Investors A can be described as fair.

Management   ★★★★★
There are 170 stocks in this $5.7 billion portfolio. The average growth and income fund today is $970 million in size. Close to 97 percent of the fund's holdings are in stocks. The stocks in this portfolio have an average price-earnings (p/e) ratio of 28 and a median market capitalization of $20 billion. The portfolio's equity holdings can be categorized as large-cap and value-oriented issues.

A team has managed this fund for the past five years. There are 138 funds besides Investors A within the MFS family. Overall, the fund family's risk-adjusted performance can be described as good.

Tax Minimization   ★★★

During the past five years, a $10,000 initial investment grew to $26,420 after taxes, assuming a 39.6 percent income tax bracket (state and federal combined) and a capital gains rate of 28 percent. This means that investors in this fund were able to preserve 78 percent of their total returns. Compared to other equity funds, this fund's tax savings are considered to be good.

Expenses   ★★★★★

Investors A's expense ratio is 0.7 percent; it has also averaged 0.7 percent annually over the past three calendar years. The average expense ratio for the 900 funds in this category is 1.3 percent. This fund's turnover rate over the past year has been 44 percent, while its peer group average has been 65 percent.

Summary

MFS Massachusetts Investors A is a special kind of growth and income fund that also likes convertibles as well as foreign and domestic equities. Managers Laupenheimer, Dynan and Parke base their purchase and sale decisions more on how well a company is being run than its current stock price or some financial ratio. The fund's risk-adjusted returns have been superb over the past three years and very good for the past five and ten years.

Profile

minimum initial investment $1,000	*IRA accounts available* . . . . yes
subsequent minimum investment . . . $50	*IRA minimum investment* $250
available in all 50 states. . . . . yes	*date of inception* . . . . July 1924
telephone exchanges. . . . . yes	*dividend/income paid* . . . . annually
number of funds in family 139	*quality of annual reports* . . . . good

Nationwide D

One Nationwide Plaza
P.O. Box 1492
Columbus, OH 43216
(800) 848-0920

total return	★★★★★
risk reduction	★★★
management	★★★★★
tax minimization	★★★★★
expense control	★★★★★
symbol MUIFX	23 points
up-market performance	fair
down-market performance	good
predictability of returns	fair

Total Return   ★★★★★

Over the past five years (all periods ending 6/30/98), Nationwide D has taken $10,000 and turned it into $29,640 ($24,630 over three years and $55,060 over the past ten years). This translates into an average annual return of 24.3 percent over the past five years, 35.1 percent over the past three years, and 18.6 percent for the decade. Over the past five years, this fund has outperformed 90 percent of all mutual funds; within its general category it has done better than 80 percent of its peers. Growth and income funds have averaged 19 percent annually over these same five years.

Risk/Volatility   ★★★

Over the past five years, Nationwide D has been safer than 90 percent of all growth and income funds. Over the past decade, the fund has had no negative years, while the S&P 500 has had one (off 3 percent in 1990). The fund has underperformed the S&P 500 five times in the last ten years.

	last 5 years		last 10 years	
worst year	1%	1994	1%	1994
best year	40%	1997	40%	1997

In the past, Nationwide D has done better than 85 percent of its peer group in up markets and outperformed 60 percent of its competition in down markets. Consistency, or predictability, of returns for Nationwide D can be described as fair.

Management   ★★★★★

There are 60 stocks in this $2 billion portfolio. The average growth and income fund today is $970 million in size. Close to 96 percent of the fund's holdings are in stocks. The stocks in this portfolio have an average price-earnings (p/e) ratio of

29 and a median market capitalization of $20 billion. The portfolio's equity holdings can be categorized as large-cap and a blend of growth and value stocks.

Charles S. Bath has managed this fund for the past 13 years. There are six funds besides Nationwide D within the Nationwide family. Overall, the fund family's risk-adjusted performance can be described as good.

Tax Minimization   ★★★★★

During the past five years, a $10,000 initial investment grew to $28,330 after taxes, assuming a 39.6 percent income tax bracket (state and federal combined) and a capital gains rate of 28 percent. This means that investors in this fund were able to preserve 88 percent of their total returns. Compared to other equity funds, this fund's tax savings are considered to be excellent.

Expenses   ★★★★★

Nationwide D's expense ratio is 0.6 percent; it has also averaged 0.6 percent annually over the past three calendar years. The average expense ratio for the 900 funds in this category is 1.3 percent. This fund's turnover rate over the past year has been 15 percent, while its peer group average has been 65 percent.

Summary

Nationwide D has had excellent risk-adjusted returns for the past three years. Manager Bath looks for companies with franchises that allow them to outperform in a variety of economic climates. He tends to own a stock for a number of years. This fund ties as the overall number two growth and income fund. The fund scores a perfect score in four out of the five categories measured.

Profile

minimum initial investment $250	*IRA accounts available* . . . . yes
subsequent minimum investment . . . $25	*IRA minimum investment* $250
available in all 50 states. . . . . yes	*date of inception.* . . . . May 1933
telephone exchanges. . . . . yes	*dividend/income paid* . . . . annually
number of funds in family 7	*quality of annual reports* . . . . good

Pioneer Equity-Income A

60 State Street
Boston, MA 02109-1820
(800) 225-6292

total return	★★
risk reduction	★★★★
management	★★★★
tax minimization	★★★★
expense control	★★★★
symbol PEQIX	18 points
up-market performance	excellent
down-market performance	n/a
predictability of returns	good

Total Return   ★★

Over the past five years (all periods ending 6/30/98), Pioneer Equity-Income A has taken $10,000 and turned it into $19,520 ($22,610 over three years). This translates into an average annual return of 17.7 percent over the past five years and 25.0 percent over the past three years. Over the past five years, this fund has outperformed 75 percent of all mutual funds; within its general category it has done better than 45 percent of its peers. Growth and income funds have averaged 19 percent annually over these same five years.

Risk/Volatility   ★★★★

Over the past five years, Pioneer Equity-Income A has been safer than 80 percent of all growth and income funds. Over the past decade, the fund has had one negative year, while the S&P 500 has had one (off 3 percent in 1990). The fund has underperformed the S&P 500 four times in the last ten years.

	last 5 years		since inception	
worst year	–1%	1994	–1%	1994
best year	35%	1997	35%	1997

In the past, Equity-Income has done better than 85 percent of its peer group in up markets. Consistency, or predictability, of returns for Equity-Income can be described as very good.

Management   ★★★★

There are 100 stocks in this $585 million portfolio. The average growth and income fund today is $970 million in size. Close to 99 percent of the fund's holdings are in stocks. The stocks in this portfolio have an average price-earnings (p/e) ratio of 24 and a median market capitalization of $15 billion. The portfolio's equity holdings can be categorized as large-cap and value-oriented issues.

John A. Carey has managed this fund for the past eight years. There are 60 funds besides Equity-Income within the Pioneer family. Overall, the fund family's risk-adjusted performance can be described as good.

Tax Minimization   ★★★★

During the past five years, a $10,000 initial investment grew to $21,260 after taxes, assuming a 39.6 percent income tax bracket (state and federal combined) and a capital gains rate of 28 percent. This means that investors in this fund were able to preserve 83 percent of their total returns. Compared to other equity funds, this fund's tax savings are considered to be very good.

Expenses   ★★★★

Equity-Income's expense ratio is 1.1 percent; it has averaged 1.2 percent annually over the past three calendar years. The average expense ratio for the 900 funds in this category is 1.3 percent. This fund's turnover rate over the past year has been 18 percent, while its peer group average has been 65 percent.

Summary

Pioneer Equity-Income A's emphasis on high dividend-paying stocks has paid off handsomely in two ways: lower risk and respectable returns. Manager Carey looks for companies that have a lengthy history of rising dividends, low price-to-dividend ratios plus strong corporate management. This is a good choice for the risk-conscious investor who is concerned with tax minimization and expense control.

Profile

minimum initial investment $1,000	*IRA accounts available* . . . . yes
subsequent minimum investment . . . $50	*IRA minimum investment* $1,000
available in all 50 states. . . . . yes	*date of inception* . . . . July 1990
telephone exchanges. . . . . yes	*dividend/income paid* . . . . annually
number of funds in family 61	*quality of annual reports* . . . . excellent

State Street Research Alpha A

One Financial Center
Boston, MA 02111
(800) 882-0052

total return	★★★
risk reduction	★★★★
management	★★★★
tax minimization	★★★★
expense control	★★★
symbol SSEAX	18 points
up-market performance	fair
down-market performance	very good
predictability of returns	good

Total Return   ★★★

Over the past five years (all periods ending 6/30/98), State Street Research Alpha A has taken $10,000 and turned it into $24,230 ($19,990 over three years and $41,310 over the past ten years). This translates into an average annual return of 19.4 percent over the past five years, 26.0 percent over the past three years, and 15.2 percent for the decade. Over the past five years, this fund has outperformed 75 percent of all mutual funds; within its general category it has done better than 65 percent of its peers. Growth and income funds have averaged 19 percent annually over these same five years.

Risk/Volatility   ★★★★

Over the past five years, State Street Research Alpha A has been safer than 90 percent of all growth and income funds. Over the past decade, the fund has had two negative years, while the S&P 500 has had one (off 3 percent in 1990). The fund has underperformed the S&P 500 seven times in the last ten years.

	last 5 years		last 10 years	
worst year	–5%	1994	–11%	1990
best year	29%	1995	29%	1995

In the past, Alpha A has done better than 35 percent of its peer group in up markets and outperformed 70 percent of its competition in down markets. Consistency, or predictability, of returns for Alpha A can be described as good.

Management   ★★★★

There are 150 stocks in this $125 million portfolio. The average growth and income fund today is $970 million in size. Close to 78 percent of the fund's holdings are in stocks. The stocks in this portfolio have an average price-earnings (p/e) ratio of 22 and a median market capitalization of $3 billion. The portfolio's equity holdings can be categorized as mid-cap and value-oriented issues.

Bartlett R. Geer has managed this fund for the past six years. There are 64 funds besides Alpha A within the State Street Research family. Overall, the fund family's risk-adjusted performance can be described as good.

Tax Minimization ★★★★
During the past five years, a $10,000 initial investment grew to $23,040 after taxes, assuming a 39.6 percent income tax bracket (state and federal combined) and a capital gains rate of 28 percent. This means that investors in this fund were able to preserve 84 percent of their total returns. Compared to other equity funds, this fund's tax savings are considered to be very good.

Expenses ★★★
Alpha A's expense ratio is 1.3 percent; it has also averaged 1.3 percent annually over the past three calendar years. The average expense ratio for the 900 funds in this category is 1.3 percent. This fund's turnover rate over the past year has been 63 percent, while its peer group average has been 65 percent.

Summary
State Street Research Alpha A's risk-adjusted returns have gone from very good to excellent. Manager Geer prefers high-yield bonds over convertibles for the more conservative part of his portfolio. Geer closely studies a company's asset replacement value and its cash flow as indicators of value. This is a good choice for the risk-averse equity investor; the portfolio is sometimes categorized as an equity-income fund.

Profile
minimum initial investment $2,500	*IRA accounts available* . . . . yes
subsequent minimum investment . . . $50	*IRA minimum investment* $2,000
available in all 50 states. . . . . yes	*date of inception* . . . . Aug. 1986
telephone exchanges. . . . . yes	*dividend/income paid* . . . . annually
number of funds in family 65	*quality of annual reports* . . . . excellent

T. Rowe Price Dividend Growth

100 East Pratt Street
Baltimore, MD 21202
(800) 638-5660

total return	★★★★
risk reduction	★★★★★
management	★★★★★
tax minimization	★★★★★
expense control	★★★★★
symbol PRDGX	24 points
up-market performance	n/a
down-market performance	n/a
predictability of returns	very good

Total Return   ★★★★

Over the past five years (all periods ending 6/30/98), T. Rowe Price Dividend Growth has taken $10,000 and turned it into $26,230 ($20,690 over three years). This translates into an average annual return of 21.3 percent over the past five years and 27.4 percent over the past three years. Over the past five years, this fund has outperformed 85 percent of all mutual funds; within its general category it has done better than 60 percent of its peers. Growth and income funds have averaged 19 percent annually over these same five years.

Risk/Volatility   ★★★★★

Over the past five years, T. Rowe Price Dividend Growth has been safer than 99 percent of all growth and income funds. Over the past decade, the fund has had no negative years, while the S&P 500 has had one (off 3 percent in 1990). The fund has underperformed the S&P 500 two times in the last ten years.

	last 5 years		since inception	
worst year	2%	1994	2%	1994
best year	32%	1995	32%	1995

Consistency, or predictability, of returns for Dividend Growth can be described as very good.

Management   ★★★★★

There are 135 stocks in this $1 billion portfolio. The average growth and income fund today is $970 million in size. Close to 83 percent of the fund's holdings are in stocks. The stocks in this portfolio have an average price-earnings (p/e) ratio of 26 and a median market capitalization of $9 billion. The portfolio's equity holdings can be categorized as large-cap and value-oriented issues.

William J. Stromberg has managed this fund for the past six years. There are 65 funds besides Dividend Growth within the T. Rowe Price family. Overall, the fund family's risk-adjusted performance can be described as very good.

Tax Minimization ★★★★★

During the past five years, a $10,000 initial investment grew to $26,220 after taxes, assuming a 39.6 percent income tax bracket (state and federal combined) and a capital gains rate of 28 percent. This means that investors in this fund were able to preserve 90 percent of their total returns. Compared to other equity funds, this fund's tax savings are considered to be excellent.

Expenses ★★★★★

Dividend Growth's expense ratio is 0.8 percent; it has averaged 1.0 percent annually over the past three calendar years. The average expense ratio for the 900 funds in this category is 1.3 percent. This fund's turnover rate over the past year has been 39 percent, while its peer group average has been 65 percent.

Summary

T. Rowe Price Dividend Growth is one of three T. Rowe Price funds to be included in the growth and income section of this book. Also categorized as an equity-income fund, this particular fund ranks as the overall best growth and income fund in the book. Its near-perfect score (24 out of 25 points) also means that it is truly the best of the best no matter how it is characterized. Risk-adjusted returns over the past three and five years have been superb. Manager Stromberg favors companies that have a history of raising their dividends.

Profile

minimum initial investment $2,500	*IRA accounts available* . . . . yes
subsequent minimum investment . . $100	*IRA minimum investment* $1,000
available in all 50 states . . . . yes	*date of inception* . . . . Dec. 1992
telephone exchanges . . . . yes	*dividend/income paid* . . . . annually
number of funds in family 66	*quality of annual reports* . . . . excellent

T. Rowe Price Equity-Income

100 East Pratt Street
Baltimore, MD 21202
(800) 638-5660

total return	★★★
risk reduction	★★★★★
management	★★★★
tax minimization	★★★★
expense control	★★★★★
symbol PRFDX	21 points
up-market performance	excellent
down-market performance	fair
predictability of returns	very good

Total Return   ★★★

Over the past five years (all periods ending 6/30/98), T. Rowe Price Equity-Income has taken $10,000 and turned it into $24,470 ($19,080 over three years and $42,650 over the past ten years). This translates into an average annual return of 19.6 percent over the past five years, 24.0 percent over the past three years, and 15.6 percent for the decade. Over the past five years, this fund has outperformed 85 percent of all mutual funds; within its general category it has done better than 60 percent of its peers. Growth and income funds have averaged 19 percent annually over these same five years.

Risk/Volatility   ★★★★★

Over the past five years, T. Rowe Price Equity-Income has been safer than 97 percent of all growth and income funds. Over the past decade, the fund has had one negative year, while the S&P 500 has had one (off 3 percent in 1990). The fund has underperformed the S&P 500 six times in the last ten years.

	last 5 years		last 10 years	
worst year	5%	1994	–7%	1990
best year	33%	1995	33%	1995

In the past, Equity-Income has done better than 90 percent of its peer group in up markets and outperformed 25 percent of its competition in down markets. Consistency, or predictability, of returns for Equity-Income can be described as very good.

Management   ★★★★

There are 160 stocks in this $15 billion portfolio. The average growth and income fund today is $970 million in size. Close to 89 percent of the fund's holdings are in stocks. The stocks in this portfolio have an average price-earnings (p/e) ratio of

25 and a median market capitalization of $12 billion. The portfolio's equity holdings can be categorized as large-cap and value-oriented issues.

Brian C. Rogers has managed this fund for the past 13 years. There are 65 funds besides Equity-Income within the T. Rowe Price family. Overall, the fund family's risk-adjusted performance can be described as very good.

Tax Minimization ★★★★
During the past five years, a $10,000 initial investment grew to $24,470 after taxes, assuming a 39.6 percent income tax bracket (state and federal combined) and a capital gains rate of 28 percent. This means that investors in this fund were able to preserve 85 percent of their total returns. Compared to other equity funds, this fund's tax savings are considered to be very good.

Expenses ★★★★★
Equity-Income's expense ratio is 0.8 percent; it has also averaged 0.8 percent annually over the past three calendar years. The average expense ratio for the 900 funds in this category is 1.3 percent. This fund's turnover rate over the past year has been 24 percent, while its peer group average has been 65 percent.

Summary
T. Rowe Price Equity-Income is the second of three T. Rowe Price funds to appear in this section alone. This equity-income fund, like the T. Rowe Price Dividend Growth Fund, boasts some of the best risk reduction numbers in the industry. Manager Rogers seeks out companies that are undervalued as measured by their p/e ratios and dividend yields. Utilities make up a modest portion of the portfolio; current income is more than twice the level of the average growth and income fund.

Profile
minimum initial investment $2,500
subsequent minimum investment . . $100
available in all 50 states. . . . . yes
telephone exchanges. . . . . yes
number of funds in family 66

IRA accounts available . . . . yes
IRA minimum investment $1,000
date of inception . . . . Oct. 1985
dividend/income paid . . . . annually
quality of annual reports . . . . excellent

T. Rowe Price Growth & Income

100 East Pratt Street
Baltimore, MD 21202
(800) 638-5660

total return	★★
risk reduction	★★★★
management	★★★★
tax minimization	★★★★★
expense control	★★★★★
symbol PRGIX	20 points
up-market performance	very good
down-market performance	poor
predictability of returns	good

Total Return   ★★

Over the past five years (all periods ending 6/30/98), T. Rowe Price Growth & Income has taken $10,000 and turned it into $23,040 ($19,130 over three years and $42,070 over the past ten years). This translates into an average annual return of 18.2 percent over the past five years, 24.1 percent over the past three years, and 15.5 percent for the decade. Over the past five years, this fund has outperformed 80 percent of all mutual funds; within its general category it has done better than 45 percent of its peers. Growth and income funds have averaged 19 percent annually over these same five years.

Risk/Volatility   ★★★★

Over the past five years, T. Rowe Price Growth & Income has been safer than 95 percent of all growth and income funds. Over the past decade, the fund has had two negative years, while the S&P 500 has had one (off 3 percent in 1990). The fund has underperformed the S&P 500 five times in the last ten years.

	last 5 years		last 10 years	
worst year	−.2%	1993	−11%	1990
best year	31%	1995	32%	1991

In the past, Growth & Income has done better than 80 percent of its peer group in up markets and outperformed only 10 percent of its competition in down markets. Consistency, or predictability, of returns for Growth & Income can be described as good.

Management   ★★★★

There are 120 stocks in this $4 billion portfolio. The average growth and income fund today is $970 million in size. Close to 88 percent of the fund's holdings are in stocks. The stocks in this portfolio have an average price-earnings (p/e) ratio of

27 and a median market capitalization of $12 billion. The portfolio's equity hold-ings can be categorized as large-cap and value-oriented issues.

Stephen W. Boesel has managed this fund for the past 11 years. There are 65 funds besides Growth & Income within the T. Rowe Price family. Overall, the fund family's risk-adjusted performance can be described as very good.

Tax Minimization ★★★★★
During the past five years, a $10,000 initial investment grew to $23,030 after taxes, assuming a 39.6 percent income tax bracket (state and federal combined) and a capital gains rate of 28 percent. This means that investors in this fund were able to preserve 89 percent of their total returns. Compared to other equity funds, this fund's tax savings are considered to be excellent.

Expenses ★★★★★
Growth & Income's expense ratio is 0.8 percent; it has also averaged 0.8 percent annually over the past three calendar years. The average expense ratio for the 900 funds in this category is 1.3 percent. This fund's turnover rate over the past year has been 16 percent, while its peer group average has been 65 percent.

Summary
T. Rowe Price Growth & Income is the third offering from this fund family to make this part of the book. What makes it different from the other two is that this port-folio is truly a growth and income fund. Risk-adjusted returns over the past three, five and ten years have consistently been very good. Manager Boesel's main crite-rion for stock selection is historical yields. In recent years the fund has not shifted its investment philosophy, and such consistency is borne out by its extremely low turnover rate. Tax reduction and expense minimization have also been envious.

Profile
minimum initial investment $2,500	*IRA accounts available* . . . . yes
subsequent minimum investment . . $100	*IRA minimum investment* $1,000
available in all 50 states. . . . . yes	*date of inception.* . . . . Dec. 1982
telephone exchanges. . . . . yes	*dividend/income paid* . . . . annually
number of funds in family 66	*quality of annual reports* . . . . excellent

Vontobel U.S. Value

1500 Forest Avenue, Suite 223
Richmond, VA 23229
(800) 527-9500

total return	★★★★
risk reduction	★★★★★
management	★★★★
tax minimization	★★★★
expense control	★
symbol VUSVX	18 points
up-market performance	excellent
down-market performance	poor
predictability of returns	good

Total Return   ★★★★

Over the past five years (all periods ending 6/30/98), Vontobel U.S. Value has taken $10,000 and turned it into $26,180 ($21,150 over three years and $38,300). This translates into an average annual return of 21.2 percent over the past five years and 28.4 percent over the past three years. Over the past five years, this fund has outperformed 85 percent of all mutual funds; within its general category it has done better than 75 percent of its peers. Growth and income funds have averaged 19 percent annually over these same five years.

Risk/Volatility   ★★★★★

Over the past five years, Vontobel U.S. Value has been safer than 95 percent of all growth and income funds. Over the past decade, the fund has had no negative years, while the S&P 500 has had one (off 3 percent in 1990). The fund has underperformed the S&P 500 three times in the last ten years.

	last 5 years		since inception	
worst year	0%	1994	0%	1994
best year	40%	1995	40%	1995

In the past, U.S. Value has done better than 95 percent of its peer group in up markets and outperformed just 10 percent of its competition in down markets. Consistency, or predictability, of returns for U.S. Value can be described as good.

Management   ★★★★

There are 20 stocks in this $235 million portfolio. The average growth and income fund today is $970 million in size. Close to 65 percent of the fund's holdings are in stocks. The stocks in this portfolio have an average price-earnings (p/e) ratio of 26 and a median market capitalization of $20 billion. The portfolio's equity holdings can be categorized as large-cap and value-oriented issues.

Edwin Walczak has managed this fund for the past eight years. There are six funds besides U.S. Value within the Vontobel family. Overall, the fund family's risk-adjusted performance can be described as good.

Tax Minimization   ★★★★
During the past five years, a $10,000 initial investment grew to $26,090 after taxes, assuming a 39.6 percent income tax bracket (state and federal combined) and a capital gains rate of 28 percent. This means that investors in this fund were able to preserve 86 percent of their total returns. Compared to other equity funds, this fund's tax savings are considered to be very good.

Expenses   ★
U.S. Value's expense ratio is 1.6 percent; it has averaged 1.5 percent annually over the past three calendar years. The average expense ratio for the 900 funds in this category is 1.3 percent. This fund's turnover rate over the past year has been 90 percent, while its peer group average has been 65 percent.

Summary
Vontobel U.S. Value gets somewhat unfairly punished with its overall rating due to its above-average expense ratio and turnover rate. However, its risk-adjusted returns over the past three and five years have been nothing short of amazing. This fund is not for the bean counter who is concerned with every administrative aspect of running a portfolio, but it is a strong candidate for anyone looking for top marks when it comes to return, minimizing taxes and caliber of management.

Profile
minimum initial investment $1,000	*IRA accounts available* . . . . yes
subsequent minimum investment . . . $50	*IRA minimum investment* $1,000
available in all 50 states. . . . . yes	*date of inception.* . . . . Mar. 1990
telephone exchanges. . . . . yes	*dividend/income paid* . . . . annually
number of funds in family 7	*quality of annual reports* . . . . good

High-Yield Funds

Sometimes referred to as "junk bond" funds, high-yield funds invest in corporate bonds rated lower than BBB or BAA. The world of bonds is divided into two general categories: "investment grade" and "high-yield." Investment grade, sometimes referred to as "bank quality," means that the bond issue has been rated AAA, AA, A, or BAA (or BBB if the rating service is Standard and Poor's instead of Moody's). Certain institutions and fiduciaries are forbidden to invest their clients' monies in anything less than investment grade. Everything less than bank quality is considered junk.

Yet the world of bonds is not black and white. There are several categories of high-yield bonds. Junk bond funds contain issues that range from BB to C; a rating less than single-C means that the bond is in default, and payment of interest and/or principal is in arrears. High-yield bond funds perform best during good economic times. Such issues should be avoided by traditional investors during recessionary periods, since the underlying corporations may have difficulty making interest and principal payments when business slows down. However, these bonds, like common stocks, can perform very well during the second half of a recession.

Although junk bonds may exhibit greater volatility than their investment-grade peers, they are safer when it comes to *interest rate risk*. Since junk issues have higher-yielding coupons and often shorter maturities than quality corporate bond funds, they fluctuate less in value when interest rates change. Thus, during expansionary periods in the economy when interest rates are rising, high-yield funds will generally drop less in value than high-quality corporate or government bond funds. Conversely, when interest rates are falling, government and corporate bonds will appreciate more in value than junk funds. High-yield bonds resemble equities at least as much as they do traditional bonds when it comes to economic cycles and certain important technical factors. Studies show that only 19 percent of the average junk fund's total return is explained by the up or down movement of the Lehman Brothers Government/Corporate Bond Index. To give an idea of how low this number is, 94 percent of a typical *high-quality* corporate bond fund's performance is explainable by movement in the same index. Indeed, even international bond funds have a higher correlation coefficient than junk, with 25 percent of their performance explained by the Lehman index.

The table below covers different periods ending 6/30/98 and compares the total return of five well known bond indexes: First Boston High Yield Index (bonds rated BBB or lower), the Lehman Aggregate Bond Index (securities from the Lehman Government/Corporate, Mortgage-Backed Securities, and Asset-Backed

Indexes), the Lehman Government Bond Index (all publicly traded domestic debt of the U.S. Government), the Lehman Municipal Bond Index and the Salomon Brothers Non-U.S. World Government Bond Index.

index	1 year	3 years	5 years	10 years	15 years
high-yield	11.0%	11.9%	10.4%	11.6%	n/a
aggregate	10.5%	7.9%	6.9%	9.1%	10.2%
government	11.3%	7.7%	6.7%	8.9%	9.9%
municipal	8.7%	7.9%	6.5%	8.3%	9.4%
foreign	0.9%	0.4%	6.4%	8.2%	n/a

The high end of the junk bond market, those debentures rated BA and BB, have been able to withstand the general beating the junk bond market incurred during the late 1980s and early 1990s. Moderate and conservative investors who want high-yield bonds as part of their portfolio should focus on funds that have a high percentage of their assets in higher-rated bonds, BB or better.

According to Salomon Brothers, the people who are responsible for the Lehman Brothers corporate, government and municipal bond indices used in this book, junk bond defaults averaged only 0.8 percent from 1980 to 1984. This rate almost tripled from 1985 to 1989 as defaults averaged 2.2 percent per year. Then, in 1990, defaults surged to 4.6 percent. Analysis based on historical data did not predict this huge increase in defaults. Bear in mind that BB-rated junk bonds can be expected to perform closer to high-quality bonds than will lower-rated junk. During 1990, for example, BB-rated bonds declined only slightly in price and actually delivered positive returns, whereas bonds rated CCC declined over 30 percent. During the mid-1990s, the default risk for the entire category had fallen to about 1.5 percent per year (well under 1 percent in the case of high-yield bond funds).

Over the past three and five years, high-yield corporate bond funds have had an average compound total return of 12.3 and 9.9 percent, respectively. The *annual* return for the past ten years has been 10.2 percent, and 10.6 percent for the last fifteen years (all figures as of 6/30/98). The standard deviation for high-yield bond funds has been 4.2 percent over the past three years. This means that these funds have been less volatile than any equity fund and similar in return variances to other types of bond funds. Two hundred and fifty funds make up the high-yield category. Total market capitalization of this category is $120 billion.

The majority of investors believe that the track record of high-yield bonds has been mixed, particularly in recent years. There was a crash in this market in 1990, but the overall track record has been quite good. These bond funds were up 13.4 percent in 1987, the year of the stock market crash. As the junk bond scare started in 1989, the fund category was still able to show a 12.9 percent return for the calendar year. The following year the group showed a negative return of just over one half percent.

Then, in 1991, high-yield bond funds suffered an almost unprecedented loss, ending the year with a 9.8 percent loss. The loss was caused by regulatory agencies putting pressure on the insurance industry, formerly the largest owner of this investment category. This, together with the demise of Drexel Burnham, the largest issuer of junk bonds, caused high-yield bonds to suffer their biggest loss in recent memory. And yet the very next two years were quite good, up 17.6 percent in 1992 and 18.9 percent in 1993. The following year, 1994, these funds fell 3.5 percent, followed by a gain of 13.8 percent in 1996, 12.9 percent in 1997, and 4.4 percent for the first half of 1998.

For stock investors, high-yield bonds can potentially smooth out performance during down markets while providing long-term volatility reduction. Because these debt instruments have historically delivered returns approaching that of the stock market, equity (stock) investors may find them a useful way to obtain diversification. Part of the beauty of high-yield bonds is that only about 50 percent of their movement (return) is correlated (related to) fluctuations in the stock market.

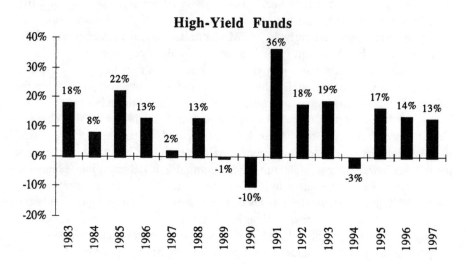

High-Yield Funds

First Investors Fund for Income A

95 Wall Street, 23rd Floor
New York, NY 10005-4297
(800) 423-4026

total return	★★★★
risk reduction	★★★★★
management	★★★★
current income	★★
expense control	★★★★
symbol FIFIX	19 points
up-market performance	very good
down-market performance	poor
predictability of returns	very good

Total Return   ★★★★

Over the past five years (all periods ending 6/30/98), First Investors Fund for Income A has taken $10,000 and turned it into $16,680 ($14,310 over three years and $24,830 over the past ten years). This translates into an average annual return of 11.0 percent over the past five years, 12.7 percent over the past three years, and 9.5 percent for the decade. Over the past five years, this fund has outperformed 60 percent of all mutual funds; within its general category it has done better than 65 percent of its peers. High-yield bond funds have averaged 10 percent annually over these same five years.

During the past five years, a $10,000 initial investment grew to $15,790 after taxes, assuming a 39.6 percent income tax bracket (state and federal combined) and a capital gains rate of 28 percent. This means that investors in this fund were able to preserve 55 percent of their total returns. Compared to other fixed-income funds, this fund's tax savings are considered to be fair.

Risk/Volatility   ★★★★★

Over the past five years, First Investors Fund for Income A has been safer than 50 percent of all high-yield bond funds. Over the past decade, the fund has had two negative years, while the Lehman Brothers Aggregate Bond Index has had one (off 3 percent in 1994); the First Boston High-Yield Bond Index fell twice (off 6 percent in 1990 and 1 percent in 1994). The fund has underperformed the Lehman Brothers Aggregate Bond Index three times and the First Boston High-Yield Bond Index five times in the last ten years.

	last 5 years		last 10 years	
worst year	1%	1994	−17%	1990
best year	18%	1993	43%	1991

In the past, Income A has done better than 75 percent of its peer group in up markets and outperformed only 15 percent of its competition in down markets.

Consistency, or predictability, of returns for Income A can be described as very good.

Management   ★★★★

There are 110 fixed-income securities in this $450 million portfolio. The average high-yield bond fund today is $475 million in size. Close to 91 percent of the fund's holdings are in bonds. The average maturity of the bonds in this account is eight years; the weighted coupon rate averages 9 percent. The portfolio's fixed-income holdings can be categorized as non-investment grade intermediate-term.

Nancy W. Jones has managed this fund for the past nine years. There are 35 funds besides Income A within the First Investors Group. Overall, the fund family's risk-adjusted performance can be described as fair.

Current Income   ★★

Over the past year, Income A had a twelve-month yield of 8.8 percent. During this same twelve-month period, the typical high-yield bond fund had a yield that averaged 8.3 percent.

Expenses   ★★★★

Income A's expense ratio is 1.2 percent; it has also averaged 1.2 percent annually over the past three calendar years. The average expense ratio for the 250 funds in this category is 1.3 percent. This fund's turnover rate over the past year has been 45 percent, while its peer group average has been 115 percent.

Summary

First Investors Fund for Income A is not the kind of high-yield bond portfolio you want to own during down markets which take place when either stocks are dropping dramatically or when we are in a severe recession. Fortunately, such events are rare. However, the overall risk level of this fund is extremely low, and total return has certainly been much higher than average. Due to the fund's tax minimization score, this portfolio is best suited for qualified retirement accounts.

Profile

minimum initial investment $1,000	*IRA accounts available* . . . . yes
subsequent minimum investment $1	*IRA minimum investment* $250
available in all 50 states. . . . . yes	*date of inception.* . . . . Dec. 1970
telephone exchanges. . . . . yes	*dividend/income paid.* . . . . monthly
number of funds in family 36	*quality of annual reports* . . . . . average

MainStay High-Yield Corporate Bond B

260 Cherry Hill Road
Parsippany, NJ 07054
(800) 624-6782

total return	★★★★
risk reduction	★★★★★
management	★★★★★
current income	★★★★
expense control	★★
symbol MKHCX	20 points
up-market performance	excellent
down-market performance	good
predictability of returns	excellent

Total Return   ★★★★

Over the past five years (all periods ending 6/30/98), MainStay High-Yield Corporate Bond B has taken $10,000 and turned it into $17,890 ($14,560 over three years and $30,210 over the past ten years). This translates into an average annual return of 12.3 percent over the past five years, 13.3 percent over the past three years, and 11.7 percent for the decade. Over the past five years, this fund has outperformed 65 percent of all mutual funds; within its general category it has done better than 75 percent of its peers. High-yield bond funds have averaged 10 percent annually over these same five years.

During the past five years, a $10,000 initial investment grew to $17,890 after taxes, assuming a 39.6 percent income tax bracket (state and federal combined) and a capital gains rate of 28 percent. This means that investors in this fund were able to preserve 67 percent of their total returns. Compared to other fixed-income funds, this fund's tax savings are considered to be very good.

Risk/Volatility   ★★★★★

Over the past five years, MainStay High-Yield Corporate Bond B has been safer than 99 percent of all high-yield bond funds. Over the past decade, the fund has had two negative years, while the Lehman Brothers Aggregate Bond Index has had one (off 3 percent in 1994); the First Boston High-Yield Bond Index fell twice (off 6 percent in 1990 and 1 percent in 1994). The fund has underperformed the Lehman Brothers Aggregate Bond Index two times and the First Boston High-Yield Bond Index four times in the last ten years.

	last 5 years		last 10 years	
worst year	2%	1994	–8%	1990
best year	22%	1993	32%	1991

In the past, Corporate Bond B has done better than 90 percent of its peer group in up markets and outperformed 60 percent of its competition in down markets. Consistency, or predictability, of returns for Corporate Bond B can be described as excellent.

Management ★★★★★

There are 165 fixed-income securities in this $3.6 billion portfolio. The average high-yield bond fund today is $475 million in size. Close to 72 percent of the fund's holdings are in bonds. The average maturity of the bonds in this account is 6 years; the weighted coupon rate averages 7 percent. The portfolio's fixed-income holdings can be categorized as intermediate-term, low-quality debt.

Steven Tananbaum and Denis Laplaige have managed this fund for the past 11 years. There are 26 funds besides Corporate Bond B within the MainStay Funds family. Overall, the fund family's risk-adjusted performance can be described as good.

Current Income ★★★★

Over the past year, Corporate Bond B had a twelve-month yield of 7.8 percent. During this same twelve-month period, the typical high-yield bond fund had a yield that averaged 8.3 percent.

Expenses ★★

Corporate Bond B's expense ratio is 1.6 percent; it has also averaged 1.6 percent annually over the past three calendar years. The average expense ratio for the 250 funds in this category is 1.3 percent. This fund's turnover rate over the past year has been 128 percent, while its peer group average has been 115 percent.

Summary

MainStay High-Yield Corporate Bond B has experienced excellent risk-adjusted returns over the past three, five and ten years. Management tends to be quite conservative, both in its security selection and tendency to keep at least a fair amount of the portfolio in cash or other securities. Tax minimization has been quite good while management and risk reduction are rated as excellent.

Profile

minimum initial investment $500	*IRA accounts available* .... yes
subsequent minimum investment ... $50	*IRA minimum investment* $500
available in all 50 states.......... yes	*date of inception*.......... May 1986
telephone exchanges.............. yes	*dividend/income paid*........ monthly
number of funds in family 27	*quality of annual reports* .... excellent

Northeast Investors

50 Congress Street
Boston, MA 02109-4096
(800) 225-6704

total return	★★★★★
risk reduction	★★★★
management	★★★★★
current income	★★★★★
expense control	★★★★★
symbol NTHEX	24 points
up-market performance	excellent
down-market performance	fair
predictability of returns	fair

Total Return   ★★★★★

Over the past five years (all periods ending 6/30/98), Northeast Investors has taken $10,000 and turned it into $18,890 ($15,310 over three years and $30,340 over the past ten years). This translates into an average annual return of 13.6 percent over the past five years, 15.3 percent over the past three years, and 11.7 percent for the decade. Over the past five years, this fund has outperformed 65 percent of all mutual funds; within its general category it has done better than 85 percent of its peers. High-yield bond funds have averaged 10 percent annually over these same five years.

During the past five years, a $10,000 initial investment grew to $18,870 after taxes, assuming a 39.6 percent income tax bracket (state and federal combined) and a capital gains rate of 28 percent. This means that investors in this fund were able to preserve 71 percent of their total returns. Compared to other fixed-income funds, this fund's tax savings are considered to be excellent.

Risk/Volatility   ★★★★

Over the past five years, Northeast Investors has been safer than 75 percent of all high-yield bond funds. Over the past decade, the fund has had one negative year, while the Lehman Brothers Aggregate Bond Index has had one (off 3 percent in 1994); the First Boston High-Yield Bond Index fell twice (off 6 percent in 1990 and 1 percent in 1994). The fund has underperformed the Lehman Brothers Aggregate Bond Index three times and the First Boston High-Yield Bond Index four times in the last ten years.

	last 5 years		last 10 years	
worst year	2%	1994	–9%	1990
best year	24%	1993	26%	1991

In the past, Northeast Investors has done better than 95 percent of its peer group in up markets and outperformed 25 percent of its competition in down markets. Consistency, or predictability, of returns for Northeast Investors can be described as fair.

Management   ★★★★★
There are 110 fixed-income securities in this $2.7 billion portfolio. The average high-yield bond fund today is $475 million in size. Close to 79 percent of the fund's holdings are in bonds. The average maturity of the bonds in this account is 7 years; the weighted coupon rate averages 9 percent. The portfolio's fixed-income holdings can be categorized as intermediate-term, low-quality debt.

Bruce H. Monrad and Ernest E. Monrad have managed this fund for the past 22 years. There is one other fund besides Northeast Investors within the Northeast Investors Group. Overall, the fund family's risk-adjusted performance can be described as excellent.

Current Income   ★★★★★
Over the past year, Northeast Investors had a twelve-month yield of 8.1 percent. During this same twelve-month period, the typical high-yield bond fund had a yield that averaged 8.3 percent.

Expenses   ★★★★★
Northeast Investors's expense ratio is 0.6 percent; it has averaged 0.8 percent annually over the past three calendar years. The average expense ratio for the 250 funds in this category is 1.3 percent. This fund's turnover rate over the past year has been 33 percent, while its peer group average has been 115 percent.

Summary
Northeast Investors is part of an elite club: it is one of the few funds, in any category, to obtain a near-perfect score (24 out of a possible 25 points). Needless to say, it is rated as the best overall high-yield corporate bond fund (it has also been categorized as a "multi-sector bond fund"). Everything about this fund is marvelous. Its tax savings also make it number one (out of 95 peers); an important consideration for the tax conscious investor. This fund is highly recommended. This is part of a very small fund family that deserves your attention.

Profile

minimum initial investment $1,000	*IRA accounts available* . . . . yes
subsequent minimum investment $1	*IRA minimum investment* $500
available in all 50 states. . . . . yes	*date of inception* . . . . Aug. 1950
telephone exchanges. . . . . yes	*dividend/income paid*. . . . . monthly
number of funds in family 2	*quality of annual reports* . . . . . average

United High-Income A

6300 Lamar Avenue
P.O. Box 29217
Shawnee Mission, KS 66201-9217
(800) 366-5465

total return	★★★
risk reduction	★★★★
management	★★★★
current income	★★★
expense control	★★★★★
symbol UNHIX	19 points
up-market performance	fair
down-market performance	good
predictability of returns	good

Total Return   ★★★

Over the past five years (all periods ending 6/30/98), United High-Income A has taken $10,000 and turned it into $16,370 ($14,450 over three years and $23,760 over the past ten years). This translates into an average annual return of 10.4 percent over the past five years, 13.1 percent over the past three years, and 9.0 percent for the decade. Over the past five years, this fund has outperformed 55 percent of all mutual funds; within its general category it has done better than 60 percent of its peers. High-yield bond funds have averaged 10 percent annually over these same five years.

During the past five years, a $10,000 initial investment grew to $15,410 after taxes, assuming a 39.6 percent income tax bracket (state and federal combined) and a capital gains rate of 28 percent. This means that investors in this fund were able to preserve 60 percent of their total returns. Compared to other fixed-income funds, this fund's tax savings are considered to be good.

Risk/Volatility   ★★★★

Over the past five years, United High-Income A has been safer than 75 percent of all high-yield bond funds. Over the past decade, the fund has had 3 negative years, while the Lehman Brothers Aggregate Bond Index has had one (off 3 percent in 1994); the First Boston High-Yield Bond Index fell twice (off 6 percent in 1990 and 1 percent in 1994). The fund has underperformed the Lehman Brothers Aggregate Bond Index four times and the First Boston High-Yield Bond Index seven times in the last ten years.

	last 5 years		last 10 years	
worst year	–4%	1994	–15%	1990
best year	18%	1995	38%	1991

In the past, High-Income has done better than 30 percent of its peer group in up markets and outperformed 50 percent of its competition in down markets. Consistency, or predictability, of returns for High-Income can be described as good.

Management   ★★★★
There are 195 fixed-income securities in this $1.2 billion portfolio. The average high-yield bond fund today is $475 million in size. Close to 88 percent of the fund's holdings are in bonds. The average maturity of the bonds in this account is 7 years; the weighted coupon rate averages 9 percent. The portfolio's fixed-income holdings can be categorized as intermediate-term, low-quality debt.

Louise D. Rieke has managed this fund for the past eight years. There are 23 funds besides High-Income within the United family. Overall, the fund family's risk-adjusted performance can be described as good.

Current Income   ★★★
Over the past year, High-Income had a twelve-month yield of 8.2 percent. During this same twelve-month period, the typical high-yield bond fund had a yield that averaged 8.3 percent.

Expenses   ★★★★★
High-Income's expense ratio is 0.9 percent; it has also averaged 0.9 percent annually over the past three calendar years. The average expense ratio for the 250 funds in this category is 1.3 percent. This fund's turnover rate over the past year has been 53 percent, while its peer group average has been 115 percent.

Summary
United High-Income A has had banner risk-adjusted returns over the past three, five and ten years. The fund does a particularly good job in minimizing tax consequences. Manager Rieke has almost the entire portfolio in B, BB and non-rated bonds, a strategy that historically has paid off the vast majority of the time.

Profile

minimum initial investment $500	*IRA accounts available* . . . . yes
subsequent minimum investment $1	*IRA minimum investment* $50
available in all 50 states. . . . . yes	*date of inception* . . . . July 1979
telephone exchanges . . . . no	*dividend/income paid*. . . . . monthly
number of funds in family 24	*quality of annual reports* . . . . good

Van Kampen American Capital High-Income A

One Parkview Plaza
Oakbrook Terrace, IL 60181
(800) 421-5666

total return	★★★
risk reduction	★★★★★
management	★★★★
current income	★★
expense control	★★★★
symbol ACHYX	18 points
up-market performance	poor
down-market performance	very good
predictability of returns	very good

Total Return   ★★★

Over the past five years (all periods ending 6/30/98), Van Kampen American Capital High-Income A has taken $10,000 and turned it into $16,140 ($14,410 over three years and $22,880 over the past ten years). This translates into an average annual return of 10.1 percent over the past five years, 12.9 percent over the past three years, and 8.6 percent for the decade. Over the past five years, this fund has outperformed 55 percent of all mutual funds; within its general category it has done better than 55 percent of its peers. High-yield bond funds have averaged 10 percent annually over these same five years.

During the past five years, a $10,000 initial investment grew to $15,400 after taxes, assuming a 39.6 percent income tax bracket (state and federal combined) and a capital gains rate of 28 percent. This means that investors in this fund were able to preserve 50 percent of their total returns. Compared to other fixed-income funds, this fund's tax savings are considered to be fair.

Risk/Volatility   ★★★★★

Over the past five years, Van Kampen American Capital High-Income A has been safer than 75 percent of all high-yield bond funds. Over the past decade, the fund has had three negative years, while the Lehman Brothers Aggregate Bond Index has had one (off 3 percent in 1994); the First Boston High-Yield Bond Index fell twice (off 6 percent in 1990 and 1 percent in 1994). The fund has underperformed the Lehman Brothers Aggregate Bond Index four times and the First Boston High-Yield Bond Index five times in the last ten years.

	last 5 years		last 10 years	
worst year	–4%	1994	–16%	1990
best year	19%	1993	41%	1991

In the past, Capital High-Income has done better than just 15 percent of its peer group in up markets but outperformed 70 percent of its competition in down markets. Consistency, or predictability, of returns for Capital High-Income can be described as very good.

Management   ★★★★

There are 160 fixed-income securities in this $570 million portfolio. The average high-yield bond fund today is $475 million in size. Close to 93 percent of the fund's holdings are in bonds. The average maturity of the bonds in this account is 7 years; the weighted coupon rate averages 10 percent. The portfolio's fixed-income holdings can be categorized as intermediate-term, low-quality debt.

Ellis Bigelow has managed this fund for the past nine years. There are 93 funds besides High-Income within the Van Kampen American Capital family. Overall, the fund family's risk-adjusted performance can be described as good.

Current Income   ★★

Over the past year, High-Income had a twelve-month yield of 9.1 percent. During this same twelve-month period, the typical high-yield bond fund had a yield that averaged 8.3 percent.

Expenses   ★★★★

High-Income's expense ratio is 1.1 percent; it has also averaged 1.1 percent annually over the past three calendar years. The average expense ratio for the 250 funds in this category is 1.3 percent. This fund's turnover rate over the past year has been 75 percent, while its peer group average has been 115 percent.

Summary

Van Kampen American Capital High-Income A is the perfect choice for the high-yield bond investor who wants better-than-average returns but substantially less risk. Risk-adjusted returns have been stunning over the past three and five years. Manager Bigelow has two-thirds of the portfolio in B rated bonds, with the balance fairly evenly divided between BB and non-rated securities. Industry group diversification is quite good.

Profile

minimum initial investment $500	*IRA accounts available* . . . . yes
subsequent minimum investment . . . $25	*IRA minimum investment* $500
available in all 50 states. . . . . yes	*date of inception* . . . . Oct. 1978
telephone exchanges. . . . . yes	*dividend/income paid.* . . . . monthly
number of funds in family 94	*quality of annual reports* . . . . excellent

Metals and Natural Resources Funds

These funds purchase metals in one or more of the following forms: bullion, South African gold stocks, and non-South African mining stocks. The United States, Canada, and Australia are the three major *stock-issuing producers* of metals outside of South Africa. Metals funds, also referred to as gold funds, often own minor positions in other precious metals stocks, such as silver and platinum.

The proportion and type of metal held by a fund can have a great impact on its performance and volatility. Outright ownership of gold bullion is almost always less volatile than owning stock in a gold mining company. Thus, much greater gains or losses occur in metals funds that purchase only gold stocks, compared to funds that hold high levels of bullion, coins, and stock. Silver, incidentally, has nearly twice the volatility of gold yet has not enjoyed any greater returns over the long term.

Gold, or metals, funds can do well during periods of political uncertainty and inflationary concerns. Over the past several hundred years, gold and silver have served as hedges against inflation. Most readers will be surprised to learn that, historically, both metals have outperformed inflation by less than one percent annually.

Metals funds are the riskiest category of mutual funds described in this book, with a standard deviation of 26.4—about 25 percent higher than the standard deviation of aggressive growth funds. And yet, although this is certainly a high-risk investment when viewed on its own, ownership of a metals fund can actually reduce a portfolio's overall risk level and often enhance its total return. Why? Because gold usually has a negative correlation to other investments. When the other investments go down in value, gold may go up. Thus, a portfolio made up strictly of government bonds will actually exhibit more risk and less return than one made up of 90 percent government and 10 percent metals funds.

There are forty-five metals funds; total market capitalization is less than $3 billion. Turnover has averaged 38 percent. The p/e ratio for metals funds is 37, while dividend yield is a little less than 1 percent. Over the past three years, these funds have averaged −17.6 percent per year, −11.1 percent for the last five years, −4.7 percent for the past decade, and −4.5 percent for the last fifteen years.

Natural resources funds invest in the stocks of companies that deal in the ownership, production, transmission, transportation, refinement, and/or storage of oil, natural gas, and timber. These funds also invest in companies that either own or are involved in real estate.

There are sixty-five natural resources funds; total market capitalization is just under $7 billion. This group has had a standard deviation of 18.7 percent over the past three years. Beta, or market-related risk, has been 0.6 percent, but do not let this low number fool you. As you can see by the standard deviation, few equity categories are riskier. Turnover has averaged 99 percent per year. The p/e ratio for natural resources funds is 25; dividend yield is a little over one half percent. Over the past three years, these funds have averaged 9.9 percent—8.1 percent for the past five years, 8.3 percent for the last ten years, and 10.0 percent for the past fifteen years.

Metals and natural resources funds should be avoided by anyone who cannot tolerate wide price swings in any single part of his portfolio. These funds are designed as an integral part of a diversified portfolio, for investors who look at the overall return of their holdings.

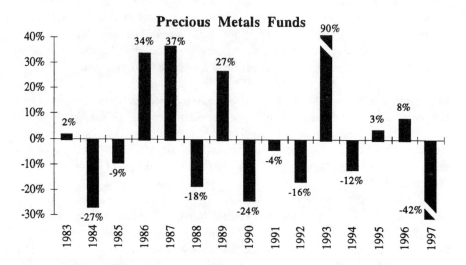

Precious Metals Funds

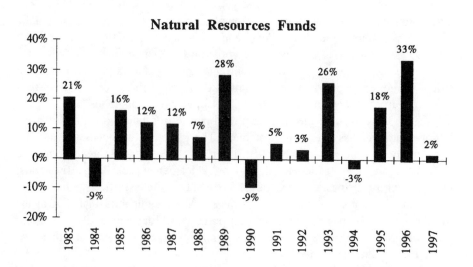

Natural Resources Funds

American Gas Index

4922 Fairmount Avenue
Bethesda, MD 20814
(800) 343-3355

total return	★★★★★
risk reduction	★★★★★
management	★★★★★
tax minimization	★★★★★
expense control	★★★★
symbol GASFX	24 points
up-market performance	n/a
down-market performance	n/a
predictability of returns	excellent

Total Return   ★★★★★
Over the past five years (all periods ending 6/30/98), American Gas Index has taken $10,000 and turned it into $17,690 ($17,640 over three years). This translates into an average annual return of 12.1 percent over the past five years and 20.8 percent over the past three years. Over the past five years, this fund has outperformed 60 percent of all mutual funds; within its general category it has done better than 70 percent of its peers. Metals and natural resources funds have averaged –1 percent annually over these same five years.

Risk/Volatility   ★★★★★
Over the past five years, American Gas Index has been safer than 80 percent of all metals and natural resources funds. Over the past decade, the fund has had two negative years, while the S&P 500 has had one (off 3 percent in 1990). The fund has underperformed the S&P 500 six times in the last ten years.

	last 5 years		since inception	
worst year	–10%	1994	–11%	1990
best year	31%	1995	31%	1995

Consistency, or predictability, of returns for Gas Index can be described as excellent.

Management   ★★★★★
There are 100 stocks in this $250 million portfolio. The average metals and natural resources fund today is $90 million in size. Close to 93 percent of the fund's holdings are in stocks. The stocks in this portfolio have an average price-earnings (p/e) ratio of 24 and a median market capitalization of $5 billion. The portfolio's equity holdings can be categorized as mid-cap and value-oriented issues.

A team has managed this fund for the past nine years. There are three funds besides American Gas Index within the Rushmore Group. Overall, the fund family's risk-adjusted performance can be described as fair.

Tax Minimization   ★★★★★
During the past five years, a $10,000 initial investment grew to $17,680 after taxes, assuming a 39.6 percent income tax bracket (state and federal combined) and a capital gains rate of 28 percent. This means that investors in this fund were able to preserve 92 percent of their total returns. Compared to other equity funds, this fund's tax savings are considered to be excellent.

Expenses   ★★★★
Gas Index's expense ratio is 0.9 percent; it has also averaged 0.9 percent annually over the past three calendar years. The average expense ratio for the 105 funds in this category is 1.8 percent. This fund's turnover rate over the past year has been 8 percent, while its peer group average has been 75 percent.

Summary
American Gas Index is not only the highest-rated natural resources fund in the book, its total point is almost perfect (24 out of a possible 25 points). This small fund is not very well known, but this kind of portfolio makes sense historically as well as conceptually. These funds are a good alternative to foreign securities for the diversification-oriented investor. Secondly, return and risk figures are dramatically better than other alternatives.

Profile
minimum initial investment $2,500	*IRA accounts available* . . . . yes
subsequent minimum investment $1	*IRA minimum investment* $500
available in all 50 states. . . . . yes	*date of inception.* . . . . May 1989
telephone exchanges. . . . . yes	*dividend/income paid* . . . . annually
number of funds in family 4	*quality of annual reports* . . . . good

Prudential Natural Resources A

One Seaport Plaza
New York, NY 10292
(800) 225-1852

total return	★★
risk reduction	★
management	★★
tax minimization	
expense control	★★★
symbol PGNAX	8 points
up-market performance	fair
down-market performance	good
predictability of returns	very good

Total Return   ★★

Over the past five years (all periods ending 6/30/98), Prudential Natural Resources A has taken $10,000 and turned it into $13,010 ($11,410 over three years). This translates into an average annual return of 5.4 percent over the past five years and 4.5 percent over the past three years. Over the past five years, this fund has outperformed 45 percent of all mutual funds; within its general category it has done better than 50 percent of its peers. Metals and natural resources funds have averaged –1 percent annually over these same five years.

Risk/Volatility   ★

Over the past five years, Prudential Natural Resources A has been safer than 35 percent of all metals and natural resources funds. Over the past decade, the fund has had two negative years, while the S&P 500 has had one (off 3 percent in 1990). The fund has underperformed the S&P 500 five times in the last ten years.

	last 5 years		since inception	
worst year	–12%	1997	–12%	1997
best year	31%	1993	31%	1993

In the past, Natural Resources A has done better than 40 percent of its peer group in up markets and outperformed 55 percent of its competition in down markets. Consistency, or predictability, of returns for Natural Resources A can be described as very good.

Management   ★★

There are 95 stocks in this $30 million portfolio. The average metals and natural resources fund today is $90 million in size. Close to 97 percent of the fund's holdings are in stocks. The stocks in this portfolio have an average price-earnings (p/e) ratio of 26 and a median market capitalization of $1 billion. The portfolio's equity holdings can be categorized as mid-cap and value-oriented issues.

Leigh R. Goehring has managed this fund for the past seven years. There are 183 funds besides Natural Resources A within the Prudential family. Overall, the fund family's risk-adjusted performance can be described as good.

Tax Minimization
During the past five years, a $10,000 initial investment grew to $12,210 after taxes, assuming a 39.6 percent income tax bracket (state and federal combined) and a capital gains rate of 28 percent. This means that investors in this fund were able to preserve 40 percent of their total returns. Compared to other equity funds, this fund's tax savings are considered to be poor.

Expenses   ★★★
Natural Resources A's expense ratio is 1.5 percent; it has averaged 1.6 percent annually over the past three calendar years. The average expense ratio for the 105 funds in this category is 1.8 percent. This fund's turnover rate over the past year has been 53 percent, while its peer group average has been 75 percent.

Summary
Prudential Natural Resources A is part of a huge fund family that includes some recommended funds. Despite the low score this particular fund has received, it is important to keep in mind that the duel-category it falls under has seen better times. More often than not, under-rated funds and categories often do quite well after experiencing a disappointing period. This natural resources fund is one of the very best.

Profile
minimum initial investment $1,000	*IRA accounts available* . . . . no
subsequent minimum investment . . $100	*IRA minimum investment* . . . . n/a
available in all 50 states . . . . yes	*date of inception* . . . . Jan. 1990
telephone exchanges . . . . yes	*dividend/income paid* . . . . annually
number of funds in family 184	*quality of annual reports* . . . . n/a

U.S. Global Investors Global Resources

P.O. Box 29467
San Antonio, TX 78229-0467
(800) 873-8637

total return	★
risk reduction	★
management	★
tax minimization	★★
expense control	★★
symbol PSPFX	7 points
up-market performance	poor
down-market performance	very good
predictability of returns	very good

Total Return   ★

Over the past five years (all periods ending 6/30/98), U.S. Global Investors Global Resources has taken $10,000 and turned it into $10,560 ($10,350 over three years and $10,770 over the past ten years). This translates into an average annual return of 1.1 percent over the past five years, 1.2 percent over the past three years, and 0.7 percent for the decade. Over the past five years, this fund has outperformed 25 percent of all mutual funds; within its general category it has done better than 30 percent of its peers. Metals and natural resources funds have averaged –1 percent annually over these same five years.

Risk/Volatility   ★

Over the past five years, U.S. Global Investors Global Resources has been safer than 35 percent of all metals and natural resources funds. Over the past decade, the fund has had five negative years, while the S&P 500 has had one (off 3 percent in 1990). The fund has underperformed the S&P 500 eight times in the last ten years.

	last 5 years		last 10 years	
worst year	–10%	1994	–16%	1990
best year	34%	1996	34%	1996

In the past, Global Resources has done better than just 10 percent of its peer group in up markets but outperformed 70 percent of its competition in down markets. Consistency, or predictability, of returns for Global Resources can be described as very good.

Management   ★

There are 50 stocks in this $25 million portfolio. The average metals and natural resources fund today is $90 million in size. Close to 93 percent of the fund's holdings are in stocks. The stocks in this portfolio have an average price-earnings (p/e) ratio of 20 and a median market capitalization of $420 million. The portfolio's equity holdings can be categorized as small-cap and value-oriented issues.

Ralph P. Aldis has managed this fund for the past six years. There are 8 funds besides Global Resources within the U.S. Global Investors family. Overall, the fund family's risk-adjusted performance can be described as fair.

Tax Minimization ★★

During the past five years, a $10,000 initial investment grew to $10,560 after taxes, assuming a 39.6 percent income tax bracket (state and federal combined) and a capital gains rate of 28 percent. This means that investors in this fund were able to preserve 69 percent of their total returns. Compared to other equity funds, this fund's tax savings are considered to be good.

Expenses ★★

Global Resources's expense ratio is 2.3 percent; it has averaged 2.5 percent annually over the past three calendar years. The average expense ratio for the 105 funds in this category is 1.8 percent. This fund's turnover rate over the past year has been 52 percent, while its peer group average has been 75 percent.

Summary

U.S. Global Investors Global Resources has done an excellent job of tax minimization—the fund's single strong suit. Natural resources funds like these often perform best during inflationary periods, something we have not experienced for a number of years. This fund is recommended as an alternative to metals funds.

Profile

minimum initial investment $100	*IRA accounts available*........... no
subsequent minimum investment ... $50	*IRA minimum investment*......... n/a
available in all 50 states......... yes	*date of inception* .... July 1983
telephone exchanges............. yes	*dividend/income paid* .... annually
number of funds in family 9	*quality of annual reports* .... n/a

Vanguard Specialized Energy

Vanguard Financial Center
P.O. Box 2600
Valley Forge, PA 19482
(800) 662-7447

total return	★★★★★
risk reduction	★★★
management	★★★★★
tax minimization	★★★★
expense control	★★★★★
symbol VGENX	22 points
up-market performance	excellent
down-market performance	excellent
predictability of returns	very good

Total Return ★★★★★

Over the past five years (all periods ending 6/30/98), Vanguard Specialized Energy has taken $10,000 and turned it into $18,160 ($16,920 over three years and $36,970 over the past ten years). This translates into an average annual return of 12.7 percent over the past five years, 19.2 percent over the past three years, and 14.0 percent for the decade. Over the past five years, this fund has outperformed 60 percent of all mutual funds; within its general category it has done better than 75 percent of its peers. Metals and natural resources funds have averaged –1 percent annually over these same five years.

Risk/Volatility ★★★

Over the past five years, Vanguard Specialized Energy has been safer than 65 percent of all metals and natural resources funds. Over the past decade, the fund has had two negative years, while the S&P 500 has had one (off 3 percent in 1990). The fund has underperformed the S&P 500 five times in the last ten years.

	last 5 years		last 10 years	
worst year	–2%	1994	–2%	1994
best year	34%	1996	43%	1989

In the past, Specialized Energy has done better than 85 percent of its peer group in up markets and outperformed 85 percent of its competition in down markets. Consistency, or predictability, of returns for Specialized Energy can be described as very good.

Management ★★★★★

There are 70 stocks in this $1.2 billion portfolio. The average metals and natural resources fund today is $90 million in size. Close to 92 percent of the fund's holdings are in stocks. The stocks in this portfolio have an average price-earnings (p/e) ratio of 25 and a median market capitalization of $5 billion. The portfolio's equity holdings can be categorized as mid-cap and value-oriented issues.

Ernst H. von Metzsch has managed this fund for the past 14 years. There are 71 funds besides Specialized Energy within the Vanguard Group. Overall, the fund family's risk-adjusted performance can be described as very good.

Tax Minimization   ★★★★

During the past five years, a $10,000 initial investment grew to $18,020 after taxes, assuming a 39.6 percent income tax bracket (state and federal combined) and a capital gains rate of 28 percent. This means that investors in this fund were able to preserve 85 percent of their total returns. Compared to other equity funds, this fund's tax savings are considered to be very good.

Expenses   ★★★★★

Specialized Energy's expense ratio is 0.4 percent; it has also averaged 0.4 percent annually over the past three calendar years. The average expense ratio for the 105 funds in this category is 1.8 percent. This fund's turnover rate over the past year has been 19 percent, while its peer group average has been 75 percent.

Summary

Vanguard Specialized Energy clearly trounces most of its natural resource and energy competition. The fund has a very impressive overall point score but does a particularly great job when it comes to total return, expense control and management; tax reduction for this fund has also been quite good. This is one of the few funds, in any category, that has done a stellar job in both up and down markets. It is highly recommended.

Profile

minimum initial investment $3,000	*IRA accounts available* . . . . yes
subsequent minimum investment . . $100	*IRA minimum investment* $1,000
available in all 50 states. . . . . yes	*date of inception.* . . . . May 1984
telephone exchanges. . . . . yes	*dividend/income paid* . . . . annually
number of funds in family 72	*quality of annual reports* . . . . excellent

Money Market Funds

Money market funds invest in securities that mature in less than one year. They are made up of one or more of the following instruments: Treasury bills, certificates of deposit, commercial paper, repurchase agreements, Euro-dollar CDs, and notes. There are four different categories of money market funds: all-purpose, government-backed, federally tax-free, and doubly tax-exempt. As of September 1998, the average maturity of taxable money market funds was 55 days; 44 days for the typical tax-exempt money fund.

All-purpose funds are the most popular and make up the bulk of the money market universe. Fully taxable, they are composed of securities such as CDs, commercial paper, and T-bills.

Government-backed money funds invest only in short-term paper, directly or indirectly backed by the U.S. government. These funds are technically safer than the all-purpose variety, but only one money market fund has ever defaulted (a fund set up by a bank for banks). The yield on government-backed funds is somewhat lower than that of its all-purpose peers.

Federally tax-free funds are made up of municipal notes. Investors in these funds do not have to pay federal income taxes on the interest earned. The before-tax yield on federally tax-free funds is certainly lower than that of all-purpose and government-backed funds, but the after-tax return can be greater for the moderate- or high-tax-bracket investor.

Double-tax-exempt funds invest in the municipal obligations of a specific state. You must be a resident of that state in order to avoid paying state income taxes on any interest earned. Nonresident investors will still receive a federal tax exemption.

All money market funds are safer than any other mutual fund or category of funds in this book. They have a perfect track record (if you exclude the one money market fund set up for banks)—investors can only make money in these interest-bearing accounts. The rate of return earned in a money market depends upon the average maturity of the fund's paper, the kinds of securities held, the quality rating of that paper, and how efficiently the fund is operated. A lean fund will almost always outperform a similar fund with high operating costs.

Investments such as United States Treasury bills and, for all practical purposes, money market funds, are often referred to as "risk-free." These kinds of investments are free from price swings and default risk because of their composition. However, as we have come to learn, there is more than one form of risk. Money market funds should never be considered as a medium- or long-term investment. The *real return* on this investment is poor. An investment's real return takes into account the effects of inflation and income taxes. During virtually every period of time, the after-tax, after-inflation return on all money market funds has been near zero or even negative.

Over the past fifty years, United States Treasury bills—an index often used as a substitute for money market funds—have outperformed inflation on average 76 percent of the time over one-year periods, 76 percent of the time over five-year periods, 73 percent of the time over ten-year periods, 89 percent of the time over fifteen-year periods, and 100 percent over any given twenty-year period of time. These figures are not adjusted for income taxes. Money market funds have rarely, if ever, outperformed inflation on an *after-tax* basis when looking at three-, five-, ten-, fifteen-, or twenty-year holding positions.

Investors often look back to the good old days of the early 1980s, when money market funds briefly averaged 18 percent, and wish such times would come again. Well, those were not good times. During the early 1980s the top tax bracket, state and federal combined, was 55 percent. If you began with an 18-percent return and deducted taxes, many taxpayers saw their 18-percent return knocked down to about 9 percent. This may look great, especially for a "risk-free" investment, but we are not through yet. During the partial year in which money market accounts paid 18 percent, inflation was 12 percent. Now, if you take the 9 percent return and subtract 12 percent for inflation; the real return was actually –3 percent for the year. So much for the good old days.

Money market funds are the best place to park your money while you are looking at other investment alternatives or if you will be using the money during the next year. These funds can provide the convenience of check writing and a yield that is highly competitive with interest rates in general. These incredibly safe funds should only be considered for short-term periods or for regular expenditures, the way you would use a savings or checking account.

Since money market funds only came into existence for the general public in the mid-1970s, Treasury bills are often used as a substitute by those who wish to analyze the performance of these funds over a long period of time. The results are instructive. Since 1948, a dollar invested in T-bills grew to $9.78 by the end of 1997. By the end of 1997, you would have needed $5.90 to equal the purchasing power of $1 at the beginning of 1948.

To give you a better sense of the cumulative effects of inflation, consider what a $100,000 investment in a money market fund would have to yield at the beginning of 1998 to equal the same purchasing power as the interest (or yield) from a $100,000 investment in a money market fund twenty years ago (1978). At the beginning of 1997, for instance, a $100,000 account held since 1978 would need to generate $17,148 to equal the same purchasing power as a $100,000 account yielding approximately 7.2 percent in 1978 (the average interest rate for money market accounts that year). The reality, however, is that at the beginning of 1998, money market funds were yielding 5 percent ($5,000 a year vs. the $17,148 that would be required to maintain purchasing power).

You may have avoided stock investing in the past because "stocks are too risky." Yet it all depends upon how you define risk. As an example, in 1969 a

$100,000 CD generated enough interest ($7,900) to buy a new, "fully loaded" Cadillac ($5,936) plus take a week-long cruise. As of the beginning of 1997, that same $100,000 CD would not generate enough income (CD rates were 4.95%) to buy 1/8th of the Cadillac ($4,950 vs. $43,000 for the cost of a 1997 Cadillac Hardtop Sedan De Ville).

As a risk-reduction tool, the addition of a money market fund may be a worthwhile strategy. For the period between 1960 and 1996, a 50–50 mix of stocks and cash delivered 79% of the S&P's return, with half the volatility. A more aggressive mix of 60% stocks and 40% cash yielded 84% of the S&P's gains, with just 60% of the risk (as measured by standard deviation).

Over the past three years, United States Treasury bills—again, similar in return to money market funds—have had an average compound return of 5.4 percent per year. The *annual return* for the past five years has been 4.6 percent; 5.4 percent for the past ten years, 6.1 percent for the last fifteen years, and 7.3 percent for the last twenty years (all periods ending 12/31/97). The standard deviation for money market funds is lower than any other mutual fund category. This means that these funds have had less return variances than any other group. Over 1,300 funds make up the money market category. Total market capitalization of this category is over $1.2 trillion.

Income Risk from Money Market Accounts

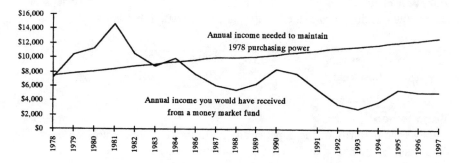

Dreyfus Basic U.S. Government Money Market

Dreyfus Service Corp.
200 Park Ave., 7th Floor
New York, NY 10166
(800) 645-6561

risk reduction	★ ★ ★ ★ ★
management	★ ★ ★ ★ ★
current income	★ ★ ★ ★ ★
expense control	★ ★ ★
symbol DBGXX	18 points

Total Return   ★ ★ ★ ★ ★

Over the past five years (all periods ending 6/30/98), Dreyfus Basic U.S. Government Money Market has taken $10,000 and turned it into $12,780 ($11,700 over three years). This translates into an average annual return of 5.0% over five years and 5.4% over the past three years. This is the number 1 performing non-institutional government securities money market fund over the past five years.

Risk/Volatility   ★ ★ ★ ★ ★

During the last three years, the fund's standard deviation has been 0.1%.

	last 5 years		since inception	
worst year	3.3%	1993	3.3%	1993
best year	6.1%	1995	6.1%	1995

Management   ★ ★ ★ ★ ★

The average maturity of the paper in the portfolio is approximately 83 days. The fund has been managed by Patricia Larkin since May 1994. The fund has outperformed its peer group average over the past one, three and five years.

Expense Control   ★ ★ ★

The expense ratio for this $1.2 billion fund is 0.5%. This means that for every $1,000 invested, $5 goes to paying overhead.

Summary

Dreyfus Basic U.S. Government Money Market is highly recommended. This money market fund is at least partially exempt from state income taxes.

Profile

minimum initial investment. . . . $25,000	IRA accounts available . . . . yes
subsequent minimum investment $1,000	IRA minimum investment. $750
available in all 50 states . . . . yes	IRA minimum additions. $1
telephone exchanges. . . . . yes	dividend/income paid . . . . monthly
number of other funds in family. . . . 100	quality of annual reports . . . . n/a

MIMLIC Cash Fund

MMLIC
400 Robert St. North
St. Paul, MN 55101
(800) 665-6005

risk reduction	★ ★ ★ ★ ★
management	★ ★ ★ ★ ★
current income	★ ★ ★ ★ ★
expense control	★ ★ ★ ★ ★
symbol MMCAE	20 points

Total Return   ★ ★ ★ ★ ★

Over the past five years (all periods ending 6/30/98), MIMLIC Cash Fund has taken $10,000 and turned it into $12,960 ($11,880 over three years). This translates into an average annual return of 5.3% over five years and 5.9% over the past three years. This is the number 1 performing taxable money market fund over the past five years and number 2 for the last three years.

Risk/Volatility   ★ ★ ★ ★ ★

During the last three years, the fund's standard deviation has been 0.3%.

	last 5 years		last 10 years	
worst year	3.2%	1993	3.2%	1993
best year	3.2%	1993	9.4%	1989

Management   ★ ★ ★ ★ ★

The average maturity of the paper in the portfolio is approximately 50 days. The fund has been managed by Wayne Schmidt since April 1991. The fund has out-performed its peer group average over the past one, three, five and ten years.

Expense Control   ★ ★ ★ ★ ★

The expense ratio for this $16 million fund is 0.1%. This means that for every $1,000 invested, $1 goes to paying overhead.

Summary

MIMLIC Cash Fund is highly recommended. This is a general-purpose money market fund that is fully taxable.

Profile

minimum initial investment	$1	IRA accounts available	yes
subsequent minimum investment	$1	IRA minimum investment	n/a
available in all 50 states	yes	IRA minimum additions	n/a
telephone exchanges	yes	dividend/income paid	monthly
number of other funds in family	11	quality of annual reports	n/a

SEI Daily Income Money Market A

SEI
530 East Swedesford Rd.
Wayne, PA 19087
(800) 342-5734

risk reduction	★ ★ ★ ★ ★
management	★ ★ ★ ★ ★
current income	★ ★ ★ ★ ★
expense control	★ ★ ★ ★ ★
symbol TCMXX	20 points

Total Return   ★ ★ ★ ★ ★

Over the past five years (all periods ending 6/30/98), SEI Daily Income Money Market A has taken $10,000 and turned it into $12,850 ($11,780 over three years). This translates into an average annual return of 5.1% over five years and 5.6% over the past three years. This is the number 7 performing taxable money market fund over the past five years and number 13 for the last three years.

Risk/Volatility   ★ ★ ★ ★ ★

During the last three years, the fund's standard deviation has been 0.1%.

	last 5 years		last 10 years	
worst year	3.0%	1993	3.0%	1993
best year	6.0%	1995	9.3%	1989

Management   ★ ★ ★ ★ ★

The average maturity of the paper in the portfolio is approximately 76 days. The fund has been managed by John Keogh (of Wellington Mgmt. Co.) since its November 1983 inception. The fund has outperformed its peer group average over the past one, three, five and ten years.

Expense Control   ★ ★ ★ ★ ★

The expense ratio for this $790 million fund is 0.2%. This means that for every $1,000 invested, $2 goes to paying overhead.

Summary

SEI Daily Income Money Market A is highly recommended. This is a general-purpose money market fund that is fully taxable.

Profile

minimum initial investment........ $1	IRA accounts available .... yes
subsequent minimum investment.... $1	IRA minimum investment....... $150
available in all 50 states .... yes	IRA minimum additions.......... $1
telephone exchanges............. yes	dividend/income paid .... monthly
number of other funds in family 36	quality of annual reports .... n/a

SEI Daily Income Treasury A

SEI Financial Mgmt. Corp.
530 East Swedesford Rd.
Wayne, PA 19087
(800) 342-5734

risk reduction	★ ★ ★ ★ ★
management	★ ★ ★ ★ ★
current income	★ ★ ★ ★ ★
expense control	★ ★ ★ ★ ★
symbol SICRE	20 points

Total Return   ★ ★ ★ ★ ★

Over the past five years (all periods ending 6/30/98), SEI Daily Income Treasury A has taken $10,000 and turned it into $12,760 ($11,740 over three years). This translates into an average annual return of 5.0% over five years and 5.5% over the past three years. This is the number 2 performing non-institutional government securities money market fund over the past three and five years.

Risk/Volatility   ★ ★ ★ ★ ★

During the last three years, the fund's standard deviation has been 0.1%.

	last 5 years		since inception	
worst year	3.0%	1993	3.0%	1993
best year	5.9%	1995	5.9%	1995

Management   ★ ★ ★ ★ ★

The average maturity of the paper in the portfolio is approximately 34 days. The fund has been managed by John Keogh since September 1992. The fund has out-performed its peer group average over the past one, three and five years.

Expense Control   ★ ★ ★ ★ ★

The expense ratio for this $225 million fund is 0.2%. This means that for every $1,000 invested, $2 goes to paying overhead.

Summary

SEI Daily Income Treasury A is highly recommended. This money market fund is at least partially exempt from state income taxes.

Profile

minimum initial investment	$1	IRA accounts available	yes
subsequent minimum investment	$1	IRA minimum investment	$150
available in all 50 states	yes	IRA minimum additions	$1
telephone exchanges	yes	dividend/income paid	monthly
number of other funds in family	36	quality of annual reports	n/a

Strong Municipal Money Market

Strong Capital Mgmt.
P.O. Box 2936
Milwaukee, WI 53201
(800) 368-1030

risk reduction	★ ★ ★ ★ ★
management	★ ★ ★ ★ ★
current income	★ ★ ★ ★ ★
expense control	★ ★ ★
symbol SXFXX	18 points

Total Return ★ ★ ★ ★ ★

Over the past five years (all periods ending 6/30/98), Strong Municipal Money Market has taken $10,000 and turned it into $11,840 ($11,140 over three years). This translates into an average annual return of 3.4% over five years and 3.7% over the past three years. This is the number 2 performing municipal money market fund over the past five years and the number 7 performer over the past three years.

Risk/Volatility ★ ★ ★ ★ ★

During the last three years, the fund's standard deviation has been 0.1%.

	last 5 years		last 10 years	
worst year	2.5%	1993	2.5%	1993
best year	4.1%	1995	6.1%	1990

Management

The average maturity of the paper in the portfolio is approximately 42 days. The fund has been managed by Steve Harrop since March 1991. The fund has outperformed its peer group average over the past one, three, five and ten years.

Expense Control ★ ★ ★

The expense ratio for this $1.9 billion fund is 0.6%. This means that for every $1,000 invested, $6 goes to paying overhead.

Summary

Strong Municipal Money Market is highly recommended. This money market fund is exempt from federal income taxes.

Profile

minimum initial investment $2,500	IRA accounts available . . . . n/a
subsequent minimum investment. . . $50	IRA minimum investment . . . . n/a
available in all 50 states . . . . yes	IRA minimum additions . . . . n/a
telephone exchanges. . . . . yes	dividend/income paid . . . . monthly
number of other funds in family 30	quality of annual reports . . . . n/a

Vanguard Municipal Money Market

Vanguard Group
P.O. Box 2600
Valley Forge, PA 19482
(800) 635-1511

risk reduction	★ ★ ★ ★ ★
management	★ ★ ★ ★ ★
current income	★ ★ ★ ★ ★
expense control	★ ★ ★ ★ ★
symbol VMSXX	20 points

Total Return   ★ ★ ★ ★ ★

Over the past five years (all periods ending 6/30/98), Vanguard Municipal Money Market has taken $10,000 and turned it into $11,750 ($11,090 over three years). This translates into an average annual return of 3.3% over five years and 3.5% over the past three years. This is the number 2 performing non-institutional municipal money market fund over the past five years.

Risk/Volatility   ★ ★ ★ ★ ★

During the last three years, the fund's standard deviation has been 0.1%.

	last 5 years		last 10 years	
worst year	2.4%	1993	2.4%	1993
best year	3.8%	1995	6.3%	1989

Management   ★ ★ ★ ★ ★

The average maturity of the paper in the portfolio is approximately 56 days. The fund has been managed by Pamela Tynan since May 1988. The fund has outperformed its peer group average over the past one, three, five and ten years.

Expense Control   ★ ★ ★ ★ ★

The expense ratio for this $5.8 billion fund is 0.2%. This means that for every $1,000 invested, $2 goes to paying overhead.

Summary

Vanguard Municipal Money Market is highly recommended. This money market fund is exempt from federal income taxes.

Profile

minimum initial investment $3,000	IRA accounts available . . . . n/a
subsequent minimum investment . . $100	IRA minimum investment . . . . n/a
available in all 50 states . . . . yes	IRA minimum additions . . . . n/a
telephone exchanges. . . . . yes	dividend/income paid . . . . monthly
number of other funds in family 70	quality of annual reports . . . . n/a

Municipal Bond Funds

Municipal bond funds invest in securities issued by municipalities, political subdivisions, and U.S. territories. The type of security issued is either a note or bond, both of which are interest-bearing instruments that are exempt from federal income taxes. There are three different categories of municipal bond funds: national, state-free, and high-yield.

National municipal bond funds are made up of debt instruments issued by a wide range of states. These funds are exempt from federal income taxes only. To determine what small percentage is also exempt from state income taxes, consult the fund's prospectus and look for the weighting of U.S. territory issues (U.S. Virgin Islands, Guam, Puerto Rico), District of Columbia items, and obligations from your state of residence.

State-free funds, sometimes referred to as "double tax-free funds" invest only in bonds and notes issued in a particular state. You must be a legal resident of that state in order to avoid paying state income taxes on the fund's return. For example, most California residents who are in a high tax bracket will only want to consider purchasing a municipal bond fund that has the name "California" in it. Residents of New York who purchase a California tax-free fund will escape federal income taxes but not state taxes.

High-yield tax-free funds invest in the same kinds of issues found in a national municipal bond fund but with one important difference. By seeking higher returns, high-yield funds look for lower-rated or nonrated notes and bonds. A municipality may decide not to obtain a rating for its issue because of the costs involved compared to the relatively small size of the bond or note being floated. Many nonrated issues are very safe. High-yield municipal bond funds are relatively new but should not be overlooked by the tax-conscious investor. These kinds of tax-free funds have demonstrated less volatility and higher return than their other tax-free counterparts.

Prospective investors need to compare tax-free bond yields to *after-tax yields* on corporate or government bond funds. To determine which of these three fund categories is best for you, use your marginal tax bracket, subtract this amount from one, and multiply the resulting figure by the taxable investment. For instance, suppose you were in the 35 percent bracket, state and federal combined. By subtracting this figure from 1, you are left with 0.65. Multiply 0.65 by the fully taxable yield you could get, let us say 9 percent. Sixty-five percent of 9 percent is 5.85 percent. The 5.85 percent represents what you get on a 9 percent investment after you have paid state and federal income taxes on it. This means that if you can get 5.85 percent or higher from a tax-free investment, take it.

Interest paid on tax-free investments is generally lower than interest paid on taxable investments like corporate bonds and bank CDs. But you should compare the yields on tax-free investments to taxable investments only after you have considered the municipal bond fund's tax-free advantage. The result will be the *taxable equivalent yield*—the yield you will have to get on a similar taxable investment to equal the tax-free yield. If the example above was not clear, look at the next table.

1997 federal income tax rates plus tax-free yields vs. equivalent taxable yields

			a tax-free yield of:			
if your taxable income is . . .			3%	4%	5%	6%
single	joint	bracket	is equivalent to a taxable yield of:			
$0–$25,350	0–$42,350	15.0%	3.5%	4.7%	5.9%	7.1%
$25,351–$61,400	$42,351–$102,300	28.0	4.2	5.6	6.9	8.3
$61,401–$128,100	$102,301–$155,950	31.0	4.3	5.8	7.2	8.7
$128,101–$278,450	$155,951–$278,450	36.0	4.7	6.3	7.8	9.4
over $278,450	over $278,450	39.6	5.0	6.6	8.3	9.9

As you can see from the table above, if you're in the 36 percent federal tax bracket, a taxable investment would have to yield 7.8 percent to give you the same after-tax income as a tax-free yield of 5.0 percent.

Municipal bond funds are not for investors who are in a low tax bracket. If such investors want to be in bonds, they would be better off in corporate or government issues. Furthermore, municipals should *never* be used in a retirement plan. There is only one way to make tax-free income taxable and that is to put it into an IRA, pension, or profit-sharing plan. Everything that comes out of these plans is fully taxable by the federal government.

Over the past three and five years, the typical municipal bond fund has had an average compounded annual return of 6.9 and 5.6 percent respectively. They have averaged a total annual return (current yield plus bond appreciation or minus bond depreciation) of 7.6 percent over the past ten years and 8.5 percent annually for the last fifteen years. Municipal bond fund returns have been fairly stable over the past three years, having a standard deviation of 3.3 percent (all periods ending 6/30/98).

Two thousand funds make up the municipal bond category. Total market capitalization of all municipal bond funds is $290 billion. Close to 98 percent of a typical municipal bond fund's portfolio is in tax-free bonds, with the balance in tax-free money market instruments. Close to 1,000 of the 2,000 municipal bond funds offered are single-state funds.

The typical municipal bond fund yields 4.5 percent in tax-free income each year. The average weighted maturity is sixteen years. Expenses for this category are 1.0 percent each year.

As you read through the descriptions of the municipal bond funds selected, you will notice a paragraph in each describing the tax efficiency of the portfolio. This may surprise you, since municipal bonds are supposed to be tax-free. Keep in mind that only the *income* (current yield) from these instruments is free from federal income taxes (and often state income taxes, depending on the fund in question and your state of residence). Since bond funds generally have a high turnover rate (which triggers a potential capital gain or loss upon each sale of a security by the portfolio manager), there are capital gains considerations with municipal bonds.

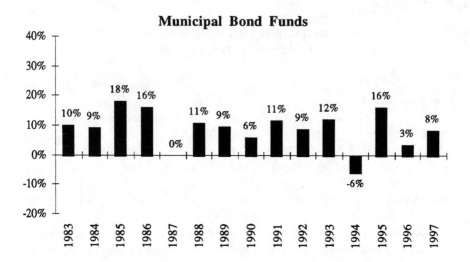

Municipal Bond Funds

Calvert Tax-Free Reserves Limited-Term A

4550 Montgomery Avenue, Suite 1000N
Bethesda, MD 20814
(800) 368-2748

total return	★★
risk reduction	★★★★★
management	★★★★
current income	★★★★★
expense control	★★★★
symbol CTFLX	20 points
up-market performance	poor
down-market performance	very good
predictability of returns	excellent

Total Return ★★

Over the past five years (all periods ending 6/30/98), Calvert Tax-Free Reserves Limited-Term A has taken $10,000 and turned it into $12,140 ($11,260 over three years and $16,230 over the past ten years). This translates into an average annual return of 4.0 percent over the past five years, 4.0 percent over the past three years, and 5.0 percent for the decade. Over the past five years, this fund has outperformed 30 percent of all mutual funds; within its general category it has done better than 45 percent of its peers. Municipal bond funds have averaged 6 percent annually over these same five years.

During the past five years, a $10,000 initial investment grew to $12,010 after taxes, assuming a 39.6 percent income tax bracket (state and federal combined) and a capital gains rate of 28 percent. This means that investors in this fund were able to preserve 99 percent of their total returns. Compared to other fixed-income funds, this fund's tax savings are considered to be excellent.

Risk/Volatility ★★★★★

Over the past five years, Calvert Tax-Free Reserves Limited-Term A has been safer than 99 percent of all municipal bond funds. Over the past decade, the fund has had no negative years, while the Lehman Brothers Aggregate Bond Index has had one (off 3 percent in 1994); the Lehman Brothers Municipal Bond Index also fell once (off 5 percent in 1994). The fund has underperformed the Lehman Brothers Aggregate Bond Index eight times and the Lehman Brothers Municipal Bond Index nine times in the last ten years.

	last 5 years		last 10 years	
worst year	2%	1994	–2%	1994
best year	6%	1995	7%	1989

In the past, Limited-Term A has done better than just 10 percent of its peer group in up markets but outperformed 70 percent of its competition in down markets. Consistency, or predictability, of returns for Limited-Term A can be described as excellent.

Management   ★★★★

There are 55 fixed-income securities in this $500 million portfolio. The average municipal bond fund today is $160 million in size. Close to 72 percent of the fund's holdings are in bonds. The average maturity of the bonds in this account is 0.9 years; the weighted coupon rate averages 5 percent. The portfolio's fixed-income holdings can be categorized as short-term, high-quality debt.

Reno J. Martini and David R. Rochat have managed this fund for the past 16 years. There are 19 funds besides Limited-Term A within the Calvert family. Overall, the fund family's risk-adjusted performance can be described as good.

Current Income   ★★★★★

Over the past year, Limited-Term A had a twelve-month yield of 3.8 percent. During this same twelve-month period, the typical municipal bond fund had a yield that averaged 4.5 percent.

Expenses   ★★★★

Limited-Term A's expense ratio is 0.7 percent; it has also averaged 0.7 percent annually over the past three calendar years. The average expense ratio for the 2,000 funds in this category is 1.0 percent. This fund's turnover rate over the past year has been 52 percent, while its peer group average has been 50 percent.

Summary

Calvert Tax-Free Reserves Limited-Term A has been safer than 99% of all other municipal bonds—quite a feat when you consider the fact that there are over 1,000 tax-free bond funds. The fund owes its risk-reduction success to its very low average maturity (less than one year). This fund is a highly recommended choice for the high bracket taxpayer whose chief concern is preservation of capital, consistency of returns, and a respectable return.

Profile

minimum initial investment $2,000	*IRA accounts available* . . . . no
subsequent minimum investment . . $250	*IRA minimum investment* . . . . n/a
available in all 50 states . . . . yes	*date of inception* . . . . Mar. 1981
telephone exchanges . . . . yes	*dividend/income paid* . . . . monthly
number of funds in family 20	*quality of annual reports* . . . . good

Colorado BondShares

1125 Seventeenth Street, Suite 1600
Denver, CO 80202
(800) 572-0069

total return	★★★★★
risk reduction	★★★★★
management	★★★★★
current income	★★★★
expense control	★★★★★
symbol HICOX	24 points
up-market performance	excellent
down-market performance	poor
predictability of returns	excellent

Total Return   ★★★★★

Over the past five years (all periods ending 6/30/98), Colorado BondShares has taken $10,000 and turned it into $14,670 ($12,770 over three years and $20,550 over the past ten years). This translates into an average annual return of 8.0 percent over the past five years, 8.5 percent over the past three years, and 7.5 percent for the decade. Over the past five years, this fund has outperformed 45 percent of all mutual funds; within its general category it has done better than 80 percent of its peers. Municipal bond funds have averaged 6 percent annually over these same five years.

During the past five years, a $10,000 initial investment grew to $13,970 after taxes, assuming a 39.6 percent income tax bracket (state and federal combined) and a capital gains rate of 28 percent. This means that investors in this fund were able to preserve 88 percent of their total returns. Compared to other fixed-income funds, this fund's tax savings are considered to be very good.

Risk/Volatility   ★★★★★

Over the past five years, Colorado BondShares has been safer than 98 percent of all municipal bond funds. Over the past decade, the fund has had no negativeyears, while the Lehman Brothers Aggregate Bond Index has had one (off 3 percent in 1994); the Lehman Brothers Municipal Bond Index also fell once (off 5 percent in 1994). The fund has underperformed the Lehman Brothers Aggregate Bond Index six times and the Lehman Brothers Municipal Bond Index six times in the last ten years.

	last 5 years		last 10 years	
worst year	6%	1994	1%	1990
best year	10%	1995	10%	1995

In the past, BondShares has done better than 90 percent of its peer group in up markets and outperformed virtually none of its competition in down markets. Consistency, or predictability, of returns for BondShares can be described as excellent.

Management   ★★★★★

There are 140 fixed-income securities in this $70 million portfolio. The average municipal bond fund today is $160 million in size. Close to 95 percent of the fund's holdings are in bonds. The average maturity of the bonds in this account is 8 years; the weighted coupon rate averages 7 percent. The portfolio's fixed-income holdings can be categorized as intermediate-term investment-grade.

Fred R. Kelly Jr. has managed this fund for the past eight years. BondShares is the only fund within the Colorado BondShares family. Overall, the fund family's risk-adjusted performance can be described as excellent.

Current Income   ★★★★

Over the past year, Colorado BondShares had a twelve-month yield of 6.4 percent. During this same twelve-month period, the typical municipal bond fund had a yield that averaged 4.5 percent.

Expenses   ★★★★★

BondShares's expense ratio is 0.7 percent; it has averaged 0.8 percent annually over the past three calendar years. The average expense ratio for the 2,000 funds in this category is 1.0 percent. This fund's turnover rate over the past year has been 28 percent, while its peer group average has been 50 percent.

Summary

Colorado BondShares has done it again. This fund rates as the overall best municipal bond fund with an almost perfect score (24 out of 25 possible points). This is an amazing accomplishment for two reasons. First, it is a "single-state" municipal bond fund (a "national" or "high-yield tax-free" fund should be in the number one spot). Second, this is not the first time that this fund has garnered the title as the best. As usual, this fund is highly recommended (again and again).

Profile

minimum initial investment $500	*IRA accounts available*........... no
subsequent minimum investment $1	*IRA minimum investment* .... n/a
available in all 50 states .... no	*date of inception*.......... June 1987
telephone exchanges .... no	*dividend/income paid*........ monthly
number of funds in family 1	*quality of annual reports* .... n/a

Franklin CA High Yield Municipal I

777 Mariners Island Boulevard
San Mateo, CA 94403-7777
(800) 342-5236

total return	★★★★★
risk reduction	★★★
management	★★★★★
current income	★★★★
expense control	★★★★★
symbol FCAMX	22 points
up-market performance	n/a
down-market performance	n/a
predictability of returns	good

Total Return   ★★★★★

Over the past five years (all periods ending 6/30/98), Franklin CA High Yield Municipal I has taken $10,000 and turned it into $14,380 ($13,140 over three years). This translates into an average annual return of 7.5 percent over the past five years and 9.5 percent over the past three years. Over the past five years, this fund has outperformed 45 percent of all mutual funds; within its general category it has done better than 90 percent of its peers. Municipal bond funds have averaged 6 percent annually over these same five years.

During the past five years, a $10,000 initial investment grew to $13,770 after taxes, assuming a 39.6 percent income tax bracket (state and federal combined) and a capital gains rate of 28 percent. This means that investors in this fund were able to preserve 88 percent of their total returns. Compared to other fixed-income funds, this fund's tax savings are considered to be very good.

Risk/Volatility   ★★★

Over the past five years, Franklin CA High Yield Municipal I has been safer than 70 percent of all municipal bond funds. Over the past decade, the fund has had one negative year, while the Lehman Brothers Aggregate Bond Index has had one (off 3 percent in 1994); the Lehman Brothers Municipal Bond Index also fell once (off 5 percent in 1994). The fund has underperformed the Lehman Brothers Aggregate Bond Index one time and the Lehman Brothers Municipal Bond Index one time in the last ten years.

	last 5 years		since inception	
worst year	–6%	1994	–6%	1994
best year	19%	1995	19%	1995

Consistency, or predictability, of returns for High Yield Municipal can be described as food.

Management   ★★★★★

There are 135 fixed-income securities in this $450 million portfolio. The average municipal bond fund today is $160 million in size. Close to 100 percent of the fund's holdings are in bonds. The average maturity of the bonds in this account is 25 years; the weighted coupon rate averages 7 percent. The portfolio's fixed-income holdings can be categorized as long-term, medium-quality debt.

A team has managed this fund for the past five years. There are 154 funds besides High Yield Municipal within the Franklin Group of Funds family. Overall, the fund family's risk-adjusted performance can be described as very good.

Current Income   ★★★★

Over the past year, High Yield Municipal had a twelve-month yield of 5.8 percent. During this same twelve-month period, the typical municipal bond fund had a yield that averaged 4.5 percent.

Expenses   ★★★★★

High Yield Municipal's expense ratio is 0.3 percent; it has also averaged 0.3 percent annually over the past three calendar years. The average expense ratio for the 2,000 funds in this category is 1.0 percent. This fund's turnover rate over the past year has been 34 percent, while its peer group average has been 50 percent.

Summary

If you are a resident of California and hate paying taxes, you are going to love Franklin CA High Yield Municipal I. Not only is this the best rated California tax-free fund (and the only one to appear in this book), its overall score shows that it is a preferred choice for anyone interested in a municipal bond fund. When it comes to bonds, whether taxable or tax-free, no one does a better job than the folks at Franklin Templeton.

Profile

minimum initial investment $100	*IRA accounts available* . . . . yes
subsequent minimum investment . . . $25	*IRA minimum investment* $100
available in all 50 states. . . . . yes	*date of inception*. . . . . May 1993
telephone exchanges. . . . . yes	*dividend/income paid*. . . . . monthly
number of funds in family 155	*quality of annual reports* . . . . n/a

Franklin High Yield Tax-Free Income I

777 Mariners Island Boulevard
San Mateo, CA 94403-7777
(800) 342-5236

total return	★★★★★
risk reduction	★★★★
management	★★★★★
current income	★★★★
expense control	★★★★★
symbol FRHIX	23 points
up-market performance	excellent
down-market performance	good
predictability of returns	very good

Total Return   ★★★★★

Over the past five years (all periods ending 6/30/98), Franklin High Yield Tax-Free Income I has taken $10,000 and turned it into $14,500 ($12,860 over three years and $23,410 over the past ten years). This translates into an average annual return of 7.7 percent over the past five years, 8.7 percent over the past three years, and 8.9 percent for the decade. Over the past five years, this fund has outperformed 45 percent of all mutual funds; within its general category it has done better than 85 percent of its peers. Municipal bond funds have averaged 6 percent annually over these same five years.

During the past five years, a $10,000 initial investment grew to $13,890 after taxes, assuming a 39.6 percent income tax bracket (state and federal combined) and a capital gains rate of 28 percent. This means that investors in this fund were able to preserve 88 percent of their total returns. Compared to other fixed-income funds, this fund's tax savings are considered to be very good.

Risk/Volatility   ★★★★

Over the past five years, Franklin High Yield Tax-Free Income I has been safer than 99 percent of all municipal bond funds. Over the past decade, the fund has had one negative year, while the Lehman Brothers Aggregate Bond Index has had one (off 3 percent in 1994); the Lehman Brothers Municipal Bond Index also fell once (off 5 percent in 1994). The fund has underperformed the Lehman Brothers Aggregate Bond Index four times and the Lehman Brothers Municipal Bond Index three times in the last ten years.

	last 5 years		last 10 years	
worst year	–3%	1994	–3%	1994
best year	16%	1995	16%	1995

In the past, Tax-Free Income I has done better than 95 percent of its peer group in up markets and outperformed 45 percent of its competition in down markets. Consistency, or predictability, of returns for Tax-Free Income I can be described as very good.

Management   ★★★★★
There are 680 fixed-income securities in this $6 billion portfolio. The average municipal bond fund today is $160 million in size. Close to 100 percent of the fund's holdings are in bonds. The average maturity of the bonds in this account is 21 years; the weighted coupon rate averages 7 percent. The portfolio's fixed-income holdings can be categorized as long-term, medium-quality debt.

A team has managed this fund for the past nine years. There are 154 funds besides Tax-Free Income I within the Franklin family. Overall, the fund family's risk-adjusted performance can be described as very good.

Current Income   ★★★★
Over the past year, Tax-Free Income I had a twelve-month yield of 5.8 percent. During this same twelve-month period, the typical municipal bond fund had a yield that averaged 4.5 percent.

Expenses   ★★★★★
Tax-Free Income I's expense ratio is 0.6 percent; it has also averaged 0.6 percent annually over the past three calendar years. The average expense ratio for the 2,000 funds in this category is 1.0 percent. This fund's turnover rate over the past year has been 16 percent, while its peer group average has been 50 percent.

Summary
Franklin California High Yield Tax-Free Income I is the answer for California residents looking for the maximum current income that is free from both federal and state income taxes. The fund's outstanding record is due to its managment, which keeps a constant eye on expenses and takes more of a buy-and-hold strategy than the vast majority of all other bond funds. This is a highly ranked fund that can be recommended without hesitation.

Profile

minimum initial investment $100	*IRA accounts available.* . . . . no
subsequent minimum investment . . . $25	*IRA minimum investment* . . . . n/a
available in all 50 states. . . . . yes	*date of inception.* . . . . Mar. 1986
telephone exchanges. . . . . yes	*dividend/income paid.* . . . . monthly
number of funds in family 155	*quality of annual reports* . . . . excellent

Franklin NY Tax-Free Income I

777 Mariners Island Boulevard
San Mateo, CA 94403-7777
(800) 342-5236

total return	★★★
risk reduction	★★★★
management	★★★★
current income	★★★
expense control	★★★★★
symbol FNYTX	19 points
up-market performance	excellent
down-market performance	fair
predictability of returns	good

Total Return   ★★★

Over the past five years (all periods ending 6/30/98), Franklin NY Tax-Free Income I has taken $10,000 and turned it into $13,490 ($12,480 over three years and $22,090 over the past ten years). This translates into an average annual return of 6.2 percent over the past five years, 7.7 percent over the past three years, and 8.3 percent for the decade. Over the past five years, this fund has outperformed 40 percent of all mutual funds; within its general category it has done better than 75 percent of its peers. Municipal bond funds have averaged 6 percent annually over these same five years.

During the past five years, a $10,000 initial investment grew to $12,900 after taxes, assuming a 39.6 percent income tax bracket (state and federal combined) and a capital gains rate of 28 percent. This means that investors in this fund were able to preserve 83 percent of their total returns. Compared to other fixed-income funds, this fund's tax savings are considered to be good.

Risk/Volatility   ★★★★

Over the past five years, Franklin NY Tax-Free Income I has been safer than 96 percent of all municipal bond funds. Over the past decade, the fund has had one negative year, while the Lehman Brothers Aggregate Bond Index has had one (off 3 percent in 1994); the Lehman Brothers Municipal Bond Index also fell once (off 5 percent in 1994). The fund has underperformed the Lehman Brothers Aggregate Bond Index six times and the Lehman Brothers Municipal Bond Index five times in the last ten years.

	last 5 years		last 10 years	
worst year	–4%	1994	–4%	1994
best year	14%	1995	14%	1995

In the past, NY Tax-Free Income has done better than 95 percent of its peer group in up markets and outperformed 35 percent of its competition in down markets. Consistency, or predictability, of returns for NY Tax-Free Income can be described as good.

Management   ★★★★

There are 410 fixed-income securities in this $5 billion portfolio. The average municipal bond fund today is $160 million in size. Close to 99 percent of the fund's holdings are in bonds. The average maturity of the bonds in this account is 19 years; the weighted coupon rate averages 6.5 percent. The portfolio's fixed-income holdings can be categorized as long-term, high-quality debt.

A team has managed this fund for the past 12 years. There are 154 funds besides NY Tax-Free Income within the Franklin family. Overall, the fund family's risk-adjusted performance can be described as very good.

Current Income   ★★★

Over the past year, NY Tax-Free Income had a twelve-month yield of 5.4 percent. During this same twelve-month period, the typical municipal bond fund had a yield that averaged 4.5 percent.

Expenses   ★★★★★

NY Tax-Free Income's expense ratio is 0.6 percent; it has also averaged 0.6 percent annually over the past three calendar years. The average expense ratio for the 2,000 funds in this category is 1.0 percent. This fund's turnover rate over the past year has been 11 percent, while its peer group average has been 50 percent.

Summary

Franklin NY Tax-Free Income I is for residents of any state looking for tax shelter. This is one of only a couple of municipal bond funds recommended for New York residents. Franklin clearly dominates the tax-free area, as evidenced by other Franklin Templeton funds that appear elsewhere in this section. Like other Franklin offerings, this fund is highly recommended for anyone trying to maximize tax-free income. This offering does a great job at keeping overhead costs to a minimum.

Profile

minimum initial investment $100	*IRA accounts available*........... no
subsequent minimum investment ... $25	*IRA minimum investment* .... n/a
available in all 50 states.......... yes	*date of inception* .... Sept. 1982
telephone exchanges............. yes	*dividend/income paid*........ monthly
number of funds in family 155	*quality of annual reports* .... excellent

Rochester Fund Municipals A

350 Linden Oaks
Rochester, NY 14625
(716) 383-1300

total return	★★★
risk reduction	★★★
management	★★★★
current income	★★★
expense control	★★★★
symbol RMUNX	17 points
up-market performance	excellent
down-market performance	excellent
predictability of returns	fair

Total Return   ★★★

Over the past five years (all periods ending 6/30/98), Rochester Fund Municipals A has taken $10,000 and turned it into $13,630 ($12,760 over three years and $23,220 over the past ten years). This translates into an average annual return of 6.4 percent over the past five years, 8.5 percent over the past three years, and 8.8 percent for the decade. Over the past five years, this fund has outperformed 40 percent of all mutual funds; within its general category it has done better than 80 percent of its peers. Municipal bond funds have averaged 6 percent annually over these same five years.

During the past five years, a $10,000 initial investment grew to $12,980 after taxes, assuming a 39.6 percent income tax bracket (state and federal combined) and a capital gains rate of 28 percent. This means that investors in this fund were able to preserve 83 percent of their total returns. Compared to other fixed-income funds, this fund's tax savings are considered to be good.

Risk/Volatility   ★★★

Over the past five years, Rochester Fund Municipals A has been safer than 75 percent of all municipal bond funds. Over the past decade, the fund has had one negative year, while the Lehman Brothers Aggregate Bond Index has had one (off 3 percent in 1994); the Lehman Brothers Municipal Bond Index also fell once (off 5 percent in 1994). The fund has underperformed the Lehman Brothers Aggregate Bond Index four times and the Lehman Brothers Municipal Bond Index two times in the last ten years.

	last 5 years		last 10 years	
worst year	–8%	1994	–8%	1994
best year	18%	1995	18%	1995

In the past, Rochester has done better than 95 percent of its peer group in up markets and outperformed 90 percent of its competition in down markets. Consistency, or predictability, of returns for Rochester can be described as fair.

Management   ★★★★

There are 975 fixed-income securities in this $3.5 billion portfolio. The average municipal bond fund today is $160 million in size. Close to 100 percent of the fund's holdings are in bonds. The average maturity of the bonds in this account is 22 years; the weighted coupon rate averages 6 percent. The portfolio's fixed-income holdings can be categorized as long-term, medium-quality debt.

Ronald H. Fielding has managed this fund for the past 12 years. There are six funds besides Municipals A within the Rochester family (which is part of the Oppenheimer Group). Overall, the fund family's risk-adjusted performance can be described as excellent.

Current Income   ★★★

Over the past year, Rochester had a twelve-month yield of 5.9 percent. During this same twelve-month period, the typical municipal bond fund had a yield that averaged 4.5 percent.

Expenses   ★★★★

Rochester's expense ratio is 0.8 percent; it has also averaged 0.8 percent annually over the past three calendar years. The average expense ratio for the 2,000 funds in this category is 1.0 percent. This fund's turnover rate over the past year has been 5 percent, while its peer group average has been 50 percent.

Summary

Now part of the Oppenheimer family of funds, Rochester Fund Municipals A takes its place as another flagship offering. This fund has appeared in numerous previous editions of the book and remains a favored choice. Management at Rochester gets it right time-and-time again. This is one of the few funds in any equity or debt category that has fared well in both bull and bear markets.

Profile

minimum initial investment $1,000	*IRA accounts available* . . . . no
subsequent minimum investment . . . $25	*IRA minimum investment* . . . . n/a
available in all 50 states . . . . yes	*date of inception* . . . . May 1986
telephone exchanges . . . . yes	*dividend/income paid* . . . . monthly
number of funds in family 7	*quality of annual reports* . . . . good

Sit Tax-Free Income

4600 Norwest Center
90 South 7th Street
Minneapolis, MN 55402-4130
(800) 332-5580

total return	★★★★
risk reduction	★★★★
management	★★★★★
current income	★★★★★
expense control	★★★★
symbol SNTIX	22 points
up-market performance	good
down-market performance	very good
predictability of returns	very good

Total Return   ★★★★

Over the past five years (all periods ending 6/30/98), Sit Tax-Free Income has taken $10,000 and turned it into $13,970 ($12,600 over three years). This translates into an average annual return of 6.9 percent over the past five years and 8.0 percent over the past three years. Over the past five years, this fund has outperformed 45 percent of all mutual funds; within its general category it has done better than 85 percent of its peers. Municipal bond funds have averaged 6 percent annually over these same five years.

During the past five years, a $10,000 initial investment grew to $13,970 after taxes, assuming a 39.6 percent income tax bracket (state and federal combined) and a capital gains rate of 28 percent. This means that investors in this fund were able to preserve 97 percent of their total returns. Compared to other fixed-income funds, this fund's tax savings are considered to be excellent.

Risk/Volatility   ★★★★

Over the past five years, Sit Tax-Free Income has been safer than 20 percent of all municipal bond funds. Over the past decade, the fund has had one negative year, while the Lehman Brothers Aggregate Bond Index has had one (off 3 percent in 1994); the Lehman Brothers Municipal Bond Index also fell once (off 5 percent in 1994). The fund has underperformed the Lehman Brothers Aggregate Bond Index four times and the Lehman Brothers Municipal Bond Index six times in the last ten years.

	last 5 years		since inception	
worst year	–1%	1994	–1%	1994
best year	13%	1995	13%	1995

In the past, Tax-Free Income has done better than 60 percent of its peer group in up markets and outperformed 80 percent of its competition in down markets.

Consistency, or predictability, of returns for Tax-Free Income can be described as very good.

Management   ★★★★★
There are 300 fixed-income securities in this $570 million portfolio. The average municipal bond fund today is $160 million in size. Close to 97 percent of the fund's holdings are in bonds. The average maturity of the bonds in this account is 18 years; the weighted coupon rate averages 6 percent. The portfolio's fixed-income holdings can be categorized as long-term, medium-quality debt.

Michael C. Brilley has managed this fund for the past 10 years. There are 9 funds besides Tax-Free Income within the Sit Group. Overall, the fund family's risk-adjusted performance can be described as good.

Current Income   ★★★★★
Over the past year, Tax-Free Income had a twelve-month yield of 5.0 percent. During this same twelve-month period, the typical municipal bond fund had a yield that averaged 4.5 percent.

Expenses   ★★★★
Tax-Free Income's expense ratio is 0.8 percent; it has also averaged 0.8 percent annually over the past three calendar years. The average expense ratio for the 2,000 funds in this category is 1.0 percent. This fund's turnover rate over the past year has been 25 percent, while its peer group average has been 50 percent.

Summary
Sit Tax-Free Income ranks in the top 16 percent of its peers over the past five years (the top 3 percent according to some neutral sources). The fund scores well in every single category. It is quite consistent and highly rated in other, lesser noticed ways. This fund is a wise choice for the skittish investor who feels uncomfortable about securities in general.

Profile

minimum initial investment $2,000	*IRA accounts available*. . . . . no
subsequent minimum investment . . $100	*IRA minimum investment* . . . . n/a
available in all 50 states. . . . . yes	*date of inception* . . . . Sept. 1988
telephone exchanges. . . . . yes	*dividend/income paid*. . . . . monthly
number of funds in family 10	*quality of annual reports* . . . . excellent

United Municipal High-Income A

6300 Lamar Avenue
P.O. Box 29217
Shawnee Mission, KS 66201-9217
(800) 366-5465

total return	★★★★★
risk reduction	★★★★
management	★★★★★
current income	★★★★
expense control	★★★★
symbol UMUHX	22 points
up-market performance	excellent
down-market performance	very good
predictability of returns	very good

Total Return   ★★★★★

Over the past five years (all periods ending 6/30/98), United Municipal High-Income A has taken $10,000 and turned it into $14,770 ($13,150 over three years and $24,400 over the past ten years). This translates into an average annual return of 8.1 percent over the past five years, 9.6 percent over the past three years, and 9.3 percent for the decade. Over the past five years, this fund has outperformed 50 percent of all mutual funds; within its general category it has done better than 90 percent of its peers. Municipal bond funds have averaged 6 percent annually over these same five years.

During the past five years, a $10,000 initial investment grew to $14,150 after taxes, assuming a 39.6 percent income tax bracket (state and federal combined) and a capital gains rate of 28 percent. This means that investors in this fund were able to preserve 88 percent of their total returns. Compared to other fixed-income funds, this fund's tax savings are considered to be very good.

Risk/Volatility   ★★★★

Over the past five years, United Municipal High-Income A has been safer than 99 percent of all municipal bond funds. Over the past decade, the fund has had one negative year, while the Lehman Brothers Aggregate Bond Index has had one (off 3 percent in 1994); the Lehman Brothers Municipal Bond Index also fell once (off 5 percent in 1994). The fund has underperformed the Lehman Brothers Aggregate Bond Index five times and the Lehman Brothers Municipal Bond Index four times in the last ten years.

	last 5 years		last 10 years	
worst year	–3%	1994	–3%	1994
best year	17%	1995	17%	1995

In the past, United Municipal has done better than 99 percent of its peer group in up markets and outperformed 75 percent of its competition in down markets. Consistency, or predictability, of returns for United Municipal can be described as very good.

Management   ★★★★★
There are 175 fixed-income securities in this $550 million portfolio. The average municipal bond fund today is $160 million in size. Close to 98 percent of the fund's holdings are in bonds. The average maturity of the bonds in this account is 9 years; the weighted coupon rate averages 7 percent. The portfolio's fixed-income holdings can be categorized as intermediate-term, medium quality debt.

John M. Holiday has managed this fund for the past 12 years. There are 23 funds besides United Municipal within the United family. Overall, the fund family's risk-adjusted performance can be described as good.

Current Income   ★★★★
Over the past year, United Municipal had a twelve-month yield of 5.5 percent. During this same twelve-month period, the typical municipal bond fund had a yield that averaged 4.5 percent.

Expenses   ★★★★
United Municipal's expense ratio is 0.8 percent; it has also averaged 0.8 percent annually over the past three calendar years. The average expense ratio for the 2,000 funds in this category is 1.0 percent. This fund's turnover rate over the past year has been 19 percent, while its peer group average has been 50 percent.

Summary
United Municipal High-Income A knows what's most important: total return with low risk. This is one of most highly rated tax-free funds, regardless of categorization. Every single rating is either very good or excellent. Only a handful of funds can lay claim to such consistently good rankings and commentary. This fund has appeared in previous editions of the book and remains a favored choice.

Profile

minimum initial investment $500	*IRA accounts available*........... no
subsequent minimum investment $1	*IRA minimum investment* .... n/a
available in all 50 states......... yes	*date of inception* .... Jan. 1986
telephone exchanges .... no	*dividend/income paid*........ monthly
number of funds in family 24	*quality of annual reports* .... good

Utility Stock Funds

Utility stock funds look for both growth and income, investing in common stocks of utility companies across the country. Historically, somewhere between a third and half of these funds' total returns come from common stock dividends. Utility funds normally stay away from speculative issues, focusing instead on well-established companies with solid histories of paying good dividends. Surprisingly, the goal of most of these funds is *long-term growth*.

Utility, metals, and natural resources funds are the only three sector, or specialty, fund categories in this book. Funds that invest in a single industry, or sector, should be avoided by most investors for two reasons. First, you limit the fund manager's ability to find attractive stocks or bonds if he or she is only able to choose securities from one particular geographic area or industry. Second, as a general category, these specialty funds represent the worst of both worlds: above-average risk and substandard returns. If you find the term "aggressive growth" unappealing, then the words "sector fund" should positively appall you.

Utility funds are the one exception. They sound safe and they are safe (–8.8 percent for 1994 notwithstanding). Any category of stocks that relies moderately or heavily on dividends generated automatically has a built-in safety cushion. A comparatively high dividend income means that you have to worry less about the appreciation of the underlying issues.

Four factors generally determine the profitability of a utility company: (1) how much it pays for energy, (2) the general level of interest rates, (3) its expected use of nuclear power, and (4) the political climate.

The prices of oil and gas are passed directly on to the consumer, but the utility companies are sensitive to this issue. Higher fuel prices mean that the utility industry has less latitude to increase its profit margins. Thus, higher fuel prices can mean smaller profits and/or dividends to investors.

Next to energy costs, interest is the industry's greatest expense. Utility companies are heavily debt-laden. Their interest costs directly affect their profitability. When rates go down and companies are able to refinance their debt, the savings can be staggering. Paying 7 percent interest on a couple of hundred million dollars worth of bonds each year is much more appealing than having to pay 10 percent on the same amount of debt. A lower-interest-rate environment translates into more money being left over for shareholders.

Depending on how you look at it, nuclear power has been an issue or problem for the United States for a few decades now. Other countries seem to have come to grips with the matter, yet we remain divided. Although new power plants have not been successfully proposed or built in this country for several years, no one knows what the future may hold. Venturing into nuclear power always seems to be much more expensive than anticipated by the utility companies and the independent experts they rely on for advice. Because of these uncertainties, mutual fund managers try to seek out utility companies that have no foreseeable plans to develop any or more nuclear power facilities. Whether this will help the nation in the long term remains to be seen, but such avoidance keeps share prices more stable and predictable.

Finally, the political climate is an important concern when calculating whether utility funds should be part of your portfolio. The Public Utilities Commission (PUC) is a political animal and can directly reflect the views of a state's government. Utility bills are something most of us are concerned with and aware of; the powers that be are more likely to be reelected if they are able to keep rate increases to a minimum. Modest, or minimum, increases can be healthy for the utility companies; freezing rates for a couple of years is a bad sign.

One hundred funds make up the utilities category. Total market capitalization of this category is close to $25 billion. Over 85 percent of a typical utility fund's portfolio is in common stocks, with the balance in bonds, convertibles, and money market instruments. The typical utilities fund has about 20 percent of its holdings in foreign utility stocks.

Over the past three years, utility funds have had an average compound return of 18.9 percent per year; the *annual* return for the past five years has been 12.1 percent. For the last ten years, these funds have averaged 13.0 percent per year; 14.3 percent per year for the last fifteen years. The standard deviation for growth funds has been 11.7 percent over the past three years. This means that these funds have been less volatile than any other stock category except equity-income funds, which have exhibited almost identical volatility.

Usually, utility stock prices closely follow the long-term bond market. If the economy surges and long-term interest rates go up, utility stock prices are likely to go down. Utility stocks are also vulnerable to a general stock market decline, although they are considered less risky than other types of common stock because of their dividends and the monopoly position of most utilities. Typically, utilities have fallen about two-thirds as much as other common stocks during market downturns.

Worldwide, there is a tremendous opportunity for growth in this industry. The average per-capita production of electricity in many developing countries is only *one-fifth* that of the United States. The electrical output per capita in the United States is 12,100 kilowatt hours, compared to 2,500 kilowatt hours for developing nations. This disparity may well be on the way out. All over the world, previously underdeveloped countries are making economic strides as they move toward free market systems.

When emerging countries become developed economically, their citizens demand higher standards of living. As a result, their requirements for electricity, water, and telephones tend to rise dramatically. Moreover, many countries are selling their utility companies to public owners, opening a new arena for investors. The net result of all of this for you, the investor, is that fund groups are beginning to offer *global utility funds*. This increased diversification—allowing a fund to

invest in utility companies all over the world instead of just in the United States—
coupled with tremendous long-term growth potential—should make this a dynamic
industry group. Utility funds are a good choice for the investor who wants a hedge
against inflation but is still afraid or distrustful of the stock market in general.

Beta, which measures the *market-related risk* of a stock, is only 0.6 percent
for utility funds as a group (compared to 1.0 for the S&P 500). This means that
when it comes to *stock market risk*, utilities have only 60 percent the risk of the
Dow Jones Industrial Average (DJIA) or the S&P 500. Keep in mind, however,
that there are other risks, such as rising interest rates, that also need to be considered whenever utilities are being considered.

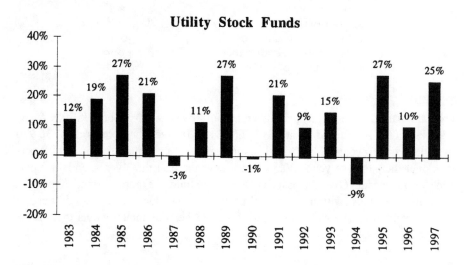

Utility Stock Funds

AIM Global Utilities A

11 Greenway Plaza, Suite 1919
Houston, TX 77046-1173
(800) 347-4246

total return	★★★
risk reduction	★★★★
management	★★★★
tax minimization	★★★★
expense control	★★★★★
symbol AUTLX	20 points
up-market performance	good
down-market performance	poor
predictability of returns	good

Total Return ★★★

Over the past five years (all periods ending 6/30/98), AIM Global Utilities A has taken $10,000 and turned it into $17,460 ($17,510 over three years and $36,970 over the past ten years). This translates into an average annual return of 11.8 percent over the past five years, 20.5 percent over the past three years, and 14.0 percent for the decade. Over the past five years, this fund has outperformed 60 percent of all mutual funds; within its general category it has done better than 50 percent of its peers. Utility stock funds have averaged 12 percent annually over these same five years.

Risk Volatility ★★★★

Over the past five years, AIM Global Utilities A has been safer than 60 percent of all utility stock funds. Over the past decade, the fund has had two negative years, while the S&P 500 has had one (off 3 percent in 1990). The fund has underperformed the S&P 500 five times in the last ten years.

	last 5 years		last 10 years	
worst year	−12%	1994	−12%	1994
best year	28%	1995	36%	1989

In the past, Global Utilities has done better than 50 percent of its peer group in up markets but outperformed just 10 percent of its competition in down markets. Consistency, or predictability, of returns for Global Utilities can be described as good.

Management ★★★★

There are 145 stocks in this $200 million portfolio. The average utility stock fund today is $250 million in size. Close to 79 percent of the fund's holdings are in stocks. The stocks in this portfolio have an average price-earnings (p/e) ratio of 28 and a median market capitalization of $7 billion. The portfolio's equity holdings can be categorized as large-cap and value-oriented issues.

A team has managed this fund for the past five years. There are 117 funds besides Global Utilities within the AIM family. Overall, the fund family's risk-adjusted performance can be described as good.

Tax Minimization   ★★★★
During the past five years, a $10,000 initial investment grew to $21,520 after taxes, assuming a 39.6 percent income tax bracket (state and federal combined) and a capital gains rate of 28 percent. This means that investors in this fund were able to preserve 75 percent of their total returns. Compared to other equity funds, this fund's tax savings are considered to be very good.

Expenses   ★★★★★
Global Utilities's expense ratio is 1.1 percent; it has averaged 1.2 percent annually over the past three calendar years. The average expense ratio for the 100 funds in this category is 1.4 percent. This fund's turnover rate over the past year has been 26 percent, while its peer group average has been 50 percent.

Summary
AIM Global Utilities A can invest up to 80 percent of its assets in foreign hold-ings—a fortunate development since domestic utilities do not offer the same divi-dends and low risk they once did. If you believe in the future of global telecommuniciations, this is a particularly wise choice. Overhead costs are extremely low and fund management is quite good. This fund ties for second place as one of the very best utilities funds.

Profile
minimum initial investment $500	*IRA accounts available* . . . . yes
subsequent minimum investment . . . $50	*IRA minimum investment* $250
available in all 50 states. . . . . yes	*date of inception* . . . . Jan. 1988
telephone exchanges. . . . . yes	*dividend/income paid* . . . . annually
number of funds in family 118	*quality of annual reports* . . . . excellent

Colonial Utilities A

One Financial Center
Boston, MA 02111
(800) 426-3750

total return	★★★
risk reduction	★★★
management	★★★★
tax minimization	★★★★
expense control	★★★★★
symbol CUTLX	19 points
up-market performance	very good
down-market performance	poor
predictability of returns	good

Total Return   ★★★

Over the past five years (all periods ending 6/30/98), Colonial Utilities A has taken $10,000 and turned it into $17,480 ($17,320 over three years and $34,190 over the past ten years). This translates into an average annual return of 11.8 percent over the past five years, 20.1 percent over the past three years, and 13.1 percent for the decade. Over the past five years, this fund has outperformed 60 percent of all mutual funds; within its general category it has done better than 60 percent of its peers. Utility stock funds have averaged 12 percent annually over these same five years.

Risk Volatility   ★★★

Over the past five years, Colonial Utilities A has been safer than 40 percent of all utility stock funds. Over the past decade, the fund has had two negative years, while the S&P 500 has had one (off 3 percent in 1990). The fund has underperformed the S&P 500 nine times in the last ten years.

	last 5 years		last 10 years	
worst year	–10%	1994	–10%	1994
best year	35%	1995	35%	1995

In the past, Colonial Utilities has done better than 70 percent of its peer group in up markets and outperformed just 10 percent of its competition in down markets. Consistency, or predictability, of returns for Colonial Utilities can be described as good.

Management   ★★★★

There are 75 stocks in this $350 million portfolio. The average utility stock fund today is $250 million in size. Close to 91 percent of the fund's holdings are in stocks. The stocks in this portfolio have an average price-earnings (p/e) ratio of 26 and a median market capitalization of $11 billion. The portfolio's equity holdings can be categorized as large-cap and value-oriented issues.

Richard Petrino and John E. Lennon have managed this fund for the past eight years. There are 104 funds besides Colonial Utilities within the Colonial family. Overall, the fund family's risk-adjusted performance can be described as good.

Tax Minimization   ★★★★
During the past five years, a $10,000 initial investment grew to $16,650 after taxes, assuming a 39.6 percent income tax bracket (state and federal combined) and a capital gains rate of 28 percent. This means that investors in this fund were able to preserve 75 percent of their total returns. Compared to other equity funds, this fund's tax savings are considered to be very good.

Expenses   ★★★★★
Colonial Utilities' expense ratio is 1.2 percent; it has also averaged 1.2 percent annually over the past three calendar years. The average expense ratio for the 100 funds in this category is 1.4 percent. This fund's turnover rate over the past year has been 7 percent, while its peer group average has been 50 percent.

Summary
Colonial Utilities A can invest up to a fifth of its assets in overseas companies. Managers Lennon and Petrino are particularly fond of telephone companies and for good reason. It is a segment of the utilities category that offers tremendous growth potential with only modest risk. The fund's strong suit is expense control; tax minimization is also quite good.

Profile

minimum initial investment $1,000	IRA accounts available . . . . yes
subsequent minimum investment . . . $50	IRA minimum investment $25
available in all 50 states. . . . . yes	date of inception . . . . Aug. 1981
telephone exchanges. . . . . yes	dividend/income paid . . . . annually
number of funds in family 105	quality of annual reports . . . . good

Franklin Global Utilities I

777 Mariners Island Boulevard
San Mateo, CA 94403-7777
(800) 342-5236

total return	★★★★★
risk reduction	★★★
management	★★★★
tax minimization	★★★★
expense control	★★★★★
symbol FRGUX	21 points
up-market performance	n/a
down-market performance	n/a
predictability of returns	fair

Total Return   ★★★★★

Over the past five years (all periods ending 6/30/98), Franklin Global Utilities I has taken $10,000 and turned it into $21,630 ($17,980 over three years). This translates into an average annual return of 16.7 percent over the past five years and 21.6 percent over the past three years. Over the past five years, this fund has outperformed 60 percent of all mutual funds; within its general category it has done better than 65 percent of its peers. Utility stock funds have averaged 12 percent annually over these same five years.

Risk Volatility   ★★★

Over the past five years, Franklin Global Utilities I has been safer than 40 percent of all utility stock funds. Over the past decade, the fund has had one negative year, while the S&P 500 has had one (off 3 percent in 1990). The fund has underperformed the S&P 500 four times in the last ten years.

	last 5 years		since inception	
worst year	–9%	1994	–9%	1994
best year	31%	1993	31%	1993

Consistency, or predictability, of returns for Global Utilities can be described as fair.

Management   ★★★★

There are 90 stocks in this $225 million portfolio. The average utility stock fund today is $250 million in size. Close to 98 percent of the fund's holdings are in stocks. The stocks in this portfolio have an average price-earnings (p/e) ratio of 29 and a median market capitalization of $6 billion. The portfolio's equity holdings can be categorized as large-cap and value-oriented issues.

A team has managed this fund for the past five years. There are 154 funds besides Global Utilities within the Franklin family. Overall, the fund family's risk-adjusted performance can be described as very good.

Tax Minimization   ★★★★
During the past five years, a $10,000 initial investment grew to $20,510 after taxes, assuming a 39.6 percent income tax bracket (state and federal combined) and a capital gains rate of 28 percent. This means that investors in this fund were able to preserve 76 percent of their total returns. Compared to other equity funds, this fund's tax savings are considered to be very good.

Expenses   ★★★★★
Global Utilities' expense ratio is 1.0 percent; it has also averaged 1.0 percent annually over the past three calendar years. The average expense ratio for the 100 funds in this category is 1.4 percent. This fund's turnover rate over the past year has been 48 percent, while its peer group average has been 50 percent.

Summary
Franklin Global Utilities I performance rates in the top 10 percent by some measures. Total return and expense control rankings are superior; management is also quite good. The folks at Franklin Templeton have had more experience (and success) than just about anyone else in the industry. This company is known for its aversion to risk. A large number of other funds in the family are also highly recommended.

Profile

minimum initial investment $100	*IRA accounts available*. . . . . no
subsequent minimum investment . . . $25	*IRA minimum investment* . . . . n/a
available in all 50 states. . . . . yes	*date of inception* . . . . July 1992
telephone exchanges. . . . . yes	*dividend/income paid* . . . . annually
number of funds in family 155	*quality of annual reports* . . . . excellent

MFS Utilities A

500 Boylston Street
Boston, MA 02116
(800) 343-2829 or (617) 954-5000

total return	★★★★★
risk reduction	★★★★
management	★★★★
tax minimization	★★★★
expense control	★★★
symbol MMUFX	20 points
up-market performance	n/a
down-market performance	n/a
predictability of returns	good

Total Return   ★★★★★

Over the past five years (all periods ending 6/30/98), MFS Utilities A has taken $10,000 and turned it into $23,630 ($20,770 over three years). This translates into an average annual return of 18.8 percent over the past five years and 27.6 percent over the past three years. Over the past five years, this fund has outperformed 75 percent of all mutual funds; within its general category it has done better than 90 percent of its peers. Utility stock funds have averaged 12 percent annually over these same five years.

Risk Volatility   ★★★★

Over the past five years, MFS Utilities A has been safer than 98 percent of all utility stock funds. Over the past decade, the fund has had one negative year, while the S&P 500 has had one (off 3 percent in 1990). The fund has underperformed the S&P 500 four times in the last ten years.

	last 5 years		since inception	
worst year	–5%	1994	–5%	1994
best year	33%	1995	33%	1995

Consistency, or predictability, of returns for Utilities A can be described as good.

Management   ★★★★

There are 145 stocks in this $175 million portfolio. The average utility stock fund today is $250 million in size. Close to 74 percent of the fund's holdings are in stocks. The stocks in this portfolio have an average price-earnings (p/e) ratio of 26 and a median market capitalization of $5 billion. The portfolio's equity holdings can be categorized as mid-cap and value-oriented issues.

Maura Shaughnessy has managed this fund for the past six years. There are 138 funds besides Utilities A within the MFS family. Overall, the fund family's risk-adjusted performance can be described as good.

Tax Minimization ★★★★
During the past five years, a $10,000 initial investment grew to $22,300 after taxes, assuming a 39.6 percent income tax bracket (state and federal combined) and a capital gains rate of 28 percent. This means that investors in this fund were able to preserve 74 percent of their total returns. Compared to other equity funds, this fund's tax savings are considered to be very good.

Expenses ★★★
Utilities A's expense ratio is 1.1 percent; it has averaged 1.0 percent annually over the past three calendar years. The average expense ratio for the 100 funds in this category is 1.4 percent. This fund's turnover rate over the past year has been 155 percent, while its peer group average has been 50 percent.

Summary
MFS Utilities A scores very well in every important category: total return, risk control, management and tax minimization. The fund's risk-adjusted returns over the past three years have been excellent. The current yield of this portfolio is one of the highest in the entire industry. Over a fourth of the portfolio's assets are in foreign utilities which have done quite well.

Profile
minimum initial investment $1,000	*IRA accounts available* . . . . yes
subsequent minimum investment . . . $50	*IRA minimum investment* $250
available in all 50 states. . . . . yes	*date of inception* . . . . Jan. 1992
telephone exchanges. . . . . yes	*dividend/income paid* . . . . annually
number of funds in family 139	*quality of annual reports* . . . . good

Putnam Utilities Growth & Income A

One Post Office Square
Boston, MA 02109
(800) 225-1581

total return	★★★★
risk reduction	★★★★★
management	★★★★★
tax minimization	★★★
expense control	★★★★
symbol PUGIX	21 points
up-market performance	n/a
down-market performance	n/a
predictability of returns	very good

Total Return   ★★★★

Over the past five years (all periods ending 6/30/98), Putnam Utilities Growth & Income A has taken $10,000 and turned it into $19,090 ($17,530 over three years). This translates into an average annual return of 13.8 percent over the past five years and 20.6 percent over the past three years. Over the past five years, this fund has outperformed 60 percent of all mutual funds; within its general category it has done better than 65 percent of its peers. Utility stock funds have averaged 12 percent annually over these same five years.

Risk Volatility   ★★★★★

Over the past five years, Putnam Utilities Growth & Income A has been safer than 95 percent of all utility stock funds. Over the past decade, the fund has had one negative year, while the S&P 500 has had one (off 3 percent in 1990). The fund has underperformed the S&P 500 six times in the last ten years.

	last 5 years		last 10 years	
worst year	–7%	1994	–7%	1994
best year	31%	1995	31%	1995

Consistency, or predictability, of returns for Utilities Growth & Income can be described as very good.

Management   ★★★★★

There are 190 stocks in this $710 million portfolio. The average utility stock fund today is $250 million in size. Close to 86 percent of the fund's holdings are in stocks. The stocks in this portfolio have an average price-earnings (p/e) ratio of 24 and a median market capitalization of $5 billion. The portfolio's equity holdings can be categorized as mid-cap and value-oriented issues.

Christopher A. Ray and Sheldon N. Simon have managed this fund for the past seven years. There are 168 funds besides Utilities Growth & Income within the Putnam Funds family. Overall, the fund family's risk-adjusted performance can be described as good.

Tax Minimization   ★★★

During the past five years, a $10,000 initial investment grew to $17,920 after taxes, assuming a 39.6 percent income tax bracket (state and federal combined) and a capital gains rate of 28 percent. This means that investors in this fund were able to preserve 71 percent of their total returns. Compared to other equity funds, this fund's tax savings are considered to be good.

Expenses   ★★★★

Utilities Growth & Income's expense ratio is 1.1 percent; it has also averaged 1.1 percent annually over the past three calendar years. The average expense ratio for the 100 funds in this category is 1.4 percent. This fund's turnover rate over the past year has been 54 percent, while its peer group average has been 50 percent.

Summary

Putnam Utilities Growth & Income A rates as the number one fund in its category. Managers Simon and Ray have little foreign exposure but still own more stocks than virtually any other utilities fund—one of the reasons why its risk level is so very low. Management is particularly fond of gas utilities. This is a highly recommended fund and is appropriate for anyone looking for utilities.

Profile

minimum initial investment $500	*IRA accounts available* . . . . yes
subsequent minimum investment . . . $50	*IRA minimum investment* $250
available in all 50 states. . . . . yes	*date of inception* . . . . Nov. 1990
telephone exchanges. . . . . yes	*dividend/income paid* . . . . annually
number of funds in family 169	*quality of annual reports* . . . . excellent

World Bond Funds

Global, or world, funds invest in securities issued all over the world, including the United States. A global bond fund usually invests in bonds issued by stable governments from a handful of countries. These funds try to avoid purchasing foreign government debt instruments from politically or economically unstable nations. Foreign, also known as international, bond funds invest in debt instruments from countries other than the United States.

International funds purchase securities issued in a foreign currency, such as the Japanese yen or the British pound. Prospective investors need to be aware of the potential changes in the value of the foreign currency relative to the U.S. dollar. As an example, if you were to invest in U.K. pound-denominated bonds with a yield of 9 percent and the British currency appreciated 12 percent against the U.S. dollar, your total return for the year would be 21 percent. If the British pound declined by 10 percent against the U.S. dollar, your total return would be −1 percent (9 percent yield minus 10 percent).

Since foreign markets do not necessarily move in tandem with U.S. markets, each country represents varying investment opportunities at different times. About 40 percent of this bond marketplace is made up of U.S. bonds; Japan ranks a distant second. The typical global bond fund has close to 40 percent of its holdings in European bonds, followed by the U.S. and Canada (30%) and Latin America (13%).

Assessing the economic environment to evaluate its affects on interest rates and bond values requires an understanding of two important factors—inflation and supply. During inflationary periods, when there is too much money chasing too few goods, government tightening of the money supply helps create a balance between an economy's cash resources and its available goods. Money supply refers to the amount of cash made available for spending, borrowing, or investing. Controlled by the central banks of each nation, it is a primary tool used to manage inflation, interest rates, and economic growth.

A prudent tightening of the money supply can help bring on disinflation—decelerated loan demand, reduced durable goods orders, and falling prices. During disinflationary times, interest rates also fall, strengthening the underlying value of existing bonds. While such factors ultimately contribute to a healthier economy, they also mean lower yields for government bond investors. A trend toward disinflation currently exists in markets around the world. The worldwide growth in money supply is at its lowest level in twenty years.

As the United States and other governments implement policies designed to reduce inflation, interest rates are stabilizing. This disinflation can be disquieting to the individual who specifically invests for high monthly income. In reality, falling interest rates mean higher bond values, and investors seeking long-term growth or high total returns can therefore benefit from declining rates. Inflation, which drives interest rates higher, is the true enemy of bond investors. It diminishes bond values and, in addition, erodes the buying power of the interest income investors receive.

Income-seeking investors need to find economies where inflation is coming under control yet where interest rates are still high enough to provide favorable bond yields. An investor who has only U.S. bonds is not taking advantage of such opportunities. If global disinflationary trends continue, those who remain invested only in the United States can lose out on opportunities for high income and total return elsewhere. The gradually decreasing yields on U.S. bonds compel the investor who seeks high income to think globally.

While not all bond markets will peak at the same level, they do tend to follow patterns. Targeting those countries where interest rates are at peak levels and inflation is falling not only results in higher income but also creates significant potential for capital appreciation as rates ultimately decline and bond prices increase. Each year since 1984, at least three government bond markets have provided yields higher than those available in the United States.

According to Lehman Brothers and Salomon Brothers, over the past ten years, international bonds have underperformed U.S. bonds by an average of 0.6 percent per year. Over the past five years, the figure drops to an average of 0.3 percent per year.

Even with high income as the primary goal, investors must consider credit and market risk. By investing primarily in mutual funds that purchase government-guaranteed bonds from the world's most creditworthy nations, you can get an extra measure of credit safety for payment of interest and repayment of principal. By diversifying across multiple markets, fund managers can significantly reduce market risk as well. Diversification is a proven technique for controlling market risk.

The long-term success of a global bond manager depends on expertise in assessing economic trends from country to country, as well as protecting the U.S. valuation of foreign holdings. The most effective way to protect the U.S. dollar value of international holdings is through active currency management. Although its affects over a ten-year period are nominal at best, currency fluctuation can substantially help returns over a one-, three-, or five-year period.

In the simplest terms, effective currency management provides exposure to bond markets worldwide, while reducing the affects of adverse currency changes that can lower bond values. If a portfolio manager anticipates that the U.S. dollar will strengthen, he or she can lock in a currency exchange rate to protect the fund against a decline in the value of its foreign holdings. (A strong dollar means that other currencies are declining in value.) This strategy is commonly referred to as hedging the exposure of the portfolio. If, on the other hand, the manager expects the U.S. dollar to weaken, the fund can stay unhedged to allow it to benefit from the increasing value of foreign currencies.

Investing in global bonds gives you the potential for capital appreciation during periods of declining interest rates. An inverse relationship exists between bond values and interest rates. When interest rates fall, as is the case in most bond markets in the world today, existing bond values climb. Conversely, as interest rates rise, the value of existing bonds declines (they are less desirable since "new" bonds have a higher current yield).

Over the past three and five years, global bond funds have had an average compound return of 8.3 and 6.1 percent per year respectively; the annual returns for the past ten and fifteen years have been 7.4 and 10.9 percent, respectively. The standard deviation for global bond funds has been 6.2 percent over the past three years (all periods ending 6/30/98). This means that these funds have been less volatile than any equity fund but more volatile than government bond funds (standard deviation of 3.3). Just 250 funds make up the global bond category. Total market capitalization of this category is over $23 billion.

Global bond funds, particularly those with high concentrations in foreign issues, can be an excellent risk-reduction tool that should be utilized by the vast majority of investors, particularly when U.S. interest rates are increasing.

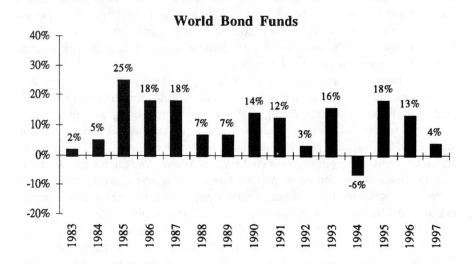

World Bond Funds

Alliance North American Government Income A

P.O. Box 1520
Secaucus, NJ 07096
(800) 227-4618

total return	★★★★★
risk reduction	★★
management	★★★
tax minimization	★★★★★
expense control	★★★
symbol ANAGX	18 points
up-market performance	n/a
down-market performance	n/a
predictability of returns	poor

Total Return   ★★★★★

Over the past five years (all periods ending 6/30/98), Alliance North American Government Income A has taken $10,000 and turned it into $14,760 ($17,320 over three years). This translates into an average annual return of 8.1 percent over the past five years and 20.1 percent over the past three years. Over the past five years, this fund has outperformed 55 percent of all mutual funds; within its general category it has done better than 70 percent of its peers. World bond funds have averaged 6 percent annually over these same five years.

During the past five years, a $10,000 initial investment grew to $14,170 after taxes, assuming a 39.6 percent income tax bracket (state and federal combined) and a capital gains rate of 28 percent. This means that investors in this fund were able to preserve 91 percent of their total returns. Compared to other fixed-income funds, this fund's tax savings are considered to be excellent.

Risk/Volatility   ★★

Over the past five years, Alliance North American Government Income A has been safer than 70 percent of all world bond funds. Over the past decade, the fund has had one negative year, while the Lehman Brothers Aggregate Bond Index has had one (off 3 percent in 1994); the Saloman Brothers World Government Bond Index fell twice (off 3 percent in 1989 and 4 percent in 1997). The fund has underperformed the Lehman Brothers Aggregate Bond Index one time and the Saloman Brothers World Government Bond Index one time in the last ten years.

	last 5 years		since inception	
worst year	–30%	1994	–30%	1994
best year	31%	1995	31%	1995

Consistency, or predictability, of returns for Alliance Government Income can be described as poor.

Management   ★★★
There are 30 fixed-income securities in this $730 million portfolio. The average world bond fund today is $95 million in size. Close to 92 percent of the fund's holdings are in bonds. The average maturity of the bonds in this account is 14 years; the weighted coupon rate averages 7 percent. The portfolio's fixed-income holdings can be categorized as intermediate-term, medium-quality debt.

Wayne D. Lyski has managed this fund for the past six years. There are 153 funds besides Alliance Government Income within the Alliance family. Overall, the fund family's risk-adjusted performance can be described as good.

Current Income   ★★★★★
Over the past year, Alliance Government Income had a twelve-month yield of 12.4 percent. During this same twelve-month period, the typical world bond fund had a yield that averaged 6.2 percent.

Expenses   ★★★
Alliance Government Income's expense ratio is 1.4 percent; it has averaged 2.1 percent annually over the past three calendar years. The average expense ratio for the 250 funds in this category is 1.4 percent. This fund's turnover rate over the past year has been 118 percent, while its peer group average has been 285 percent.

Summary
Alliance North American Government Income A has had returns over the past three years that trounce all of its competition. This fund has turned in phenomenal results for a global bond fund (20% per year). The fund does a good job in virtually every other area, but its performance deserves praise again. The portfolio's average maturity makes it a good candidate for extremely positive risk-adjusted returns in the future.

Profile

minimum initial investment $250	*IRA accounts available* . . . . yes
subsequent minimum investment . . . $50	*IRA minimum investment* $250
available in all 50 states. . . . . yes	*date of inception.* . . . . Mar. 1992
telephone exchanges. . . . . yes	*dividend/income paid.* . . . . monthly
number of funds in family 154	*quality of annual reports* . . . . n/a

Global Total Return A

One Seaport Plaza
New York, NY 10292
(800) 225-1852

total return	★★★★★
risk reduction	★★★★★
management	★★★★★
tax minimization	★★★★
expense control	★★★★★
symbol GTRAX	24 points
up-market performance	n/a
down-market performance	n/a
predictability of returns	very good

Total Return   ★★★★★

Over the past five years (all periods ending 6/30/98), Global Total Return A has taken $10,000 and turned it into $15,340 ($13,300 over three years and $24,350 over the past ten years). This translates into an average annual return of 8.9 percent over the past five years, 10.0 percent over the past three years, and 8.9 percent for the decade. Over the past five years, this fund has outperformed 45 percent of all mutual funds; within its general category it has done better than 75 percent of its peers. World bond funds have averaged 6 percent annually over these same five years.

During the past five years, a $10,000 initial investment grew to $14,340 after taxes, assuming a 39.6 percent income tax bracket (state and federal combined) and a capital gains rate of 28 percent. This means that investors in this fund were able to preserve 88 percent of their total returns. Compared to other fixed-income funds, this fund's tax savings are considered to be very good.

Risk/Volatility   ★★★★★

Over the past five years, Global Total Return A has been safer than 90 percent of all world bond funds. Over the past decade, the fund has had two negative years, while the Lehman Brothers Aggregate Bond Index has had one (off 3 percent in 1994); the Saloman Brothers World Government Bond Index fell twice (off 3 percent in 1989 and 4 percent in 1997). The fund has underperformed the Lehman Brothers Aggregate Bond Index five times and the Saloman Brothers World Government Bond Index three times in the last ten years.

	last 5 years		last 10 years	
worst year	–7%	1994	–7%	1994
best year	25%	1995	25%	1995

Consistency, or predictability, of returns for Global Total Return A can be described as very good.

Management   ★★★★★

There are 35 fixed-income securities in this $180 million portfolio. The average world bond fund today is $95 million in size. Close to 90 percent of the fund's holdings are in bonds. The average maturity of the bonds in this account is seven years; the weighted coupon rate averages 8 percent. The portfolio's fixed-income holdings can be categorized as very high quality intermediate-term.

J. Gabriel Irwin and Simon J. Wells have managed this fund for the past 12 years. There are 183 funds besides Global within the Prudential family. Overall, the fund family's risk-adjusted performance can be described as good.

Current Income   ★★★★

Over the past year, Global had a twelve-month yield of 6.8 percent. During this same twelve-month period, the typical world bond fund had a yield that averaged 6.2 percent.

Expenses   ★★★★★

Global's expense ratio is 1.4 percent; it has averaged 1.2 percent annually over the past three calendar years. The average expense ratio for the 250 funds in this category is 1.4 percent. This fund's turnover rate over the past year has been 43 percent, while its peer group average has been 285 percent.

Summary

Global Total Return A is in a three-way tie for first place; however, the fund does beat its competition over the past three and ten-year periods. This is one of a few funds that has obtained a close-to-perfect score (23 out of a possible 25 points). The portfolio has no weak areas and has managed to keep true costs down by minimizing turnover—something most of its peers cannot claim.

Profile

minimum initial investment $1,000	*IRA accounts available* . . . . yes
subsequent minimum investment . . $100	*IRA minimum investment* $1,000
available in all 50 states. . . . . yes	*date of inception* . . . . July 1986
telephone exchanges . . . . no	*dividend/income paid.* . . . . monthly
number of funds in family 184	*quality of annual reports* . . . . n/a

Payden & Rygel Global Fixed-Income R

333 South Grand Avenue, 32nd Floor
Los Angeles, CA 90071-0000
(800) 572-9336

total return	★★★★
risk reduction	★★★★★
management	★★★★★
tax minimization	★★★★★
expense control	★★★★
symbol PYGFX	23 points
up-market performance	n/a
down-market performance	n/a
predictability of returns	excellent

Total Return   ★★★★

Over the past five years (all periods ending 6/30/98), Payden & Rygel Global Fixed-Income R has taken $10,000 and turned it into $14,700 ($12,880 over three years). This translates into an average annual return of 8.0 percent over the past five years and 8.8 percent over the past three years. Over the past five years, this fund has outperformed 50 percent of all mutual funds; within its general category it has done better than 70 percent of its peers. World bond funds have averaged 6 percent annually over these same five years.

During the past five years, a $10,000 initial investment grew to $14,700 after taxes, assuming a 39.6 percent income tax bracket (state and federal combined) and a capital gains rate of 28 percent. This means that investors in this fund were able to preserve 63 percent of their total returns. Compared to other fixed-income funds, this fund's tax savings are considered to be excellent.

Risk/Volatility   ★★★★★

Over the past five years, Payden & Rygel Global Fixed-Income R has been safer than 95 percent of all world bond funds. Over the past decade, the fund has had one negative year, while the Lehman Brothers Aggregate Bond Index has had one (off 3 percent in 1994); the Saloman Brothers World Government Bond Index fell twice (off 3 percent in 1989 and 4 percent in 1997). The fund has underperformed the Lehman Brothers Aggregate Bond Index three times and the Saloman Brothers World Government Bond Index two times in the last ten years.

	last 5 years		since inception	
worst year	–3%	1994	–3%	1994
best year	18%	1995	18%	1995

Consistency, or predictability, of returns for Fixed-Income can be described as excellent.

Management   ★★★★★

There are 15 fixed-income securities in this $500 million portfolio. The average world bond fund today is $95 million in size. Close to 100 percent of the fund's holdings are in bonds. The average maturity of the bonds in this account is 7 years; the weighted coupon rate averages 7 percent. The portfolio's fixed-income holdings can be categorized as intermediate-term, high-quality debt.

A team has managed this fund for the past six years. There are 17 funds besides Fixed-Income within the Payden & Rygel Investment Group. Overall, the fund family's risk-adjusted performance can be described as good.

Current Income   ★★★★★

Over the past year, Fixed-Income had a twelve-month yield of 8.1 percent. During this same twelve-month period, the typical world bond fund had a yield that averaged 6.2 percent.

Expenses   ★★★★

Fixed-Income's expense ratio is 0.5 percent; it has also averaged 0.5 percent annually over the past three calendar years. The average expense ratio for the 250 funds in this category is 1.4 percent. This fund's turnover rate over the past year has been 289 percent, while its peer group average has been 285 percent.

Summary

Payden & Rygel Global Fixed-Income R ties for first place as the best overseas or world bond fund. Its returns have been more predictable than the other two winners, and tax minimization has been quite a bit better. This fund becomes the number one choice for investors looking for current income by investing in U.S. as well as foreign debt instruments.

Profile

minimum initial investment $5,000	*IRA accounts available* . . . . yes
subsequent minimum investment . $1,000	*IRA minimum investment* $2,000
available in all 50 states . . . . yes	*date of inception* . . . . Sept. 1992
telephone exchanges . . . . yes	*dividend/income paid* . . . . monthly
number of funds in family 18	*quality of annual reports* . . . . excellent

Prudential International Bond A

One Seaport Plaza
New York, NY 10292
(800) 225-1852

total return	★★★★★
risk reduction	★★★★★
management	★★★★★
tax minimization	★★★★
expense control	★★★★★
symbol GGPAX	24 points
up-market performance	n/a
down-market performance	n/a
predictability of returns	very good

Total Return ★★★★★

Over the past five years (all periods ending 6/30/98), Prudential International Bond A has taken $10,000 and turned it into $15,320 ($13,210 over three years and $23,590 over the past ten years). This translates into an average annual return of 8.9 percent over the past five years, 9.7 percent over the past three years, and 9.0 percent for the decade. Over the past five years, this fund has outperformed 45 percent of all mutual funds; within its general category it has done better than 75 percent of its peers. World bond funds have averaged 6 percent annually over these same five years.

During the past five years, a $10,000 initial investment grew to $14,350 after taxes, assuming a 39.6 percent income tax bracket (state and federal combined) and a capital gains rate of 28 percent. This means that investors in this fund were able to preserve 87 percent of their total returns. Compared to other fixed-income funds, this fund's tax savings are considered to be very good.

Risk/Volatility ★★★★★

Over the past five years, Prudential International Bond A has been safer than 90 percent of all world bond funds. Over the past decade, the fund has had two negative years, while the Lehman Brothers Aggregate Bond Index has had one (off 3 percent in 1994); the Saloman Brothers World Government Bond Index fell twice (off 3 percent in 1989 and 4 percent in 1997). The fund has underperformed the Lehman Brothers Aggregate Bond Index six times and the Saloman Brothers World Government Bond Index four times in the last ten years.

	last 5 years		last 10 years	
worst year	–5%	1994	–5%	1994
best year	25%	1995	25%	1995

Consistency, or predictability, of returns for International Bond can be described as very good.

Management ★★★★★
There are 35 fixed-income securities in this $95 million portfolio. The average world bond fund today is $95 million in size. Close to 85 percent of the fund's holdings are in bonds. The average maturity of the bonds in this account is 8 years; the weighted coupon rate averages 8 percent. The portfolio's fixed-income holdings can be categorized as high quality intermediate-term.

J. Gabriel Irwin and Simon J. Wells have managed this fund for the past 11 years. There are 183 funds besides International Bond within the Prudential family. Overall, the fund family's risk-adjusted performance can be described as good.

Current Income ★★★★
Over the past year, International Bond had a twelve-month yield of 6.6 percent. During this same twelve-month period, the typical world bond fund had a yield that averaged 6.2 percent.

Expenses ★★★★★
International Bond's expense ratio is 1.6 percent; it has averaged 1.4 percent annually over the past three calendar years. The average expense ratio for the 250 funds in this category is 1.4 percent. This fund's turnover rate over the past year has been 53 percent, while its peer group average has been 285 percent.

Summary
Prudential International Bond A ties for first place as the number one foreign and/or global bond fund. Its close-to-perfect score (23 out of a possible 25 points) is quite impressive. Turnover for the fund is comparatively quite low, and such minimal trading helps keep the real costs of running a fund down as well as enhancing total return figures. Its five-year performance figures clearly beat the competition as well as the other two funds that have tied for this top position. This fund is highly recommended.

Profile

minimum initial investment $1,000	*IRA accounts available* . . . . yes
subsequent minimum investment . . $100	*IRA minimum investment* $1,000
available in all 50 states. . . . . yes	*date of inception* . . . . July 1987
telephone exchanges . . . . no	*dividend/income paid*. . . . . monthly
number of funds in family 184	*quality of annual reports* . . . . n/a

XII.
Summary

Aggressive Growth Funds (10)
1. Acorn
2. Ariel Growth
3. Babson Enterprise II
4. Eclipse Equity
5. FAM Value
6. Fasciano
7. Galaxy Small Cap Value Return A
8. Nicholas II
9. Stratton Small Cap Value Return A
10. T. Rowe Price Small Cap Stock

Balanced Funds (10)
11. American Balanced
12. Columbia Balanced
13. Eclipse Balanced
14. Gabelli ABC
15. Gabelli Westwood Balanced Retail
16. Income Fund of America
17. MFS World Total Return A
18. Preferred Asset Allocation
19. T. Rowe Price Balanced
20. Vanguard STAR

Corporate Bond Funds (5)
21. Bond Fund of America
22. Forum Investors Bond
23. FPA New Income
24. Phoenix Multi-Sector Short-Term A
25. Pillar Short-Term Investment A

Global Equity Funds (13)
26. AIM Global Growth and Income A
27. Bartlett Europe A
28. Capital World Growth and Income
29. Fidelity Europe
30. GAM Europe A

31. Idex Global A
32. Janus Worldwide
33. Merrill Lynch Eurofund B
34. Oppenheimer Quest Global Value A
35. Scout Worldwide
36. T. Rowe Price European Stock
37. Tweedy, Browne Global Value
38. Vanguard International Equity European

Government Bond Funds (5)
39. Cardinal Government Obligation
40. Franklin Strategic Mortgage
41. Lexington GNMA Income
42. SIT U.S. Government Securities
43. Smith Breeden Short Duration Government

Growth Funds (14)
44. Ariel Appreciation
45. Clipper
46. Dreyfus Appreciation
47. First Eagle Fund of America Y
48. GAM North America A
49. Hilliard Lyons Growth A
50. MAP-Equity
51. MFS Capital Opportunities
52. Oak Value
53. Oppenheimer Quest Value A
54. Performance Large Cap Equity
55. T. Rowe Price Blue Chip Growth
56. Torray
57. Weitz Value

Growth & Income Funds (11)
58. American Mutual
59. Capital Income Builder
60. Mairs and Power Balanced
61. MFS Massachusetts Investors A
62. Nationwide D
63. Pioneer Equity-Income A
64. State Street Research Alpha A
65. T. Rowe Price Dividend Growth
66. T. Rowe Price Equity-Income
67. T. Rowe Price Growth & Income
68. Vontobel

High-Yield Funds (5)
69. First Investors Fund for Income A
70. MainStay High-Yield Corporate Bond B
71. Northeast Investors
72. United High-Income A
73. Van Kampen American Capital High-Income A

Metals and Natural Resources Funds (4)
74. American Gas Index
75. Prudential Natural Resources A
76. U.S. Global Investors Global Resources
77. Vanguard Specialized Energy

Money Market Funds (6)
78. Dreyfus Basic Money Market
79. MIMLIC Cash Fund
80. SEI Daily Income Money Market A
81. SEI Daily Income Treasury A
82. Strong Municipal Money Market
83. Vanguard Municipal Money Market

Municipal Bond Funds (8)
84. Calvert Tax-Free Reserves Limited-Term A
85. Colorado BondShares
86. Franklin California High-Yield Income I
87. Franklin High-Yield Tax-Free Income I
88. Franklin New York Tax-Free Income I
89. SIT Tax-Free Income
90. Rochester Fund Municipals A
91. United Municipal High Income A

Utility Stock Funds (5)
92. AIM Global Utilities A
93. Colonial Utilities A
94. Franklin Global Utilities I
95. MFS Utilities A
96. Putnam Utilities Growth and Income A

World Bond Funds (4)
97. Alliance North American Government Income A
98. Global Total Return A
99. Payden and Rygel Global Fixed-Income R
100. Prudential International Bond A

Appendix A
Glossary of Mutual Fund Terms

Advisor—The individual or organization employed by a mutual fund to give professional advice on the fund's investments and asset management practices (also called the "investment advisor").

Asked or Offering Price—The price at which a mutual fund's shares can be purchased. The asked, or offering, price means the current net asset value per share plus sales charge, if any.

BARRA Growth Index—An index of 152 large-capitalization stocks that are all part of the S&P 500; specifically those with above-average sales and earnings growth.

BARRA Value Index—An index of 363 large-capitalization stocks that are all part of the S&P 500; specifically those with above-average dividend yields and relatively low prices considering their book values.

Bid or Sell Price—The price at which a mutual fund's shares are redeemed (bought back) by the fund. The bid or redemption price usually means the current net asset value per share.

Board Certified—Designation given to someone who has become certified in: insurance, estate planning, income taxes, securities, mutual funds, or financial planning. To obtain additional information about the board certified programs or to get the name of a board certified advisor in your area, call (800) 848-2029.

Bottom Up—Refers to a type of security analysis. Management that follows the bottom-up approach is more concerned with the company than with the economy in general. (For a contrasting style, see **Top Down.**)

Broker/Dealer—A firm that buys and sells mutual fund shares and other securities to the public.

Capital Gains Distributions—Payments to mutual fund shareholders of profits (long-term gains) realized on the sale of the fund's portfolio securities. These amounts are usually paid once a year.

Capital Growth—An increase in the market value of a mutual fund's securities, as reflected in the net asset value of fund shares. This is a specific long-term objective of many mutual funds.

Broker/Dealer—A firm that buys and sells mutual fund shares and other securities to the public.

Cash Reserves—Short-term, interest-bearing securities that can easily and quickly be converted to cash. Some funds keep cash levels at a minimum and always remain in stocks and/or bonds; other funds hold up to 25% or more of their assets in cash reserves (money market instruments) as either a defensive play or as a buying opportunity to be used when securities become depressed in price.

CFS—Also known as Certified Fund Specialist, this is the only designation awarded to brokers, financial planners, CPAs, insurance agents, and other investment advisors who either recommend or sell mutual funds. Fewer than 7,000 people across the country have passed this certification program. To obtain additional information about the CFS program or to get the name of a CFS in your area, call (800) 848-2029.

CPI—The Consumer Price Index (CPI) is the most commonly used yardstick for measuring the rate of inflation in the United States.

Custodian—The organization (usually a bank) that keeps custody of securities and other assets of a mutual fund.

Derivatives—A financial contract whose value is based on, or "derived," from a traditional security, such as a stock or bond. The most common examples of derivatives are futures contracts and options.

Diversification—The policy of all mutual funds to spread investments among a number of different securities in order to reduce the risk inherent in investing.

Dollar-Cost Averaging—The practice of investing equal amounts of money at regular intervals regardless of whether securities markets are moving up or down. This procedure reduces average share costs to the investor, who acquires more shares in the periods of lower securities prices and fewer shares in periods of higher prices.

EAFE—An equity index (EAFE stands for Europe, Australia, and the Far East) used to measure stock market performance outside of the United States. The EAFE is a sort of S&P 500 Index for overseas or foreign stocks. As of the middle of 1997, the EAFE was weighted as follows: 59.5% Europe, 28.8% Japan, 10.6% Pacific Rim, and 1.1% "other."

Exchange Privilege—An option enabling mutual fund shareholders to transfer their investment from one fund to another within the same fund family as their needs or objectives change. Typically, funds allow investors to use the exchange privilege several times a year for a low fee or no fee per exchange.

Expense Ratio—A figure expressed as a percentage of a fund's assets. The main element is the management fee. Administrative fees cover a fund's day-to-day operations, including printing materials, keeping records, paying staff, and renting office space. Sometimes administrative fees are included in the management fee; a number of funds list such fees separately. Roughly half of all funds charge a 12b-1 fee, which pays for a fund's distribution and advertising costs. The 12b-1 fee can be higher than the management or administrative fee.

Indexing—In contrast to the traditional approach to investing that tries to outperform market averages, index investing is a strategy that seeks to match the performance of a group of securities that form a recognized market measure, known as an index.

Investment Company—A corporation, trust, or partnership that invests pooled funds of shareholders in securities appropriate to the fund's objective. Among the benefits of investment companies, compared to direct investments, are professional management and diversification. Mutual funds (also known as open-ended and close-ended investment companies) are the most popular type of investment company.

Investment Objective—The goal that the investor and mutual fund pursue together (e.g., growth of capital or current income).

Large-Cap Stocks—Equities issued by companies with a net worth of at least $7.5 billion dollars.

Long-Term Funds—An industry designation for funds that invest primarily in securities with remaining maturities of more than one year. In this book the term means fifteen years or more. Long-term funds are broadly divided into bond and income funds.

Management Fee—The amount paid by a mutual fund to the investment advisor for its services. The average annual fee industrywide is about 0.7 percent of fund assets.

"Market-Neutral" Funds—A strategy that seeks to neutralize market movements by running two portfolios simultaneously—one buys stocks that are predicted to rise, and the other invests an equal amount in a similar assortment of other stocks that are predicted to decline.

Mid-Cap Stocks—Equities issued by companies with a net worth between $1 billion and $7.5 billion dollars.

Mutual Fund—An investment company that pools money from shareholders and invests in a variety of securities, including stocks, bonds, and money market instruments. A mutual fund stands ready to buy back (redeem) its shares at their current net asset value; this value depends on the market value of the fund's portfolio securities at the time of redemption. Most mutual funds continuously offer new shares to investors.

Net Asset Value Per Share—The market worth of one share of a mutual fund. This figure is derived by taking a fund's total assets—securities, cash, and any accrued earnings—deducting liabilities, and dividing by the number of shares outstanding.

No-Load Fund—A mutual fund selling its shares at net asset value without the addition of sales charges.

Passive Management—A portfolio that tries to match the performance of a target index, such as the S&P 500.

Portfolio—A collection of securities owned by an individual or an institution (such as a mutual fund). A fund's portfolio may include a combination of stocks, bonds, and money market securities.

Portfolio Diversification—The average U.S. stock fund has about 30% of its assets invested in its 10 largest holdings.

Prospectus—The official booklet that describes a mutual fund, which must be furnished to all investors. It contains information required by the U.S. Securities and Exchange Commission on such subjects as the fund's investment objectives, services, and fees. A more detailed document, known as "Part B" of the prospectus or the "Statement of Additional Information," is available at no charge upon request.

Redemption Price—The amount per share (shown as the "bid" in newspaper tables) that mutual fund shareholders receive when they cash in the shares. The value of the shares depends on the market value of the fund's portfolio securities at the time. This value is the same as net asset value per share.

Reinvestment Privilege—An option available to mutual fund shareholders in which fund dividends and capital gains distributions are automatically turned back into the fund to buy new shares, without charge (meaning no sales fee or commission), thereby increasing holdings.

Russell 2000—An index that represents 2,000 small domestic companies (less than 8 percent of the U.S. equity market).

Sales Charge—An amount charged to purchase shares in many mutual funds sold by brokers or other sales agents. The maximum charge is 8.5 percent of the initial investment; the vast majority of funds now have a maximum charge of 4.75 percent or less. The charge is added to the net asset value per share when determining the offering price.

Short-Term Funds—An industry designation for funds that invest primarily in securities with maturities of less than one year; the term means five years or less in this book. Short-term funds include money market funds and certain municipal bond funds.

Small-Cap Stocks—Equities issued by companies with a net worth of less than $1 billion.

Top Down—Refers to a type of security analysis. Management that follows the top-down approach is very concerned with the general level of the economy and any fiscal policy being followed by the government.

Turnover—The percentage of a fund's portfolio that is sold during the year, a percentage rate that can range from 0% to 300% or more. The average turnover rate for U.S. stock funds is approximately 80% (10% for domestic stock index funds).

Transfer Agent—The organization employed by a mutual fund to prepare and maintain records relating to the accounts of its shareholders. Some funds serve as their own transfer agents.

12b-1 Fee—The distribution fee charged by some funds, named after a federal government rule. Such fees pay for marketing costs, such as advertising and dealer compensation. The fund's prospectus outlines 12b-1 fees, if applicable.

280 The 100 Best Mutual Funds You Can Buy, 1999

Underwriter—The organization that acts as the distributor of a mutual fund's shares to broker/dealers and investors.

Value Stocks—Stocks that most investors view as unattractive for some reason. They tend to be priced low relative to some measure of the company's worth, such as earnings, book value or cash flow. Value stock managers try to identify companies whose prices are depressed for temporary reasons, and that may bounce back strongly if investor sentiment improves.

■ ■ ■

The Securities Act of 1933 requires a fund's shares to be registered with the Securities and Exchange Commission (SEC) prior to their sale. In essence, the Securities Act ensures that the fund provides potential investors with a current prospectus. This law also limits the types of advertisements that may be used by a mutual fund.

The Securities Exchange Act of 1934 regulates the purchase and sale of all types of securities, including mutual fund shares.

The Investment Advisors Act of 1940 is a body of law that regulates certain activities of the investment advisors to mutual funds.

The Investment Company Act of 1940 is a highly detailed regulatory statute applying to mutual fund companies. This act contains numerous provisions designed to prevent self-dealing by employees of the mutual fund company, as well as other conflicts of interest. It also provides for the safekeeping of fund assets and prohibits the payment of excessive fees and charges by the fund and its shareholders.

Appendix B
Who Regulates Mutual Funds?

Mutual funds are highly regulated businesses that must comply with some of the toughest laws and rules in the financial services industry. All funds are regulated by the U.S. Securities and Exchange Commission (SEC). With its extensive rule-making and enforcement authority, the SEC oversees mutual fund compliance chiefly by relying on the four major federal securities statutes mentioned in Appendix A.

Fund assets must generally be held by an independent custodian. There are strict requirements for fidelity bonding to ensure against the misappropriation of shareholder monies. In addition to federal statutes, almost every state has its own set of regulations governing mutual funds.

Although federal and state laws cannot guarantee that a fund will be profitable, they are designed to ensure that all mutual funds are operated and managed in the interests of their shareholders. Here are some specific investor protections that every fund must follow:

- Regulations concerning what may be claimed or promised about a mutual fund and its potential.
- Requirements that vital information about a fund be made readily available (such as a prospectus, the "Statement of Additional Information," also known as "Part B" of the prospectus, and annual and semiannual reports).
- Requirements that a fund operate in the interest of its shareholders, rather than any special interests of its management.
- Rules dictating diversification of the fund's portfolio over a wide range of investments to avoid too much concentration in a particular security.

Appendix C
Dollar-Cost Averaging

Investors often believe that the market will go down as soon as they get in. For these people, and anyone concerned with reducing risk, the solution is dollar-cost averaging.

Dollar-cost averaging is a simple yet effective way to reduce risk, whether you are investing in stocks or bonds. The premise behind dollar-cost averaging (DCA) is that if several purchases of a fund are made over an extended period of time, the unpredictable highs and lows will average out. The investor ends up with buying some shares at a comparatively low price, others at perhaps a much higher price.

DCA assumes that investors are willing to sacrifice the possibility of having bought all of their shares at the lowest price in return for knowing that they did not also buy every share at the highest price. In short, we are willing to accept a compromise—a sort of *risk-adjusted* decision.

DCA is based on investing a fixed amount of money in a given fund at specific intervals. Typically, an investor will add a few hundred dollars at the beginning of each month into the XYZ mutual fund. DCA works best if you invest and continue to invest on an established schedule, *regardless of price fluctuations*. You will be buying more shares when the price is down than when it is up. Most investors do not mind buying shares when prices are increasing, since this means that their existing shares are also going up. When this program is followed, losses during market declines are limited, while the ability to participate in good markets is maintained.

Another advantage of DCA is that it increases the likelihood that you will follow an investment program. As with other aspects of our life, it is important to have goals. However, DCA is not something that should be universally recommended. Whether or not you should use dollar-cost averaging depends upon your risk level.

From its beginnings well over one hundred years ago, there has been an upward bias in the performance of the stock market. More often than not, the market goes up, not down. Therefore, it hardly makes sense to apply dollar-cost averaging to an investment vehicle, knowing that historically one would be paying a higher and higher price per share over time.

Studies done by the Institute of Business & Finance (800-848-2029) show that over the past fifty years, a dollar-cost averaging program produced inferior returns compared to a lump-sum investment. The Institute's studies conclude the following: (1) a DCA program is a good idea for a conservative investor (the person or couple who gives more weight or importance to risk than reward); (2) for investor's whose risk level is anything but conservative, an immediate, one-time investment resulted in better returns the great majority of the time; and (3) there have certainly been periods of time when a DCA program would have benefitted even the extremely aggressive investor—but such periods have not been very common over the past half century and have been quite rare over the past twenty, fifteen, ten, five, and three years.

Example of Dollar-Cost Averaging
($1,000 invested per period)

Period	Cost per share	Number of shares bought with $1,000	Total shares owned	Total amount invested	Current value of shares (2) x (4)	Net gain or loss (percentage) (6) x (5)
(1)	(2)	(3)	(4)	(5)	(6)	(7)
1	$100	10.0	10.0	$1,000	$1,000	0
2	$80	12.5	22.5	$2,000	$1,800	−10.0%
3	$70	14.3	36.8	$3,000	$2,576	−14.1%
4	$60	16.7	53.5	$4,000	$3,210	−19.7%
5	$50	20.0	73.5	$5,000	$3,675	−26.5%
6	$70	14.3	87.8	$6,000	$6,146	+2.4%
7	$80	12.5	100.3	$7,000	$8,024	+14.6%
8	$100	10.0	110.3	$8,000	$11,030	+37.9%

Appendix D
Systematic Withdrawal Plan

A systematic withdrawal plan (SWP) allows you to have a check for a specified amount sent monthly or quarterly to you, or anyone you designate, from your mutual fund account. There is no charge for this service.

This method of getting monthly checks is ideal for the income-oriented investor. It is also a risk reduction technique—a kind of dollar-cost averaging in reverse. A set amount is sent to you each month. In order to send you a check for a set amount, shares of one or more of your mutual funds must be sold, which, in turn, will most likely trigger a taxable event, but only for those shares redeemed.

When the market is low, the number of mutual fund shares being liquidated will be higher than when the market is high, since the fund's price per share will be lower. If you need $500 a month and the fund's price is $25.00 per share, 20 shares must be liquidated; if the price per share is $20.00 per share, 25 shares must be sold.

Shown below is an example of a SWP from the Investment Company of America (ICA), a conservative growth and income fund featured in previous editions of this book. The example assumes an initial investment of $100,000 in the fund at its inception, the beginning of 1934. A greater or smaller dollar amount could be used. The example shows what happens to the investor's principal over a 65-year period (Jan. 1, 1934 through June 30, 1998). It assumes that $10,000 is withdrawn from the fund at the end of the first year. At the end of the first year, the $10,000 withdrawal *is increased by 4 percent each year thereafter* to offset the effects of inflation, which averaged less than 4 percent during this 65-year period. This means that the withdrawal for the second year was $10,400 ($10,000 multiplied by 1.04), for the third year $10,816 ($10,400 x 1.04), and so on.

Compare this example to what would have happened if the money had been placed in an average fixed-income account at a bank. The $100,000 depositor who took out only $9,000 each year would be in a far different situation. His (or her) original $100,000 was fully depleted by the end of 1948. All the principal and interest payments could not keep up with an annual withdrawal of $9,000.

The difference between ICA and the savings account is over $5.8 million. The savings account had a total return of $26,300 (plus distribution of the original $100,000 principal); the ICA account had a total return of $6,012,000 ($2,827,000 distributed over sixty-five years plus a remaining principal, or account balance, of $4,716,000). This difference becomes even more disturbing when you consider that the bank depositor's withdrawals were not increasing each year to offset the effects of inflation. The interest rates used in this example came from the *U.S. Savings & Loan League Fact Book*.

SWP from The Investment Company of America (ICA)
initial investment: $100,000
annual withdrawals of: $10,000 (10%)
the first check is sent: 12/31/34
withdrawals annually increased by: 4%

date	amount withdrawn	value of remaining shares
12/31/34	$10,000	$109,000
12/31/35	$10,400	$185,000
12/31/40	$12,700	$151,000
12/31/45	$15,400	$241,000
12/31/50	$18,700	$204,000
12/31/55	$22,800	$354,000
12/31/60	$27,700	$431,000
12/31/65	$33,700	$612,000
12/31/70	$41,000	$649,000
12/31/75	$50,000	$552,000
12/31/80	$60,700	$762,000
12/31/85	$73,900	$1,225,000
12/31/86	$76,900	$1,415,000
12/31/87	$79,900	$1,411,000
12/31/88	$83,100	$1,515,000
12/31/89	$86,500	$1,872,000
12/31/90	$89,900	$1,794,000
12/31/91	$93,500	$2,170,000
12/31/92	$86,500	$2,224,000
12/31/93	$101,200	$2,379,000
12/31/94	$105,200	$2,277,000
12/31/95	$109,400	$2,865,000
12/31/96	$113,780	$3,900,000
12/31/97	$118,330	$4,200,000
6/30/98	———	$4,716,000

If the ICA systematic withdrawal plan were 8 percent annually instead of 10 percent (but still increased by 4 percent each year to offset the effects of inflation), the investor would have ended up with remaining shares worth $87 million, plus withdrawals that totaled $2.2 million.

Next time some broker or banker tells you that you should be buying bonds or CDs for current income, tell them about a systematic withdrawal plan (SWP), a program designed to maximize your income and offset something the CD, T-bill, and bond advocates never mention: inflation.

Appendix E
Load or No-Load—Which is Right for You?

As the amount of information available on mutual funds continues to grow almost exponentially, the load versus no-load debate has intensified. What makes the issue difficult to evaluate is the continued absence of neutrality on either side. Before you learn the real truth, let us first examine who is advocating what, what their biases are, and how each side argues its point.

A number of publications, including *Money, Forbes, Fortune, Kiplinger Personal Investor*, and *Business Week*, favor the no-load camp. Although these publications appear neutral, they are not. First, each one derives the overwhelming majority of its mutual fund advertisements from funds that charge no commission. Second, all of these publications are trying to increase readership; they are in the business of selling copy, not information. A good way to increase or maintain a healthy circulation is by having their readership rely on them for advice—instead of going to a broker or investment advisor.

On the other side is the financial services industry, whose most vocal load supporters include the brokerage, banking, and insurance industries. That's not much of a surprise. These groups are also biased. Like the publication that only makes money by getting you to purchase a copy or having an editorial board whose policy favors no-load funds, much of the financial services community supports a sales charge because that is how they are compensated.

No-load proponents argue that a fund that charges any kind of commission or ongoing marketing fee (which is known as a 12-b-1 charge) inherently cannot be as good as a similar investment that has no entry or exit fee or ongoing 12-b-1 charge. On its surface, this argument appears logical. After all, if one investor starts off with a dollar invested and the other starts off with somewhere between 99 and 92 cents (commissions range from 1 to 8.5 percent; most are in the 3 to 5 percent range), all other things being equal, the person who has all of his money working for him will do better than someone who has an initial deduction. The press and the no-load funds say that there is no reason to pay a commission because you can do as well or better than the broker or advisor whose job it is to provide you with suggestions and guidance.

The commission-oriented community says you should pay a sales charge because you get what you pay for—good advice and ongoing service. After all, brokers, financial planners, banks that include mutual fund desks, and insurance agents are all highly trained professionals who know things you do not. Moreover, they study the markets on a continuous basis, ensuring that they have more information than any weekend investor. In short, they ask, do you want someone managing your money who has experience and works full-time in this area, or someone such as yourself who has no formal training and whose time and resources are limited?

There is no clear-cut solution. Valid points are raised by both sides. To gain more insight into what course of action (or type of fund) is best for you, let us take a neutral approach. I believe I can give you valid reasons why both kinds of funds make sense, because I have no hidden agenda. True, I am a licensed broker and branch manager of a national securities firm; however, it is also true that the great majority of my compensation is based on a fee for service, meaning that clients who invest solely in no-load funds pay me an annual management fee.

First, you should never pay a commission to someone who knows no more about investing than you do. There is no value added in such a situation, except perhaps during uncertain or negative periods in the market. (This point will be discussed later.) After all, if your broker's advice and mutual fund experience are based solely on the same financial publications you have access to, you are not getting your money's worth by paying a sales charge. I raise this point first because the financial services industry is filled with a tremendous number of inexperienced and ignorant brokers. These people may make a lot of money, but this is usually the result of their connections (they know a lot of people) or marketing skills (they know how to get new business)—neither of which have anything to do with your money.

Brokerage firms, banks, and insurance companies hire stockbrokers based on their sales ability, not their knowledge or analytical ability. The financial analysts at the home office are the ones involved in research and managing money. The fact that your broker has a couple of dozen years' experience in the securities industry or is a vice president may actually be hazardous to your financial health. Extensive experience could mean that the advisor is less inclined to learn about new products or studies, because he already has an established client base. Brokers obtain titles such as "vice president" because they outsell their peers. Contests (awards, trips, prizes, and enhanced payouts) are based on how much is sold, period. There has never been an instance of a brokerage firm, bank, or insurance company giving an award to someone based on knowledge or how well a client's account performed.

Second, if your investment time horizon is less than a couple of years, it is a mistake to pay anything more than a nominal fee, something in the 1 percent range. Even though the advice you are receiving may be great, it is hard to justify a 3 to 5 percent commission over the short haul. Sales charges in this range can only be rationalized if they can be amortized over a number of years. Thus, worthwhile advice becomes a bargain if you stay with the investment, or within the same family of mutual funds, for at least three years.

Third, if you are purchasing a fund that charges a fee, find out what you are getting for your money. Question the advisor; find out about his or her training, experience, education, and designations. Equally important, get a clear understanding as to what you will be receiving on an ongoing basis. What kind of continuing education does the broker engage in (attending conferences, reading books, seeking a designation, and so forth)? Finally, make sure your advisor or broker tells you how your investments will be monitored. It is important to know how often you will be contacted and how a buy, hold, or sell decision will be made.

So far, it looks as if I've been pretty tough on my fellow brokers. Well, believe me, I'm even harder on about 99 percent of those do-it-yourself investors. I have been in this business for close to twenty years, and I can tell you that I have rarely met an investor who was better off on his or her own. Here's why.

First, it is extremely difficult to be objective about your own investments. Decisions based on what you have read from a newsletter or magazine or what you learned at a seminar are often a response to current news, such as trade relations with Japan, the value of the U.S. dollar, the state of the economy, or the direction of interest rates. This kind of knee-jerk reaction has proven to be wrong in most cases.

Mind you, out of fairness to those who manage their own investments, amateurs aren't the only ones who make investment errors. As an example, the majority of the major brokerage firms gave a sell signal just before the war in the Persian Gulf. It turned out that this would have been about the perfect time to buy. E.F. Hutton was forced to merge with another brokerage firm because they incorrectly predicted the direction of interest rates (and lost tens of millions of dollars in their own portfolio).

The mutual fund industry itself deserves a healthy part of the blame, as evidenced by their timing of new funds. Take my advice: When you see a number of new mutual funds coming out with the same timely theme (government plus or optioned-enhanced bond funds in the mid-eighties, Eastern European funds after German reunification, health care funds a few years ago, derivatives and hedge funds last year), run for cover. By the time these funds come out, the party is about to end. Investors who got into these funds often do well for a number of months but soon face devastating declines.

Your favorite financial publications are also to blame. Their advice is based on a herd instinct—What do our readers think? Instead of providing leadership, they simply reinforce what is most likely incorrect information. For example, for over a year after the 1987 stock market crash, the most popular of these mainstream publications, *Money*, had cover stories that recommended (and extolled the virtues of) safe investments. For almost a year and a half after the crash, this magazine was giving out bad advice. When something goes on sale (stocks, in this case) you should be a buyer, not a seller. Since *Money* routinely surveys (or polls) their readers for feature articles, such behavior (the herd instinct) is understandable but not forgivable.

Besides the lack of objectivity and the constant bombardment of what I call "daily noise" (what the market is doing at the moment, comments from the financial gurus, etc.), there is also the question of your competence. Presumably, you and I could figure out how to fix our own plumbing, sew our own clothes, fix the car when it breaks down, or avoid paying a lawyer by purchasing "do-it-yourself" books. The question then becomes whether it is worth going through the learning curve, and, even supposing we are successful, whether the task would have been better accomplished by someone else—perhaps for less money or better use of our own time. I think the answer is obvious. Each of us has our own area or areas of expertise or skill. You and I rely on others either because they know more than we do about the topic or task at hand or because having someone else help is a more efficient use of our time.

If you're going to seek the services of an investment advisor or broker, it should be because he or she knows more than you do, because he or she is more objective, or because you can make more money doing whatever you do than in taking the time to make complex investment decisions yourself. This is what makes sense. The fact that there are brokers and advisors who put their interests before yours is simply a reality that you must deal with. And the proper way to deal with these conflicts of interest or ignorant counselors is by doing your homework. Ask questions. Just as there are great plumbers, mechanics, lawyers, and doctors, so too are there exceptional investment advisors and brokers. Your job is to find them.

Eliminating load or no-load funds from your investing universe is not the answer. If you are determined never to pay a commission, then you may miss out on the next John Templeton (the Franklin-Templeton family of funds), Peter Lynch (Fidelity Magellan Fund), or Jean-Marie Eveillard (SoGen Funds). You will also miss out on some of the very best mutual fund families: American Funds (large), Fidelity-Advisor (medium), and SoGen (small). A better way to proceed is to try to separate good funds from bad ones. After all, an investor is clearly far better off in a good load fund than in a bad no-load one.

The bottom line is that performance, as well as *risk-adjusted returns*, for load funds often exceeds the returns on no-load funds, and vice versa. The "top ten" list (or whatever number you want to use) for one period may have been dominated by funds that charge a commission, but in just a year or two the top ten list may be heavily populated by mutual funds with no sales charge or commission.

It might seem strange to be questioning the benefits of financial planning when our society places professions like law and accountancy in such high regard. And certainly I am not suggesting that investors should consider only load funds. But with all the load-fund bashing in recent years, it is important to recognize that no-load funds are not the perfect answer for a large percentage of investors. Approaching the mutual fund industry with an us vs. them mentality results in a great deal of misleading information and unfairly discredits the work of skilled financial planners and brokers.

Appendix F
The Best and Worst Days

Many would-be stock investors fear investing at the wrong time—when market prices are *highest*. Suppose you invested $5,000 in the Dow Jones Industrial Average (which is comprised of just thirty stocks) every year for the last twenty years during the month the market peaked. How much would your total investment of $100,000 be worth versus an investment made each year during the month when prices were *lowest*? The results may surprise you.

Month of Market High	Cumulative Investment	Value of Acct. on 12/31	Month of Market Low	Cumulative Investment	Value of Acct. on 12/31
1/77	$5,000	$4,587	11/77	$5,000	$5,089
9/78	10,000	9,447	2/78	10,000	10,986
10/79	15,000	15,669	11/79	15,000	17,329
11/80	20,000	24,067	4/80	20,000	27,336
4/81	25,000	27,803	9/81	25,000	31,593
12/82	30,000	40,340	8/82	30,000	46,123
11/83	35,000	55,804	1/83	35,000	64,227
1/84	40,000	61,756	7/84	40,000	70,640
12/85	45,000	87,473	1/85	45,000	100,625
12/86	50,000	116,182	1/86	50,000	134,155
8/87	55,000	126,246	10/87	55,000	146,411
10/88	60,000	152,367	1/88	60,000	175,787
10/89	65,000	206,575	1/89	65,000	238,498
7/90	70,000	210,081	10/90	70,000	242,607
12/91	75,000	265,895	2/91	75,000	306,962
6/92	80,000	290,645	10/92	80,000	334,857
8/93	85,000	345,084	4/93	85,000	397,164
8/94	90,000	367,517	11/94	90,000	422,428
12/95	95,000	507,898	1/95	95,000	584,861
11/96	$100,000	659,369	1/96	$100,000	759,672
1997	$105,000		1997	$105,000	

As you can see, even if you had the worst luck in the world, by investing $5,000 at the high point of the market each year, you would still end up with $659,369 after twenty years. This is not as good as having perfect timing (buying at the market low each year), but the difference is certainly not as great as one might first suspect. Perfect timing resulted in an average annual rate of return of 16.35 percent over each of the past twenty years. Investing on each of the worst possible days still resulted in an average annual rate of return of 15.48 percent.

Appendix G
Investing in the Face of Fear

What do you do when the market declines? When the Iraqis invaded Kuwait, the market retreated from fears of rising interest rates and inflation. The Dow Jones Industrial Average (DJIA) had reached a new high on July 16, 1990, at 2999.75, and by August 22, 1990, had fallen to 2560—a decline of almost 15 percent. For some insight on how to respond to a drop in the market, let us look back at the first Arab oil embargo in 1973. Oil prices tripled, as did the Consumer Price Index and interest rates. And the DJIA fell from 947 on September 30, 1973, to 616 on December 31, 1974, a drop of 35 percent.

Suppose you had placed $10,000 in AIM Weingarten Fund (a fund featured in a previous edition of this book) on September 30, 1973. By December 31, 1974, your investment had dropped in value to $5,725—a decrease of 43 percent. What would you have done with your shares, and how would you have fared?

Let's look at several scenarios:
1. Sell now! Take the loss and put the money in a bank certificate of deposit.
2. Wait until the mutual fund breaks even, then sell it, and put the money in a certificate of deposit.
3. Hold on to your shares. It was a long-term investment, and time will win out.
4. Invest an additional $10,000 in Weingarten, capitalizing on the opportunity to buy more shares at a lower price.

Which scenario did you choose?
1. If you sold your AIM Weingarten Fund shares on December 31, 1974 in reaction to the declining market and placed the remaining money in a bank CD, your investment as of June 30, 1998 would have been worth (depending on the interest rate): $21,868 at 6 percent, $27,135 at 7 percent, and $33,631 at 8 percent.
2. If you had waited for Weingarten's value to return to $10,000, sold the shares on December 31, 1977, and then placed the money in a bank CD, the $10,000 as of June 30, 1998 would have been worth: $32,076 at 6 percent, $38,702 at 7 percent, and $46,613 at 8 percent.
3. If you had sat tight and left your money in the fund, your $10,000 would have been worth $475,047 as of June 30, 1998.

4(a). If you had an additional $10,000 to invest in Weingarten on December 31, 1974, your $20,000 total investment would have been worth $1,259,294 as of June 30, 1998.

4(b). Assuming you did not have another $10,000 lump sum to place in Weingarten, but started investing $100 each month beginning December 31, 1974, your total investment of $32,300 would have been worth $901,323 as of June 30, 1998.

Did you end up with $21,868, $32,076, $475,047, $1,259,294 or $901,323? Smart money does not panic! When confidence is low and emotion is high, there are opportunities for the smart investor.

Appendix H
Is Bigger Better?

There is constant debate within the financial services community and mutual fund industry as to whether a large fund is better than a small one. According to the *Wall Street Journal*, if you "stick with the fund industry's major players, you're far less likely to end up with a real turkey." According to a study by Morningstar, Inc. (which includes each of the past five calendar years ending 12/31/93 and covers the twenty-five best and worst performers among diversified U.S. stock funds), small is both better and worse.

The Morningstar study indicates that the worst performers, on average, were over 40% smaller than the typical mutual fund, which has assets of approximately $500 million. On the other hand, the top twenty-five, for the calendar years from 1989 through 1993, were, on average, 60% smaller than the typical fund. In other words, as the study points out, the majority of each extreme came from small fund families. Only 22% of the worst performers and 35% of the best performers came from the thirty-nine biggest fund groups. In this study, the largest fund families were described as those companies that managed more than $10 billion by the end of 1993. (As a side note, these thirty-nine groups control over 75% of all mutual fund assets; total assets for the mutual fund industry as of the middle of 1998 were approximately $5.0 trillion.)

When viewing each of the ten years through 1994, Morningstar divided the domestic stock group (aggressive growth, small company, growth, growth and income, and equity-income) into four groups, based solely on size. On average, the smallest funds, those in the bottom 25%, turned in the best results for calendar years 1984, 1991, and 1992. However, the three smallest funds each year showed the biggest losses in nine of those ten years.

There are a number of explanations for these results. As a fund or fund family gets larger, it has the money available to hire a management team with more depth. Smaller fund groups may have management performing multiple jobs, including research and administrative tasks. On a positive note, smaller funds can be more nimble in exploiting investment opportunities.

A small fund is less likely to have to answer to a large investment committee or to have other forms of restriction. This is a double-edged sword, since it often allows the fund's manager to load up heavily on a comparatively small number of issues. This decisiveness sounds good, but if management is wrong, the losses can be substantial.

A favored argument against small funds has to do with economies of scale, specifically, expenses. The average domestic stock fund has expenses that average 1.4 % annually; a few small funds have yearly costs that range from 6 to 18 percent.

A big fund has other advantages. First, when an existing manager leaves, it is very likely that his or her replacement will be at least pretty good, if not very good. Second, knowledge is power. Big fund groups have large numbers of researchers, traders, analysts, and other support personnel to help out the money managers.

The table below lists the ten largest equity funds, as of June 30, 1998. The funds are listed in order of largest to smallest; size is in billions of dollars. The returns shown in the final column are annualized.

The 10 Largest Equity Funds (as of 6/30/98)

name of fund	size (in billions)	returns		
		3-year	5 year	10 year
Fidelity Magellan Fund	$74	22.1%	19.3%	18.8%
Vanguard Index 500	$61	30.1%	22.9%	18.4%
Washington Mutual	$46	29.2%	21.6%	17.4%
Fidelity Growth & Income	$45	28.5%	21.9%	19.6%
Investment Co. of America	$44	25.4%	19.6%	16.6%
Fidelity Contrafund	$35	25.7%	20.4%	23.0%
Vanguard/Windsor II	$30	30.2%	22.3%	17.9%
Amer. Cent.—20th Century Ultra	$27	25.7%	19.8%	22.2%
Fidelity Equity-Income	$25	25.9%	20.2%	15.8%
Fidelity-Advisor Growth Opportunity T	$24	23.7%	20.6%	19.1%
Average stock fund	**$0.6**	**23.0%**	**18.3%**	**15.6%**
S&P 500 (dividends reinvested)	—	**30.2%**	**23.1%**	**18.6%**

It is difficult to draw any definitive conclusions from this one, somewhat limited, study. However, there are some important inferences or recommendations that can be made. Unless you know what you are doing, stay away from small funds and small mutual fund families—except those mentioned in this book. If you want to do better than the market averages, you may also want to stay away from the very biggest funds, even though there is safety in numbers. One guideline might be to choose mutual funds that have assets that range in size from $500 million to less than $3 billion. And, as always, diversify by category. Do not load up too heavily on a single category (such as growth, small-cap, foreign stock, etc.), no matter how impressive the results or how convincing the study.

Appendix I
U.S. Compared to Foreign Markets

Investing worldwide gives you exposure to different stages of economic market cycles—which has given international investors an advantage in the past. Foreign equities and bonds have generally offered higher levels of short-, intermediate-, and long-term growth than their domestic counterparts. Not once during the past eleven years was the U.S. stock market the world's top performer.

Top-Performing World Stock Markets: An Eleven-year Review: 1987–1997

year	1st	2nd	3rd	4th	5th
1997	Portugal + 47%	Switzerland + 45%	Italty + 36%	Denmark +35%	**USA + 34%**
1996	Spain 41.3%	Taiwan 40.3%	Sweden 38%	Hong Kong 33.1%	Ireland 32.0%
1995	Switzerland 44.1%	**USA 33.4%**	Sweden 33.4%	Spain 29.8%	Netherlands 27.7%
1994	Finland 52.2%	Norway 23.6%	Japan 21.4%	Sweden 18.3%	Ireland 14.5%
1993	Hong Kong 109.9%	Malaysia 107.3%	Finland 81.3%	Singapore 65.5%	New Zealand 62.6%
1992	Hong Kong 27.4%	Switzerland 15.6%	Sing./Malaysia 4.4%	**USA 4.2%**	France 1.0%
1991	Hong Kong 49.5%	Australia 33.6%	**USA 30.1%**	Sing./Malaysia 25.0%	New Zealand 18.3%
1990	United Kingdom 10.1%	Hong Kong 9.2%	Austria 6.3%	Norway 0.7%	Denmark –0.9%
1989	Austria 103.9%	Germany 46.3%	Norway 45.5%	Denmark 43.9%	Sing./Malaysia 42.3%
1988	Belgium 53.6%	Denmark 52.7%	Sweden 48.3%	Norway 42.4%	France 37.8%
1987	Japan 43.0%	Spain 41.3%	United Kingdom 35.1%	Canada 13.9%	Denmark 13.2%

The U.S. stock market has ranked among the five top performers only four times in the past eleven years. During this same period, the U.S. bond market has never claimed the number one spot against other world markets.

Appendix J
The Power of Dividends

The table below shows how important common stock dividends can be. The figures assume a one-time investment of $100,000 in the S&P 500 at the beginning of 1977. The table shows that dividends have increased for each of the past twenty-one years.

Viewed from a different perspective, if you were strictly income-oriented and invested $100,000 in the S&P 500 at the beginning of 1977, you would have received a 4.3% return on your investment ($4,310 divided by $100,000). For the 1996 calendar year, this same investment returned 31.2% for the year ($31,234 divided by $100,000); for 1997 the figure increases to 31.9% ($31,934 divided by $100,000). These figures assume that dividends received each year were spent and not reinvested. Moreover, these numbers do not include the over *fifteenfold* growth of capital (the original $100,000 grew to $1,611,000 without dividends) that also took place.

As a point of comparison for the figures described in the previous paragraph, consider what would have happened if the same investor had invested in a twenty-year U.S. government bond in 1977. By the end of 1996, twenty years later, the original $100,000 worth of bonds would have matured and had an ending value of $100,000. Additionally, the investor would have received approximately 7% for each of these twenty years—a far cry from the increased dividend stream and capital appreciation the S&P 500 experienced over the same period. Perhaps more important, the bond investor could have taken his $100,000 at the beginning of 1997 and invested the money for another twenty years, getting a 6.5% return for each of those years (versus the S&P 500 investor who just finished receiving over 31.9%, based on $100,000, and presumably will be receiving even greater dividend returns for each or most of the next twenty years).

Annual Dividends from $100,000 Invested in the S&P 500

year	S&P 500 dividend	year	S&P 500 dividend
1977	$4,310	1987	$13,286
1978	$4,946	1988	$16,017
1979	$5,647	1989	$17,275
1980	$9,798	1990	$19,824
1981	$7,564	1991	$21,824
1982	$8,112	1992	$22,598
1983	$8,955	1993	$22,725
1984	$10,005	1994	$24,906
1985	$11,893	1995	$26,039
1986	$11,523	1996	$31,234
		1997	$31,934

Appendix K
Growth Stocks vs. Value Stocks

Throughout the different equity sections (e.g., growth, growth and income, global equity, etc.), the end of each stock fund's "Management" paragraph often mentions whether the fund manager seeks out "growth" or "value" issues. The differences and possible consequences of these two forms of equity selection are shown in the table below.

Value means that the stocks are inexpensive relative to their earnings potential. *Growth* refers to stocks of companies whose earnings per share are expected to grow significantly faster than the market average.

As you can see by the table, the performance of these two types of stocks can vary from year to year. On a monthly or quarterly basis, the difference is often much more significant than on an annual basis.

The table below shows performance of the S&P Barra Value Index and the S&P Barra Growth Index (dividends reinvested in both indexes). Over the past 13+ years, an investment in both growth stocks and value stocks would have been less volatile than an investment in only one equity style.

Year	Growth Stocks	Value Stocks
1985	33.3%	29.7%
1986	14.5%	21.7%
1987	6.5%	3.7%
1988	12.0%	21.7%
1989	36.0%	26.1%
1990	.2%	–6.9%
1991	38.4%	22.6%
1992	5.1%	10.5%
1993	1.7%	18.6%
1994	3.1%	–.6%
1995	38.1%	37.0%
1996	24.0%	22.0%
1997	36.5%	30.0%
1998 (1st half)	23.1%	12.1%

Source: S&P 500 Barra Value Index and the S&P 500 Barra Growth Index.

The table below shows the annualized returns of growth versus value funds, as categorized by Morningstar.

Total Returns through 6/30/98

mutual fund category	3 year	5 year	10 year
large growth	25.8%	20.1%	17.5%
large value	23.5%	18.6%	15.4%
mid-cap growth	20.0%	16.9%	15.9%
mid-cap value	21.6%	17.1%	14.4%
small growth	17.6%	15.7%	15.3%
small value	21.0%	16.9%	13.3%

Appendix L
Stock Volatility in Perspective

As of the middle of 1998, U.S. households held over to $25 trillion in financial assets, which represents an 80% increase from $13.8 trillion at year-end 1991. Currently, stocks comprise about 45% of household financial assets, up from earlier this decade but still below the level seen in the early 1970s, when interest rates were at comparable levels. And, although there have certainly been quite a few negative years for stocks during the twentieth century, the number of really bad years has been modest (as shown in the following table).

Since 1900, U.S. stocks have had 31 down years, averaging a negative 13.4% return per year—but the 66 positive years have averaged 22.2% annually. Furthermore, the market has had back-to-back negative years only once since World War II.

U.S. Stocks: The Bad Years from 1900 to 1997

up to a 5% loss		5–10% loss		10–25% loss		more than a 25% loss	
1939	−0.4%	1914	−5.11%	1966	−10.1%	1974	−26.5%
1953	−1.0	1977	−7.2	1913	−10.3	1920	−32.9
1934	−1.4	1946	−8.1	1957	−10.8	1937	−35.0
1906	−1.9	1932	−8.2	1941	−11.6	1907	−37.7
1990	−3.2	1929	−8.4	1973	−14.7	1931	−43.3
1923	−3.3	1969	−8.5	1910	−17.9		
1916	−4.2	1901	−8.7	1917	−21.7		
1981	−4.9	1962	−8.7	1903	−23.6		
		1940	−9.8	1930	−24.9		

Since 1900 there have been 54 occassions (not necessarily calendar years) when stocks have "corrected"—meaning that they fell by ten percent or more from their most recent peak. In the past 40 years, there have been fourteen bear markets—drops of fifteen percent or more. The average duration of these fourteen bear markets has been just eight months; in most cases, the market fully recovered in less than one year (the average recovery period was thirteen months).

Sometimes the question is asked, "If the stock market is going down (or "expected" to go down in the near future), why not sit on the sidelines until it passes?" The reason you do not want to try and time the stock market is that missing out on just a few good days can make a tremendous difference to a portfolio's performance. According to a study by the University of Michigan, an investor who was on the sidelines during the best 1.2 percent of all trading days from 1963 to 1993 missed 95% of the market's gains.

Appendix M
Does Foreign Diversification Really Reduce Risk?

As you can see by the table below, whether you are looking at a purely U.S. port-folio (the S&P 500) or one that has 30% of its holdings in foreign stocks (as mea-sured by the EAFE Index), being "global" has done little to enhance returns or reduce risk. The best case for a global portfolio under the heading "average annual return" shows only a 0.2% advantage for the more diversified portfolio (100% stocks). Looking at the "largest 1-year gain," the best one-year period for a global portfolio was a portfolio that was evenly divided between stocks and bonds (25.0% for USA vs. 27.3% for global).

Looking at risk reduction over all one-year calendar periods over the past twenty-five years (ending 12/31/96), the "best" global portfolio only reduced the loss by just 0.6% (100% stock). Looking back at the October 19, 1987 stock market crash, one of the few benefits of owning foreign stocks was that each country bounced back at different times; Japanese stocks took just over a year to recover while U.S. stocks took nineteen months. Evidence suggests that a rising market is local, while a declining market is global. A large decline in U.S. stocks has fre-quently caused a big loss in foreign markets.

During the 1973–74 bear market, the biggest cumulative loss U.S. stocks have suffered since the Great Depression, the S&P 500 dropped 14.7% in 1973 and 26.4% in 1974. The EAFE (Europe, Australia, Far East) Index fell 14.2% in 1973 and 22.2% in 1974.

By owning just domestic companies, U.S. investors may already be getting quite a bit of international diversification: about 80% of Coca-Cola's profits come from its foreign operations, and McDonald's is a similar situation.

The table below covers the twenty-five-year period ending 12/31/96 (all fig-ures are in U.S. dollars).

allocation	average annual return	largest 1-year gain	largest 1-year loss
100% stock	13.7% USA	41.9% USA	−24.5% USA
	3.9% global	40.3% global	−23.9% global
90% stocks/10% bonds	13.3% USA	38.4% USA	−21.4% USA
	13.4% global	37.0% global	−20.8% global
80% stocks/20% bonds	12.8% USA	35.0% USA	−18.3% USA
	12.9% global	33.7% global	−17.8% global
70% stocks/30% bonds	12.3% USA	31.5% USA	−15.2% USA
	12.4% global	31.6% global	−14.8% global
60% stocks/40% bonds	11.8% USA	28.0% USA	−12.2% USA
	11.9% global	29.4% global	−11.8% global

allocation	average annual return	largest 1-year gain	largest 1-year loss
50% stocks/50% bonds	11.3% USA	25.0% USA	−9.1% USA
	11.4% global	27.3% global	−8.7% global
40% stocks/60% bonds	10.7 USA	23.5% USA	−6.0% USA
	10.8% global	23.0% global	−5.7% global
30% stocks/70% bonds	10.2% USA	23.5% USA	−2.9% USA
	10.2% global	23.0% global	−2.7% global
20% stocks/80% bonds	9.6% USA	23.5% USA	−1.6% USA
	9.6% global	22.0% global	−1.2% global
10% stocks/90% bonds	8.9% USA	23.5% USA	−2.0% USA
	8.9% global	22.8% global	−1.8% global
100% bonds	8.3% USA	23.5% USA	−2.4% USA
	8.3% bonds	23.5% global	−2.4% global

Notes:
1. USA = 70% S&P 500 + 30% U.S. small-company stocks
2. Global = 50% S&P 500 + 30% EAFE Index + 20% U.S. small-company stocks
3. Bonds = 70% medium-term government + 30% U.S. T-bills

Appendix N
Asset Categories:
Total Returns for the Last Ten Years

The table below shows the year-by-year returns for eight different asset categories. All of the returns are in U.S. dollars, expressed as percentages, and include the reinvestment of any dividends, interest, and capital gains. The boldface type indicates the best-performing category for the year (source: Micropal).

category	'87	'88	'89	'90	'91	'92	'93	'94	'95	'96	'97
S&P 500	5.2	16.8	31.5	–3.2	30.6	7.7	10.0	1.3	**37.5**	**23.1**	**33.4**
small U.S. stocks	–8.8	24.9	16.2	–19.5	46.1	**18.4**	18.9	–1.8	28.4	16.5	22.4
foreign stocks (EAFE)	24.6	28.3	10.5	–23.5	12.1	–12.2	32.6	**7.8**	11.2	6.1	1.8
emerging mkt. stocks	13.6	**58.2**	**54.7**	–29.9	17.6	0.3	**67.5**	–0.5	–12.5	7.9	–14.8
U.S. gov't/ corp. bonds	2.8	7.9	14.5	9.0	16.0	7.4	9.6	–2.9	18.5	3.6	9.7
high-yield bonds	5.0	12.5	0.8	–9.6	**46.2**	15.8	17.1	–1.0	19.2	11.1	12.8
foreign gov't bonds	**35.2**	2.3	–3.4	**15.3**	16.2	4.8	15.1	6.0	19.6	4.1	–4.3
U.S. T-bills	5.8	6.8	8.2	7.5	5.4	3.5	3.0	4.3	5.4	5.0	5.2

Appendix O
Alphabetical Index of the Funds

Pioneer Equity-Income A
Preferred Asset Allocation
Prudential International Bond A
Prudential Natural Resources A
Putnam Utilities Growth and Income A
Rochester Fund Municipals A
Scout Worldwide
SEI Daily Income Money Market A
SEI Daily Income Treasury A
SIT Tax-Free Income
SIT U.S. Government Securities
Smith Breeden Short Duration U.S.
   Government
State Street Research Alpha A
Stratton Small Cap Yield
Strong Municipal Money Market
T. Rowe Price Balanced
T. Rowe Price Blue Chip Growth
T. Rowe Price Dividend Growth
T. Rowe Price Equity-Income

T. Rowe Price European Stock
T. Rowe Price Growth and Income
T. Rowe Price Small Cap Stock
Torray
Tweedy, Browne Global Value
U.S. Global Investors Global
   Resources
United High Income A
United Municipal High Income A
Van Kampen American Capital
   High-Income A
Vanguard International Equity
   European
Vanguard Municipal Money Market
Vanguard Specialized Energy
Vanguard STAR
Vontobel U.S. Value
Weitz Value

Appendix P
Stock Market Declines

If you are a relatively new investor, you may not have had first-hand experience with a bear market. Since corrections are a natural part of the stock market cycle, it is important to ask yourself how you would react. Would you panic or would you be patient? It is difficult to know for sure. Stock market fire drills do not really work, because it is one thing to ponder your reaction to a market meltdown—another to live through one with your financial goals at stake. However, an historical perspective may help you gain a better perspective and, more importantly, may help you remain patient.

The table below shows all of the periods when the U.S. stock market dropped 15% or more from 1953 through the end of 1997 (a "bear market" is defined as a drop of 20% or more; a "correction" is a decline of 10% or more). Of these 14 down markets, the worst took place during the 1973–74 recesssion, resulting in the greatest loss since the Great Depression. Surprisingly, half of the 48% loss that took place during the 1973–74 decline was recovered within five months after the drop.

U.S. Market Declines of 15% or More [1953–1997]

bear year	% decline	# of down months	months to recovery
1953	15%	9	6
1956–57	16%	6	5
1957	20%	3	12
1961–62	29%	6	14
1966	22%	9	6
1968–70	37%	18	22
1973–74	48%	21	64
1975	15%	2	4
1977–78	18%	14	6
1978	17%	2	10
1980	22%	2	4
1981–82	22%	13	3
1987	34%	2	23
1990	20%	3	23
average	24%	8	13

One possible strategy to avoiding market declines is to sit on the sidelines until the volatility passes. According to a study by the University of Michigan, this is a bad idea. An investor who was on the sidelines during the best 1.2% of all trading days from 1963 to 1993 missed 95% of the market's gains.

These included investors who were sidelined in 1995 by the poor showing in 1994 for both stocks and bonds as well as those stock market investors who bailed out in 1996 because the 37% gain in 1995 made them nervous about a downturn. Those who bailed out in 1997 because the 22% gain in 1996 made them nervous missed another 33% gain!

Being in the market when it falls is not the greatest risk most stock investors face, it is being out of the market when it soars. The best strategy is to keep investing through any market environment.

The problem is that no one rings a bell when the market hits bottom. Similarily, you do not get any advance notice that the market is turning around. Stocks tend to gain significant ground in short periods; missing out on the first, brief phase of a recovery can be costly. For example, when the stock market took off in August 1982, ending years of mediocre performance, the market jumped 42% in just three months. From the October low of the 1987 crash to the end of December, just two months later, stocks rebounded 22%. And in the four months after the October 1990 Gulf War low, with the U.S. still mired in recession, the stock market shot up more than 30%.

Trying to get out of the market and get back in calls for two right decisions. There is no evidence that professional investors, market timers, brokers, financial analysts, or anyone else can get these calls right with any degree of consistency. One bad market timing call can seriously handicap lifetime performance.

The question then becomes, if stock prices fall hard, should you cut your losses and play it safe? Of all the options that investors have, this one may be the worst solution and the most devastating. An investment of $10,000 in common stocks, as measured by the S&P 500, on the day before the October 1987 crash would have fallen to $7,995 in a single day. Leaving the account intact would have resulted in a whopping 445% gain through June 30, 1998. Taking the $7,995 and reinvesting it in U.S. Treasury bills would have resulted in a gain of just 79% over the same period.

Appendix Q
A Reason Not to Index

Appendix D showed a systematic withdrawal program (SWP) for Investment Company of America (ICA), a growth and income portfolio from the American Funds Group, starting with its first full year through the middle of 1998. Let us now look at two more examples of a SWP, comparing results from Washington Mutual, another growth and income fund offered through the American Funds Group with the S&P 500.

For this example, a different time frame (1/1/73 through 6/30/98) will be used, showing radically different results. Like the ICA example, it is assumed that a single $100,000 investment is made and that all capital gains and dividend payments are automatically reinvested into the fund. Also less money is taken out in this example (8%, or $8,000 per year).

As you can see, applying an SWP to the S&P 500 (or an index fund that matches the S&P 500) and a SWP results in the investor being flat broke by December 1996 (all of the $100,000 and its resulting growth has been depleted). Yet, by using professional management like that found with Washington Mutual (abbreviated as WM below), not only are the cumulative distributions greater ($200,000 vs. $188,700), so is the remaining principal ($886,320 vs. zero).

Systematic Withdrawal Program Using a
Growth & Income Fund (Washington Mutual) vs. the S&P 500
$100,000 Invested in Each Portfolio on Jan. 1st, 1973

date	cumulative withdrawal from WM	cumulative withdrawal from S&P 500	remaining value of Washington Mutual (WM)	remaining value of S&P 500
1/1/73	0	0	$100,000	$100,000
12/31/73	$8,000	$8,000	$79,280	$76,890
12/31/74	$16,000	$16,000	$57,460	$48,370
12/31/75	$24,000	$24,000	$74,830	$58,050
12/31/80	$64,000	$64,000	$89,980	$52,930
12/31/85	$104,000	$104,000	$170,740	$42,890
12/31/90	$144,000	$144,000	$260,020	$28,520
12/31/95	$184,000	$184,000	$503,180	$3,910
12/31/96	$192,000	$188,700	$596,530	$0
12/31/97	$200,000		$787,050	
6/30/98	$200,000		$886,320	

For the S&P 500, the average annual total return for this illustration was 6.0% (Jan. 1, 1973 through Dec. 15, 1996 when the money ran out) and 18.5% for the last 10 years. For Washington Mutual Fund (WM), the average annual total return for this illustration was 12.9% (Jan. 1, 1973 through June 30, 1998) and 16.7% for the last 10 years.

Two conclusions can be reached from this illustration. First, there is a benefit to professional management versus a passively managed portfolio such as the S&P 500 (which as an index fund is also considered to be a growth and income fund). Second, moderate gains or advances in some early years can make a great difference later on (compare the value of both portfolios at the end of 1974 and 1975 versus what happened in later years, such as 1980 and 1985, when the gaps become huge due to earlier gains by Washington Mutual).

Appendix R
Using Index Funds

The vast majority of mutual funds buy and sell securities based on the fund management's judgment about which securities are likely to provide the greatest return to investors, given any restrictions as described by the fund's literature or prospectus (e.g., "at least two-thirds of the portfolio will be invested in . . ."). An index fund, on the other hand, simply buys a large number, or all, of the securities listed in a particular index or market average—seeking to duplicate that index's or average's performance.

For most mutual funds, the "active" approach typically gives management latitude in managing assets. As a result, investors in these funds are often not entirely sure how their money is being invested at a given moment. Fund performance, which is dependent on the advisor's strategies and parameters as described in the prospectus (e.g., "U.S. large-cap growth stocks," "foreign bonds from mature economies," etc.), comes at a significant yearly cost: typically 1–2% or more of the value of the portfolio.

Indexing's "passive" approach is more objective and can be more predictable, with costs that are roughly half to one-sixth (expense ratios as low as 0.25%) the yearly cost. Perhaps a more important savings is the dramatically lower turnover rates that are common with index funds; the cost of buying and selling securities (trading costs plus the difference between the bid and the ask price) can easily be much greater than a fund's expense ratio (note: the expense ratio does not include the cost of acquiring or getting rid of securities).

Active management does not mean you will outperform passive management, even during a market decline. According to Lipper Analytical Services, in five of the past seven downturns (ending 8/4/98), S&P 500 index funds held up better than actively managed U.S. stock funds.

Passive vs. Active Domestic Equity Mutual Funds During a Downturn

downturn	S&P 500 Index funds	active mgmt. general equity	downturn	S&P 500 Index funds	active mgmt. general equity
7/17/98–8/4/98	–9.6%	–10.7%	6/5/96–7/24/96	–7.4%	–10.7%
10/7/97–10/27/97	–10.8%	–9.8%	2/2/94–4/20/94	–7.8%	–8.7%
2/18/97–3/31/97	–7.1%	–7.4%	7/12/90–10/11/90	–18.3%	–20.7%
			8/13/87–12/3/87	–32.2%	–29.8%

By its very nature, indexing emphasizes broad diversification, minimal trading activity, and usually razor-thin costs. As a result, index investors benefit from a reduction of certain investment risks, the possibility of lower taxable distributions, and the ability to keep a higher percentage of investment returns.

Twenty years ago, index investing was available only to pension funds. Not until The Vanguard Group introduced the 500 Portfolio (which is identical to the S&P 500) in 1976 could individual investors index. Today, Vanguard remains the most recognizable name in indexing and offers a broad array of index choices including:

- **Total Stock Market Portfolio**—seeks to match the performance of all U.S. stocks, from large, established companies to small firms. This fund tracks the Wilshire 5000 Equity Index, which includes all stocks traded regularly on the nation's largest exchanges. The fund invests in a representative sample of approximately 2,800 stocks in the Wilshire 5000 (which, in fact, includes more than 7,000 stocks).
- **500 Portfolio**—invests in all 500 stocks in the S&P 500 Index in proportions that match the Index's composition. The S&P 500 Index represents 500 of the largest publicly traded companies in the U.S., accounting for about 75% of the market's value.
- **Extended Market Portfolio**—tracks the Wilshire 4500 Equity Index, a benchmark of all U.S. stocks excluding the S&P 500. Designed for investors who wish to extend their stock exposure into small and medium-size companies; the portfolio accounts for about 25% of U.S. stock valuation.
- **Mid Capitalization Stock Portfolio**—invests in 400 mid-cap stocks; stocks whose market values, or capitalization, is between approximately $1 billion and $7.5 billion. The fund's target index is the S&P MidCap 400 Index.
- **Small Capitalization Stock Portfolio**—1,700 stocks whose market capitalization is usually less than $1 billion. The fund tracks the Russell 2000 Index, a barometer of the U.S. small-cap market.
- **Value Portfolio**—large company stocks that have familiar names, historically below-average volatility, and above-average dividend yields. The fund invests in all 363 stocks listed in the S&P/BARRA Value Index.
- **Growth Portfolio**—stocks of companies that have above-average earnings growth, above-average sales, and below-average dividend yields. The fund invests in all 152 stocks listed in the S&P/BARRA Growth Index.
- **Small Capitalization Value Stock Portfolio**—seeks to match the performance of the S&P Small Cap 600/BARRA Value Index, a benchmark of small company stocks that are classified as value stocks because they have below-average p/e and price-to-book ratios. These stocks are often considered to be out of favor with investors.
- **Small Capitalization Growth Stock Portfolio**—seeks to match the performance of the S&P Small Cap 600/BARRA Growth Index that are clas-

sified as growth stocks because they have above-average price-to-book and p/e ratios.

- **European Portfolio**—tracks the Morgan Stanley Capital International (MSCI) Europe Index by investing in more than 550 stocks in 15 countries including: the U.K. (32% of the portfolio), Germany (15%), France (12%), Switzerland (12%), Netherlands (8%), Italy (6%) and Sweden (4% of the portfolio).
- **Pacific Portfolio**—tracks the MSCI Pacific Free Index by investing in approximately 500 stocks in six countries: Japan (77% of the portfolio), Hong Kong (9%), Australia (8%), Singapore (3%), Malaysia (3%) and New Zealand (1% of the portfolio).
- **Emerging Markets Portfolio**—tracks the MSCI Select Emerging Markets Free Index by investing in more than 600 stocks in 16 countries, including: Brazil (20% of the portfolio), Mexico (16%), Hong Kong (15%), South Africa (13%), Malaysia (7%), Argentina (6%), and Singapore (5% of the portfolio).
- **Total International Portfolio**—a "fund of funds" that invests in the European, Pacific, and Emerging Markets Portfolios, offering exposure to some 1,700 stocks in 34 countries. This portfolio is designed to track the performance of the MSCI Total International Index.

Vanguard (800-662-7447) also has a number of bond index funds plus a REIT index portfolio and a balanced index fund.

Appendix S
Tax Basics for Mutual Fund Investors

This appendix provides you with an introduction to mutual fund taxation, including a list of necessary year-end tax forms and statements plus a discussion of mutual fund distributions. You will also learn about the four methods of calculating cost basis and capital gains or losses. Finally, the tax consequences of wash sales and gifts as well as inheritances will be covered.

Forms and statements

The following year-end tax forms and statements are sent to mutual fund shareholders in January and include information applicable to the preceding year:

- Annual statements list all account activity during the year, including purchases, redemptions, and fund distributions.
- Form 1099-B reports any redemptions or exchanges from your account during the year. You will need this information to complete Schedule D of your federal tax return; this information is reported to both you and the IRS.
- Form 1099-DIV reports the taxable ordinary income and capital gains distributed to your account(s) during the year; this information is reported to both you and the IRS.

It is a good idea to keep all of your annual statements and 1099 forms, even after you close your account(s). The statements may be needed to calculate cost basis and capital gains or losses. 1099 forms may be requested by the IRS if you are audited.

Mutual fund distributions

Mutual funds distribute two types of income to their shareholders—ordinary income and capital gains. As an investor (shareholder), you have a choice of receiving distributions as cash or opting to have such distributions automatically reinvested in additional shares. Taxation is the same, whether you receive such distribution(s) or reinvest such monies. Distributions declared in October, November or December but paid in January of the following year are taxable as if paid on December 31st.

- **Ordinary income distributions:** A fund earns dividends and/or interest on the securities in which it invests. Once a fund subtracts its expenses from such income, the remainder is distributed to shareholders as ordinary income distributions. Ordinary income distributions, which are taxed at a maximum rate of just under 40%, also include any short-term capital gains earned by the fund (when the fund sells a security it has owned for less than a year for a profit).
- **Capital gain distributions:** When a fund makes a profit from selling its investments, it passes the profit on to its shareholders as capital gains distributions. Profits from the sale of securities held for more than a year qualify as long-term with a maximum federal tax rate of 20%.
- **Tax Exempt Dividends:** Interest from U.S. Government securities is exempt from state taxes. Interest from municipal bonds is exempt from federal taxes and is also exempt from staste taxes in the state in which the bond was issued. Short-term capital gains distributions are treated as ordinary income for federal tax purposes.

Calculating capital gains and losses

When you sell or exchange shares of a mutual fund, the sale price is usually different from the original purchase price (*cost basis*) of the shares. When the sale price is greater, your profit is called a *capital gain*; if the sale price is less than the purchase price, your loss is called a *capital loss*. Although it appears straightforward, you may have had many different purchases, including your adding new money to the account, as well as reinvested dividends and/or capital gains. Furthermore, you might only sell some of the shares you own or make multiple sales at different times at various prices per share. To calculate a capital gain or loss for a particular sale, you must determine which shares were sold and how much you paid for those shares.

Four methods of calculating cost basis

In order to calculate your cost basis, you must first determine the purchase price for all of the shares you own in a particular fund. Over the year(s), you may have purchased shares at different prices and in differing amounts. In addition, any reinvested dividend and capital gain distributions are considered purchases and must be included in your calculations.

You may need all of your annual statements to ascertain every purchase made for a particular account. Once you have determined the purchase price for the different shares you own, you can determine your cost basis using one of the four acceptable methods: the FIFO method (First In, First Out), the Share Identification method, the Average-Cost, single category method, or the Average-Cost, double category method.

Deciding which method works to your advantage may require you to perform the calculations for each method before you make your first sale. Each method has advantages and disadvantages, depending on your tax situation. Your cost basis needs to reflect the price of all of your purchases, including any reinvested dividend and capital gains distributions.

Once you choose one of the four cost basis methods, you must use the same method for all of your accounts in a particular fund. You can use a different method for your other mutual fund accounts.

To illustrate the four methods for calculating cost basis, let us say that the numbers below represent your account activity in the XYZ Fund, through November 1997.

date	transaction	$ amount	share price	# of shares	share balance
11/2/97	purchase by check	$7,700	$11.00	700	700
11/30/97	reinvest dividends	$240	$12.00	20	720
1/9/98	purchase by exchange from other fund	$9,000	$10.00	900	1,620
6/27/98	purchase by check	$5,600	$14.00	400	2,020
	Total invested	$22,540			2,020 shares

On December 1, 1998 you have decided to sell 400 shares and expect to sell at a price of $13.00 per share, for a total sale of $5,200. Before you make this redemption (or exchange), you want to know whether it will result in a capital gain or loss. Based on this hypothetical example, we will calculate a cost basis using each of the four methods.

The FIFO method

Using FIFO, the first shares you sell are the first ones you bought. If you do not specify another method, the IRS will assume that you have used this method.

Applying FIFO to your account in the XYZ Fund, you are selling 400 of the 700 original shares you bought in November 1994. Your cost basis for those 400 shares is 400 multiplied by the $11 purchase price, for a total of $4,400. In this example, your sale of 400 shares resulted in a long-term capital gain (you held the shares for more than one year) of $800. Your capital gain would be reported as follows:

security description	purchase date	sale date	sales price	cost basis	loss	gain
300 shares of XYZ	11/2/97	12/1/98	$5,200	$4,400	—	$800

The Share Identification or Specific Shares method

This method allows you to choose which shares are sold, as long as you identify the shares *in writing before you sell them.* For each such redemption or exchange, you must send a dated letter to the fund identifying which shares are to be redeemed. The letter must specify the number of shares to be sold, the date the shares were purchased, and the purchase price of the shares.

While this method allows you to minimize or maximize gains and losses, it also requires you to keep written records confirming which shares were sold. You should keep a copy of all redemption letters; the IRS may request them. A number of mutual fund companies do not keep copies of redemption letters. Other funds stamp such letters with the date it was received and then return the original letter to the shareholder.

When choosing which shares to sell, investors can decide to redeem or exchange shares that have losses rather than shares that have gains. Capital losses offset capital gains dollar-for-dollar; there is no dollar limit. If, after offsetting capital losses with capital gains there is a remaining "net" loss, up to $3,000 per year of any remaining capital loss can be used to offset ordinary income (e.g., salary, bonuses, commissions, interest, dividends, redemptions from annuities). Any still remaining capital losses are then carried forward to the next year. You never lose your losses, they can be carried forward indefinitely.

In the XYZ Fund, you will have a capital loss if you sell the 400 shares you purchased in June 1998. Your cost basis for those 400 shares is 400 multiplied by the $14 purchase price, for a total of $5,600. Your sale of 400 shares resulted in a short-term capital loss of $400 (short-term because the shares were held for less than a year).

security description	purchase date	sale date	sales price	cost basis	loss	gain
400 shares of XYZ	5/7/98	12/1/98	$5,200	$5,600	$400	—

The Average-Cost methods

Both of the average-cost methods have special requirements: (1) you must state on your tax return, or on an attachment to your return, which method you have chosen; (2) *once selected, you must use the same method for all of your accounts in that particular mutual fund*; (3) you cannot later change methods for that account without permission from the IRS; (4) average-cost methods can only be used for mutual funds.

If you trade often, these two methods can be very labor intensive—every time you buy new shares at a different price (including the reinvestment of dividends, interest and/or capital gains), you must recalculate your average cost. However, if you have made regular, infrequent purchases over a long period of time, you may be able to use one of the average cost methods to your advantage.

Single Category method

This average cost method allows you to average the cost of all of your shares, regardless of the amount of time you have held them. On your tax return, you need to declare whether your holding period was short or long term. The IRS requires you to decide this on a FIFO basis. In our example, you bought your first 400 shares on November 2, 1997 (over a year ago); therefore you must declare a long-term capital gain.

For the XYZ Fund, your total cost, including reinvested dividends, was $22,540, and you owned a total of 2,020 shares. Your average cost is $22,450 divided by 2,020, or $11.16 per share. Your resulting cost basis for 400 shares is $11.16 multiplied by 400, or $4,464. In this example, your sale of 400 shares resulted in a long-term capital gain of $736.

security description	purchase date	sale date	sales price	cost basis	loss	gain
400 shares of XYZ	11/2/97	12/1/98	$5,200	$4,464	—	$736

The cost basis for the remaining shares in your account is now equal to the average cost you calculated ($11.16 a share). In the above example, 1,620 shares remain in the account after the sale; the purchase price of all 1,620 shares is now $11.16 (the average cost), regardless of the original purchase price. If additional shares are purchased in the future, you must recalculate your average cost. For example, if you purchased 500 additional shares at $12.00 per share, you would need to calculate a new average cost using 1,620 shares at $11.16 and 500 shares at $12.00.

Double Category method

This average-cost method requires you to calculate two average-cost basis: a short-term cost basis for shares bought less than a year ago, and a long-term cost basis for shares bought a year ago or more. Despite the extra work, some investors prefer this method because it allows them to choose whether their gains and losses are short or long term.

In the XYZ Fund, you have held 720 shares—your 700 original shares plus 20 shares bought on November 30, 1997—for more than a year. When you divide $7,940 (the total cost of these shares) by 720 (the total number of shares), you get an average long-term share cost of $11.03.

Additionally, you have held 1,300 shares—900 shares purchased on January 1998, and 400 shares purchased on June 27, 1998—for less than a year. When you divide $14,600 (the total cost of the shares) by 1,300 (the total number of shares), you get an average short-term cost of $11.23 per share.

Since you have made this separation, the IRS allows you to specify whether you are selling short- or long-term shares. However, you must identify the shares *in writing before you sell them*. For each redemption or exchange, you must send a dated letter to the fund, specifying the number of shares to be sold, the date the shares were purchased, the purchase price of the shares, and whether the shares are short or long term. If you fail to specify whether the shares are short- or long-term, their holding period will be determined by the IRS on a FIFO basis.

Suppose you decide you will sell your long-term shares. Your 400 shares at $11.03 give you a cost basis of $4,412. In our example, your sale of 400 shares resulted in a long-term capital gain of $788; if you had chosen to sell your short-term shares, you short-term capital gain would have totaled $708.

security description	purchase date	sale date	sales price	cost basis	loss	gain
400 shares of XYZ	11/2/97	12/1/98	$5,200	$4,412	—	$788

Special tax issue: Capital losses

For individuals and couples, a net capital loss on the sale of mutual fund shares, or any other security, can be used to offset income in two ways: (1) the loss can offset gains, or (2) the loss can be deducted dollar-for-dollar against ordinary income (up to $3,000 whether you are married or single). Any unused capital losses may be carried forward to offset future income. In order to discourage loss-oriented selling, the IRS created several complex rules related to capital losses:

Wash sales

If you purchase shares of the same fund, including reinvested dividends, interest and/or capital gains, within 30 days before or after you sell shares at a loss, the sale is considered a "wash sale." In this case, the shares purchased offset any realized capital losses on a share-by-share basis. The IRS does allow an adjustment to the cost basis of the purchased shares, compensating you for the disallowed loss.

Long-term capital gain distributions

If you hold mutual fund shares for six months or less and receive a long-term capital gain distribution during that period, any short-term capital loss you realized from the sale of those shares must be treated as a long-term capital loss to the extent of the capital gain distribution.

Losses after receipt of tax-exempt dividends

If you hold shares in a municipal or other tax-free mutual fund for six months or less and receive tax-exempt dividends (interest) during that period, any loss you realize from the sale of those shares will be reduced by the amount of the tax-exempt distribution.

Special tax issue: Inheritances or gifts

Your cost basis for inherited shares is usually the value of the shares on the day the decedent passed away. However, for gifts, your cost basis is the lesser of the value of the shares on the date the gift was made or the donor's cost basis, adjusted for any federal gift tax paid.

Appendix T
A Benefit of Balanced Funds

Prudence can pay off. Even though stocks usually outperform bonds, there have been extensive periods of time when a balanced portfolio (30% to 70% in bonds and the balance in stocks) can be a better way to go than a pure stock portfolio (represented by the S&P 500 below)—especially when current income is needed.

The table below shows a systematic withdrawal program (SWP) for Income Fund of America (a balanced portfolio from the American Funds Group) versus a similar SWP using the S&P 500. Both withdrawal programs assume a one-time investment of $200,000 made on January 1st, 1972, annual withdrawals made at the end of each year, and a first-year withdrawal of $15,000 (7.5% of $200,000) that is then increased by 3.5% for each subsequent year (in order to offset the effects of inflation). As you can see, the balanced fund comes out ahead.

Systematic Withdrawal Program Using a Balanced Fund (IFA) and the S&P 500 $200,000 Invested in Each Portfolio on Jan. 1st, 1972

date	cumulative withdrawal from IFA	cumulative withdrawal from S&P 500	remaining value of IFA	remaining value of S&P 500
1/1/72	0	0	$200,000	$200,000
12/31/72	$15,000	$15,000	$197,040	$222,840
12/31/73	$30,525	$30,525	$162,340	$173,760
12/31/74	$46,593	$46,593	$135,530	$111,390
12/31/75	$63,224	$63,224	$166,820	$135,560
12/31/80	$155,527	$155,527	$172,060	$126,140
12/31/85	$265,154	$265,154	$277,640	$82,080
12/31/90	$395,356	$383,214	$287,370	$0
12/31/95	$549,997	—	$366,070	
12/31/96	$584,247	—	$386,960	
12/31/97	$619,696	—	$436,920	
6/30/98	—	—	$464,690	

For the S&P 500, the average annual total return for this illustration was 6.9% (Jan. 1, 1972 through Dec. 15, 1996 when the money ran out) and 18.5% for the last 10 years. For Income Fund of America (IFA), the average annual total return for this illustration was 10.9% (Jan. 1, 1972 through June 30, 1998) and 13.2% for the last 10 years.

Appendix U
Realistic Expectations

Successful investing is not just about managing money; it is about managing expectations as well. It is about understanding the realities of the ups and downs of the market. And it is about understanding the impact of your emotions on your investment results. The following are brief observations about the market:

- The past 15-year period (ending 6/30/98) has been an exceptionally good one for stocks. In fact, since June 30, 1984, the S&P 500's average has been 50% higher than the long-term average (18% vs. 13% for the past 50 years).
- Until August 1998, the market had experienced its longest ever period without going through a 10% correction: over 2,500 days (1990 to Aug., 1998) compared to 1,127 days (1984 to 1987), 1,053 days (1962 to 1965), 955 days (1987 to 1990) and 912 days (1943 to 1946).
- A 1997 survey (1,014 investors) conducted by Liberty Financial shows that 85% of those polled expect market performance over the next decade to meet or beat the past 10 years; 78% of those surveyed expect no declines of −20% over the next decade; and 41% of those polled expect no declines of −10% over the next decade.
- As the table from InvesTech Research below suggests, a loss of 10% or more since 1900, as measured by the Dow Jones Industrial Average (DJIA) has been fairly commonplace.

Frequency and Extent of Market Declines (1990–1997)

DJIA loss	number of times in past 97 years	average occurrence	time since last occurrence
−10%	65	every 1.5 years	7 years
−20%	39	every 2.5 years	7 years
−30%	21	every 4.6 years	10 years
−40%	11	every 8.8 years	23 years

- Even people who are not wildly optimistic about stocks seem to look at the long-term average annual 10% return of stocks as some kind of minimum—almost a floor, if you will. But any number gets to be an average because reality spends just about as much time below it as above it. Looking at all of the rolling 10-year periods since 1936 (e.g., 1937–1946, 1938–1947, etc.), the market has averaged less than 10% about 45% of the time (ending 12/31/97).
- Another popular misconception is that professional management and broad diversification protect mutual fund investors from major market declines. They do nothing of the kind. Indeed, because most funds stay virtually fully invested all the time—generally 85% or more in stocks through bull and bear markets—declines as great as or even greater than the overall market are quite commonplace. As an example, during the bear market of 1987, the S&P 500 dropped 32.6% while the average growth fund declined 31.3%; and during the 1990 bear market, the average growth fund dropped 20.0% while the S&P 500 declined 17.6%.
- Even a well-diversified portfolio of mutual funds is generally not effective in blunting major stock price declines. The table below shows how different cateories of domestic equity funds fared during the two worst markets over the past 12 years.

Is Diversification Effective in a Bear Market?
(1986-1997)

U.S. Equity Fund Types	8/25/87–12/4/87	7/16/90–10/11/90
large-cap growth	–30.2%	–19.2%
large-cap value	–25.4%	–16.0%
mid-cap growth	–33.7%	–22.5%
mid-cap value	–27.1%	–17.5%
small-cap growth	–35.3%	–26.3%
small-cap value	–32.0%	–22.0%

- Another school of thought believes that there is significant downside protection by diversifying overseas, but again, the numbers do not bear this out. The table below shows the declines of international and global equity funds on the same dates as the previous table.

Is Global Diversification Effective in a Bear Market?
(1986-1997)

U.S. Equity Fund Types	8/25/87–12/4/87	7/16/90–10/11/90
large-cap growth	–26.9%	–16.3%
large-cap value	–25.1%	–15.4%
mid-cap growth	–27.3%	–17.0%
mid-cap value	–16.9%	–14.5%
small-cap growth	n/a	–20.4%
small-cap value	n/a	–16.6%

- The impact of a single bear market (the average bear market decline so far this century has been 35%) can greatly vary, depending on when the bear strikes. As an example, assume that you invested $5,000 each year for 16 years ($80,000 total invested). If there was a bull market throughout this 16-year period, your ending value would have been $382,000 (assumes a 16.8% return). If you went through a bear market the first year (a drop of 35% but just on the first $5,000 invested), and then there was a bull market thereafter (again, assume 16.8% for all "bull" years), you would end up with $355,000. However, if you went through a bull market for the first fifteen years and then experienced a bear market in the 16th year, you would end up with less than $213,000.
- The average bear market recovery period since 1900 has been 5.4 years. The average bear market recovery period excluding 1929 has been 4.4 years. The longest bear market recovery period since 1900, excluding 1929, has been 9.8 years. (Note: all of these figures are based on the DJIA and do not include the effects of reinvested dividends.)
- Sometimes you can achieve the same result with less risk. As an example, suppose an aggressive investor averaged 19.5% for each of the first three years of investing but suffered a 20% loss in the fourth year. A more moderate investor averaged 15% for each of the first three years but suffered only a 19% loss in the fourth year. Both investors end up with a total return of 37%.

Appendix V
Global Market Performance

Twenty years ago, the U.S. represented 57% of the world's stock market capitalization; today, that figure has dropped to 43%—although the size of the pie is substantially bigger. By limiting a portfolio to just U.S. stocks, an investor would be ignoring: (a) 10 of the world's 10 largest real estate companies; (b) 9 of the world's 10 largest construction and housing companies; (c) 8 of the world's largest electrical and electronics companies; (d) 8 of the world's largest insurance companies; and (e) 7 of the world's largest automobile companies.

The table below shows the average annual total returns, in U.S. dollars, of many of the world's major equity markets for the 10-year period ending December 31, 1997.

country	returns	country	returns
Netherlands	19.8%	United Kingdom	14.0%
Switzerland	19.4%	France	13.9%
Hong Kong	19.2%	Spain	11.6%
United States	**19.4%**	Singapore	10.7%
Sweden	18.4%	Australia	10.6%
Belgium	15.7%	Canada	10.0%
Germany	14.3%	Italy	7.0%

Appendix W
A Balanced Approach

A balanced fund will never be one of the top-performing funds; in fact, the overall category will never be number one or two. When stocks are doing well, which is most years, one or more equity categories will dominate the top of the lists. When stocks are doing poorly, one or more bond or money market categories will be the winners.

For patient investors who have the time to wait out the stock market's rough periods, equities are certainly the way to go—history has proved that over and over again. Yet, there can be a huge difference between history and human nature—particularly when the element of fear or uncertainty is part of the equation.

Over the past 25 years, the U.S. stock and bond markets have often offset each other, as the table below shows (note: "U.S. stocks" = the S&P 500 and "U.S. bonds" = a Lehman Brothers bond index). During the past 25 years, stocks outperformed bonds 18 times. The two worst years for stocks were 1973 (–14.6%) and 1974 (–26.5%); the two worst years for bonds were 1994 (–2.4%) and 1978 (+1.4%). As you can see, when bonds have a really bad year, the loss is only a small fraction of what stocks go through during their worst years. Prudent investors try to take advantage of this by diversifying their holdings across the investment spectrum.

year	U.S. stocks	U.S. bonds	year	U.S. stocks	U.S. bonds
1973	− 14.6%	+ 2.3%	1985	+ 31.7%	+ 22.1%
1974	− 26.5%	+ 0.2%	1986	+ 18.6%	+ 15.3%
1975	+ 37.2%	+ 12.3%	1987	+ 5.3%	+ 2.8%
1976	+ 24%	+ 15.6%	1988	+ 16.6%	+ 7.9%
1977	+ 6.5%	+ 1.4%	1989	+ 31.6%	+ 14.5%
1978	+ 6.5%	+ 1.4%	1990	− 3.1%	+ 9.0%
1979	+ 18.6%	+ 1.9%	1991	+30.4%	+ 16.0%
1980	+ 32.3%	+ 2.7%	1992	+ 7.6%	+ 7.4%
1981	− 5.1%	+ 6.2%	1993	+ 10.0%	+ 9.7%
1982	+ 21.5%	+ 32.6%	1994	+ 1.3%	− 2.9%
1983	+22.6%	+ 8.4%	1995	+ 37.5%	+ 18.5%
1984	+ 6.3%	+ 15.1%	1996	+ 22.9%	+ 3.6%
			1997	+ 33.3%	+ 9.7%

Appendix X
Performance as a Contrary
Predictor of the Future

The main reason I do not just use performance as a criteria for selecting "the 100 best" each year is that there is truly no relationship between past, present and future returns. However, when it comes to risk measurement, past numbers are fairly, and often, quite similar to a fund's present risk profile.

A 1997 research report by the Smith Barney Consulting Group (302-888-4109) covering different periods ending Dec. 31, 1996, titled "Why Past Performance is a Poor Indicator of Future Performance" shows that top-ranked money managers tend to underperform in subsequent periods. The period covered for all of the tables below was from January 1, 1987 through December 31, 1996 and is based on the track records of 72 stock investment managers.

Average Change in Subsequent Performance

manager ranking	subsequent 1-year change	subsequent 2-year change	subsequent 3-year change	subsequent 4-year change
top quintile	− 9.3%	− 9.7%	− 10.4%	− 7.1%
2nd quintile	− 2.2%	− 2.8%	− 4.4%	− 2.8%
3rd quintile	+ 0.7%	+ 0.5%	− 1.7%	− 0.7%
4th quintile	+ 5.0%	+ 3.5%	+ 1.4%	+ 1.1%
5th quintile	+ 12.0%	+ 10.8%	+ 5.2%	+ 6.3%

Average 3-Year Annualized Returns

manager ranking	years 1–3	years 4–6
top quintile	+ 23.7%	+ 13.4%
2nd quintile	+ 19.1%	+ 14.7%
3rd quintile	+ 16.1%	+ 14.4%
4th quintile	+ 14.1%	+ 15.6%
5th quintile	+ 10.1%	+ 15.3%

Average 2-Year Annualized Returns

manager ranking	years 1–2	years 3–4
top quintile	+ 23.6%	+ 13.9%
2nd quintile	+ 18.0%	+ 15.2%
3rd quintile	+ 14.8%	+ 15.4%
4th quintile	+ 12.5%	+ 15.7%
5th quintile	+ 7.0%	+ 17.7%

Over the 10 years studied (1987–1996), only 15 managers remained in the top quintile for two successive two-year periods; 27 managers fell from the top to the bottom quintile. Looking at all two-year periods, 11 out the 72 managers were in top quintile two successive (or more) times; 28 fell from the top to the bottom quintile over two successive three-year periods.

The real conclusion of the Smith Barney study is not that good managers turn bad, but that investment style (growth vs. value, small cap vs. large cap, etc.) has a lot more to do with performance than most people think.

Appendix Y
Stock Gains, Losses and Averages

In the five calendar years ending December 1932, the S&P 500 had a cumulative loss of almost 49%. Although this is quite a depressing figure (particularly since similar losses took place during the 1973–74 recession), basing your stock market strategy on a couple of terrible periods is foolish.

To get a better feel for the likely range of returns you will experience, let us examine what happens when you throw out the worst 10% and best 10% of the years and then look at performance for the remaining 80% of the time. Here is what you would find, looking at rolling calendar year periods from 1871 through 1997 (all figures are from *Stocks for the Long Run* by Jeremy Siegel):

- for 5-year periods (123 observations) and then eliminating the 12 best and 12 worst such periods, annualized returns ranged from 0.1% to 18.5%;
- for 10-year periods (118 observations), annualized returns ranged from 2.8% to 15.9%;
- for 20-year periods (108 observations), annualized returns ranged from 5.3% to 13.8%;
- for 30-year periods (98 observations), annualized returns ranged from 6.0% to 11.8%.

Note: If you earned 5.3% a year for 20 years, your money would grow 181%. If you earned 6.0% a year for 30 years, you would end up with 474%.

Looking at returns and variability from a different perspective Jeffrey Schwartz, a senior consultant at Ibbotson, provides an even wider range of returns. According to his figures, since the end of World War II (throwing out the best 5% and the worst 5% of the years):

- 5-year returns vary from 2.5% to 22.7% a year;
- 10-year returns vary from 4.0% to 20.4% a year;
- 20-year returns vary from 6.0% to 15.8% a year.

About the Author

Gordon K. Williamson, JD, MBA, MS, CFP, CLU, ChFC, RP is one of the most highly trained investment counselors in the United States. Williamson, a former tax attorney, is a Certified Fund Specialist and branch manager of a national brokerage firm. He has been admitted to the Registry of Financial Planning Practitioners, the highest honor one can attain as a financial planner. He holds the two highest designations in the life insurance industry, Chartered Life Underwriter and Chartered Financial Consultant. He is also a real estate broker with an MBA in real estate.

Mr. Williamson is the founder and Executive Director of the Institute of Business & Finance, a professional education program that leads to the designations "CFS" and "Board Certified" (800/848-2029).

He is also the author of more than twenty-five books, including: *Building & Managing an Investment Portfolio, Making the Most of Your 401(k), The 100 Best Annuities You Can Buy, All About Annuities, How You Can Survive and Prosper in the Clinton Years, Investment Strategies under Clinton/Gore, The Longman Investment Companion, Investment Strategies, Survey of Financial Planning, Tax Shelters, Advanced Investment Vehicles and Techniques, Your Living Trust, Sooner Than You Think, Getting Started in Annuities, Big Decisions—Small Investor, Building & Managing an Investment Portfolio,* and *Low Risk Investing.* He has been the financial editor of various magazines and newspapers and a stock market consultant for a television station.

Gordon K. Williamson is an investment advisory firm located in La Jolla, California. The firm specializes in financial planning for individuals and institutions ($100,000 minimum account size). Additional information can be obtained by phoning (800) 748-5552 or (619) 454-3938.